Belief and Beyond

MUKUNDA RAO is the author of several insightful philosophical works including *The Buddha*, and several works of fiction. After taking voluntary retirement from a teaching job in a college in 2000, he now lives on a farm outside Bengaluru. He can be contacted at mukunda53@gmail.com.

Also by the author

Fiction

Confessions of a Sanyasi
The Mahatma: A Novel
The Death of an Activist
Rama Revisited and Other Stories
Chinnamani's World
In Search of Shiva

Non-fiction

Babasaheb Ambedkar: Trials with Truth
The Other Side of Belief: Interpreting U.G. Krishnamurti
The Penguin U.G. Krishnamurti Reader (Ed.)
The Biology of Enlightenment: Unpublished Early Conversation of U.G. Krishnamurti After He Came Into the Natural State (1967–71) (Ed.)
Between the Serpent and the Rope: Ashrams, Traditions, Avatars, Sages and Con Artists
The Buddha: An Alternative Narrative of His Life and Teaching
Sky-clad: The Extraordinary Life and Times of Akka Mahadevi
Shambuka Rama: Three Tales Retold

Plays

Mahatma: Khuda ka Hijra
Babasaheb Ambedkar

Belief and Beyond

Adventures in Consciousness from the Upanishads to Modern Times

Mukunda Rao

HarperCollins *Publishers* India

First published in India by
HarperCollins *Publishers* in 2019
A-75, Sector 57, Noida, Uttar Pradesh 201301, India
www.harpercollins.co.in

2 4 6 8 10 9 7 5 3 1

P-ISBN: 978-93-5302-847-3
E-ISBN: 978-93-5302-848-0

Typeset in 11.5/15 Dante MT Std at
Manipal Digital Systems, Manipal

Printed and bound at
Thomson Press (India) Ltd

Contents

             Akka Mahadevi   155
             Lalleshwari   175
             Anandamayi Ma   184
             The Mother   196

Eight   Modern Sages   203
             Sri Ramakrishna Paramahamsa   205
             Sri Aurobindo   221
             Ramana Maharshi   228
             Nisargadatta Maharaj   238
             Jiddu Krishnamurti   245
             U.G. Krishnamurti   255

         Acknowledgements   279
         References   281
         A Reading List   291
         Copyright Acknowledgements   301

Preface

On the first day as a student of the intermediate course at the then reputed National College in Bengaluru, I discovered Sri Ramakrishna Ashram, a ten-minute walk down an avenue from our campus. The street was aflame with flowers, the Gul Mohur trees were in full bloom. It was June 1970. I was seventeen then; a phase in life when the world looks infinite with immense possibilities. But I took a path, rather I found myself on the path that was not so much worldly as spiritual; I chose *adhyatma* or spirituality. When I had no classes, sometimes even bunking them, I would go and sit in the meditation hall for a while and then spend several hours in the ashram library, reading books on the lives of spiritual masters and their teachings.

Thus started my spiritual journey, which took me into unknown realms of consciousness—there was more to life than what I saw on the surface. I needed to go deeper, both inwardly and outwardly. It was at once a simultaneous and unitary process, the quest. And yet, the propensity to see life, our living, in terms of religious, political and secular, in terms of spiritual and material only divided it up into almost irreconcilable binaries; a hopeless duality, the falsity of which had to be seen through. Once I was able to see through this falsity, life, rather one's living and the world, turned into a seamless whole, no longer solid, tangible and measurable. It freed me from the ideological narratives and boundaries which fixed the meaning and purpose of human existence.

In other words, it was a quest, rather an adventure in consciousness that put me on the telling yet deceptive road of Advaitic philosophy and then eventually led me into the backstreets of subversive political and religious schools of thought. I quit my family and studies to join an ashram to pursue my sadhana, spiritual discipline. This was a blunder, for I soon realized that a genuine search for truth could not be transacted within the ashram's already established pattern of life, study and sadhana. What one witnessed there was not the agony of search, but only a trained confirmation of answers to all questions already given by traditions.

After a month at the ashram I returned home, completed my studies and turned into a college teacher. Then came love, marriage, and children, agonies and ecstasies, joys and sorrows, rather telling and disquieting discoveries and transformative experiences. During these years, inevitably as it seemed then, I poured out my insights not discounting my many doubts and questions and prayers and authored philosophical works as well as works of fiction, biographies and plays. Perhaps it would not be out of place to share here a few baffling yet revealing experiences that I went through during this long period of gestation, resolution, creative thinking and writing.

One fine day in the early period of this long journey, when still a college student, I was overcome by a terrible fear of death. Everything around me blanked out and I felt engulfed by a great, palpable darkness. I began to descend into a dark, moving bottomless pit. How I came out of it remains a blur to this day. Days later, I started to feel a burning sensation throughout my body and my head went missing. That sensation lasted for quite some days.

During another episode (years later), driving back home from my sister's house, I saw a white car in a roadside ditch surrounded by a small crowd of bystanders. The car I was driving was a similar model, and white. I drove on, but was seized by a trembling thought that I was dead, that it was I who was lying dead inside the car that had tumbled into the ditch. I reached home but this inexplicable feeling persisted. For about a week or so I felt light and bright, like a spirit, rather like a witness to the happenings around me and my own being. Weeks later, I was overcome with *bhava*, emotion, an overwhelming feeling of love flowing towards others and a great urge to hug and kiss people, which of course I did not. At all hours of the day, on roads, at shops and restaurants, everywhere the sight of children, men and women and beggars, moved me to tears.

Then, in 2010, shortly before my wife and I moved to live on a farm outside Bengaluru, a tremendous silence opened up one day as I lay under a huge mango tree taking in the leaves gently swaying in the breeze and the blue emptiness beyond. The great silence seemed to me like the cosmic womb in which everything played around and rested.

I have recounted these experiences briefly, deliberately avoiding words loaded with spiritual meanings. And I have chosen these experiences (from among many over the years), to make a point. That is, these have changed me in many ways but not fundamentally. I have not kept a record of my experiences nor tried to probe their spiritual significance, for there is no need to mystify them or attribute great spiritual values to them. These experiences happen now and then, indicating the transient nature of our separateness and giving us a glimpse of the oneness of reality. And they happen differently to different people, perhaps more intensely and frequently than in my case. However, what is more important is to let go these experiences, as they can be imprisoning rather than liberating if we cling to them. It is important to be attentive to the tremendous flow and interconnectedness of all things in the universe and to understand that our sense of separation is false, that it is only a historical-cum-psychological fiction put together over centuries.

In this way, after questing and being on the road and alleyways of consciousness for over four decades, I cannot pinpoint and declare when I found myself on a plateau. It is where I have been for quite some years now, living on a farm outside Bengaluru, growing vegetables,

writing when I have to, interacting with the villagers, or gazing at the
hills as they subtly change colour from dawn to dusk.

The texts that figure in this narrative have been my companions almost
all my life, although I don't commune with them any more. I have
travelled outside these texts many a time in search of new pastures,
but have always returned to them to be succoured again and again,
only to eventually let go the search, the enquiry and even the need for
clarity and resolution.

Some years ago, I thought I must put together these texts and share
them with fellow seekers and those interested in ideas and insights. It
has taken me about five years to complete the task and I must reiterate
that I have done this in the spirit of sharing, and not as an instructor.
So this narrative ought not to be seen as an instruction manual or as
a handbook on spirituality, though you'll find here a cornucopia of
spiritual insights, awe-inspiring stories, and proclamations that provoke
and inspire. On a journey such as this all we need is an open, quiet
mind and the patience and rigour to hold on till the end, which shall
be no end but an utterly new beginning, although what that would be
for each one of us cannot be predicted.

It is interesting to note here that more than three thousand years
ago, the Indian mind was already engaged in tackling what are
even today considered the hard problems in both philosophy and
psychology. Discussions and debates about the nature of the world
and the self, the distinction of the soul, mind and body, if there is
a beyond, a life after death and so on were widespread. There was
indeed a tremendous explosion and battle of ideas; dialecticians,
controversialists, materialists, sceptics, transcendentalists, advocates
of immanence and non-duality, complemented and contradicted yet
deepened each other's enquiry in turns.

A veritable bazaar of beliefs and ideas, insights and revelations,
an incredibly large number of creeds and sects—all of these, in

many varied ways, exist in India to this day. Truly an adventure in consciousness that eventually led to the discovery and realization of the state of being where all conflicts and fears, ideas and beliefs cease, where the divided mind has gone quiet, and the body, cleansed of animal passion and established in its pristine state, begins to live in a rhythm natural to it and in tune with life without boundaries.

A word about the notion of spiritual authority, especially Vedic authority, is in order here. Vedic hymns were transmitted orally from guru to disciple, being written down only about two thousand years after they were first composed. Nevertheless, and despite a long, complex and problematic history, these texts came to be fixed as divine revelation, valid for all time. Several schools of Hindu thought and tradition claim to have been derived from the Vedas, including the various schools of Vedanta, and acknowledge their authority. To date there are thousands of stubborn believers who vehemently argue for the spiritual authority of the Vedas and their divine origin, reproducing chapter and verse from these as well as other religious texts, to justify their stand.

On the other hand, the enlightenment traditions in India have always held a rather ambivalent stance with regard to spiritual authority. It is possible to adduce against one textual citation, or tradition, that apparently affirms faith in the Vedic authority two or three that deny it with vehemence. Indeed, we could produce evidence of several texts and traditions that question, reject and subvert Vedic authority. The different *agamas* ('traditions' or 'that which has come down'), such as the Buddhist, Jain, or Virashaivism, Shaktism, Tantrism, even certain Advaitic traditions, for instance, not only question but reject the Vedas as the sole criterion and source of valid knowledge.

As Daya Krishna, in his polemical yet instructive work *Indian Philosophy, a Counter Perspective*, would ask—are the Upanishads composed as late as the thirteenth century to be included in the Vedic corpus? What about, 'the *Manduka*, the *Mandukya*, the *Prasna* and the *Svetasvatara* Upanishads which are not supposed to form a part of any of them' (Krishna 1996). The *Mantras* and *Brahmanas* are said to constitute the Vedas. Do the *Brahmanas* include or exclude the *Aranyakas* and the Upanishads? Daya Krishna asserts that the four Vedas not only borrowed from one another and emulated one another, but that there was continuous one-upmanship amongst them. Given this, he maintains, it is difficult to establish that the Vedas have 'distinctive specific content' and it 'would be difficult to argue for the so-called *apauruseyatva* or revelation of the Vedas' (Ibid.).

With regard to Vedic authority therefore, one is not sure *whose* authority is invoked and *what* exactly is the source of the inspiration. The argument on the authority of the Vedas, and their divine origin, has been raised here to point out that this tradition has been accepted unquestioningly for too long and that it is time—especially in the context of the spiritual texts and lives and teachings of the sages that we are going to discuss—to either jettison the belief or delink the notion of *sruti* (literally, 'what is heard'), and *apauruseyatva*, from the Vedas and even from the Upanishads, which are supposed to form the end part of the Vedas.

More importantly, the Vedas, the Upanishads—even the different schools of thought such as Sankhya, Vedanta, Yoga and so on—should not be seen or taken as finished and final, providing answers to all our questions or solutions to our problems. If anything, these texts and schools of thought are profound beginnings, not final arbiters. Over the centuries there have been significant changes, new developments and radical departures.

In short, these (and other texts) are great, insightful and illuminating, seeking to reflect the teachings of terrific, enlightening sages and thinkers, but none can be vested with exclusive and absolute divine authority. It is not necessary—for the very idea of divine authority is incorrect and runs counter to *jnana* or enlightenment. The following lines from a *vachana* (prose-poem) by the twelfth-century mystic–social reformer Basavanna should amply demonstrate this supreme fact:

Listen, O Kudalasangamadeva,
things standing shall fall,
but the moving ever shall stay—

Basavanna's prophetic lines not only capture the spirit of the counter culture or schools of thought that questioned and rejected Vedic authority over the centuries, but also the core of Indian philosophy.

Elsewhere in the above *vachana*, Basavanna 'calls for a return to the original of all temples, preferring the body to the embodiment'. By questioning the spiritual authority of the Brahmin priests, he opens a path away from the Vedic religion and its tyranny, simultaneously giving a call to return to what the Shiva *saranas* (devotees) called '*anubhaava*', the unmediated experience or vision of the Absolute Infinite Principle.

Such spiritual upsurge within the enlightenment traditions of India was deeply inspired and informed by *lived experiences*, which led not only to the rejection of Brahminical discourses and authority, but in fact sought to move beyond all texts—Vedic or non-Vedic. Allama Prabhu, Akka Mahadevi, Lalleshwari and Kabir epitomized this vital, cleansing stream within the Bhakti Movement.

'Your Vedas are mere words, your Shastras and Puranas a gossip,' chided Allama Prabhu; Akka Mahadevi moved and lived the way she did, in the light of her own experiences. To Kabir, the Vedas and Puranas, yajnas and mantras, reading the scriptures or believing in the spiritual authority of the mullahs and pandits, were all flawed and misleading beliefs and practices, which had become substitutes for the real thing. Amidst the cacophony of Hindu and Muslim voices entombed in regressive traditions, Kabir's was a radical yet refreshing voice nudging us to move away from institutionalized, restrictive religiosities and their regime, and to return to the unmediated vision or experience of *that* which has no name nor form.

Sri Ramana had not studied any religious texts, let alone the Vedas or the Upanishads, nor had he performed any sadhana as per any religious tradition, before he came into the *sahaja sthithi* (the natural state). His utterances became the living scripture, the breathing, living Upanishad. The Vedas had to be validated in the light of his experience and not the other way round.

This is the most beautiful and cleansing fact about the enlightenment traditions in India. The utterance of a sage—and not of the gurus, bhagavans, paramahamsas and avatars in the marketplace— becomes the mantra that can open a quester up to the possibility of self-realization, which cannot be gotten from, or be found in, spiritual texts. Hence, J. Krishnamurti urged his listeners not to depend on gurus and books, to reject all forms of spiritual authority, to look within and take the inward journey of self-discovery. U.G. Krishnamurti put it differently when he said:

> Several people have come into this state and they have expressed it in different ways. But what I am trying to point out is you must reject not only that but also what I am saying. It has to be your path. The essence is not different; it can't be, because the movement of life and its functions are exactly the same in everybody. But its expression is bound to be different, because it's your path and you come to a point where you reject your own path as well. This is a pathless one. (Rao [ed.] 2010)

This enlightened state of being or nirvana is not something that can be transmitted from one to another, it is not achieved by treading a beaten path, because it is not an experience that can be replicated. So the best a sage can do is to point out errors, offer techniques or *upayas* to a quester to surge ahead and carve a path of his or her own and ultimately, having realized the divided nature of the search, to abandon it.

Enlightenment or nirvana or *sahaja sthithi* or the fourth state or *turiya avastha* is not the end result of the quest. Rather, it is the consequence or aftermath of total surrender towards the end of the quest. For, it is not an experience at all but the end of the experiencing structure, end of the feeling–thinking subject. In other words, nirvana or *turiya avastha* is a state not beyond the mind but a state that is *not of the mind*, where the experiencing structure, the self, is absent, where there is Awareness with no frontiers or boundaries.

In mystical experiences or higher states of consciousness, the binary mind is still in operation, there is recognition, and the sense of separation, however subtle, persists. When the mind goes silent, our sense of time and space collapse and we experience an expansion of consciousness, as if the horizon is expanding endlessly, there is what is called oceanic feeling, you feel connected to everything, even a speck of dust seems to sparkle with divinity. Such experiences do alter the way we see and perceive and experience the world, the problems of living dissolve into nothing and there is a great sense of being. This is beautiful, truly an adventure in consciousness that gives us a glimpse of the oneness of reality, but it is only a beginning, for it is not entirely free of what the Buddha called 'becoming'.

So the sages point to a state of being where 'becoming' has completely come to an end, a state of being which is not put together by experience, whether oceanic or something else. Sages use different expressions—*turiya*, fourth state—to bring home this wonder and mystery, to point out that it is possible to gain freedom from conflict and authority, fear and sorrow; that there is a state of being that human beings are capable of, a state of being that is the answer, the solution, the change, the goal that we have been yearning and struggling for over centuries.

The texts I have put together here, starting from the Upanishads to those on the Buddha, to those of Anandamayi Ma and U.G. Krishnamurti, trace at least about three thousand years of robust, cathartic and illuminating spiritual history. But unlike scientific discipline, the enlightenment tradition (which in actuality is no tradition at all in the conventional sense), does not build on the past and there isn't any necessary or inevitable logical connection between and amongst them. Science, being progressive, maintains the new theory cannot emerge without the old, there's a logical connection and growth between theories and they become part of the scientific structure. No such concept of progress is applicable to enlightenment. It is not a linear movement or progress, rather it is an explosion of consciousness.

The Buddha did not build upon the past or upon Upanishadic insights, in order to come into the state of nirvana. Anandamayi Ma had no guru and followed no spiritual method, Akka Mahadevi was exposed to the teachings of the *saranas*, Lalleshwari probably had a guru, but ultimately they both too went beyond the teachings, beyond texts, and driven by their own inner experiences attained the state of tranquillity. The same could be said of Kabir, Ramana, U.G. Krishnamurti and other sages.

We can understand this conundrum better in the light of what U.G. Krishnamurti has said of his coming into the natural state:

After his 'near death experience', U.G.'s life had been somewhat bound up with J. Krishnamurti and he had struggled to free himself over many years. Using a traditional metaphor, but without meaning any disrespect to J. Krishnamurti, U.G. Krishnamurti said, '...but this monkey on my back continued to stay there however much I tried to free myself from it, but now (on his forty-ninth year when the biological mutation occurred) I freed myself: how the monkey jumped off by itself I don't really know.' He had actually freed himself not from J. Krishnamurti so much as from himself. The monkey jumping off by itself was nothing but the experiencing structure, the self, knocking itself off. In his words again, 'It took fourteen years to free—not from Krishnamurti—but to free myself from my own experience' (Rao [ed.] 2010).

The past has to go, cleaned up for the new to emerge. In other words, you surrender, let go and then suddenly it's all over. This is the mystery, or what I call the 'second missing link', for we do not know what exactly catapults an individual into the natural state.

The different forms of reflection and meditation, yoga, bhakti, *jnana*, Vedanta and so on are all methods, *upayas* or techniques offered by sages in order to break that link, the chain, or, 'bondage', if you like. These *upayas* or techniques may work in loosening the grip of the binary mind, but ultimately what actually breaks the continuity remains unknown. However, what we know is that once this link or chain is broken, the division in consciousness, the separation, disappears, and the human finds himself or herself in a state where there is no conflict, no becoming, no *dukkha* or grief, because the continuity, which is what samsara is all about, is gone.

The Buddha once used the raft as a simile to emphasize the purely instrumental and relative nature of the dhamma (Pali), dharma (Sanskrit), and indeed of all concepts used by him—the dhamma was something to be left behind, not something to be lugged along. He spoke of a traveller who, after covering a long distance, reached a river and wanted to reach the other side. With no other means of crossing it, he began gathering grass, twigs, branches and leaves, built a raft and crossed the river. Now, what should the traveller do with the raft, the Buddha asked the monks. Should he hoist it on his head or carry it on his back, just because it had brought him safely to the other shore? Obviously not, he would instead drag it onto dry land and leave it there, or sink it in the river and go his way. That would be the most sensible and wise thing to do.

> 'Similarly,' said the Buddha to the monks, 'I have taught the Dhamma compared to a raft, for the purpose of crossing over, not for the purpose of holding onto. Understanding the Dhamma as taught compared to a raft, you should let go even of Dhammas, to say nothing of non-Dhammas.' (Bhikkhu 2004)

In the same way, readers have to remember that all concepts and ideas in this narrative possess not an absolute, but only a relative and functional value. So what we are going to say or discuss about the texts or the sages and their teachings in the following pages should be understood in the spirit of the parable of the raft: that they are only pointers, signposts.

It is important to point out here yet again that this work is in the form of a narrative and not in the format of a logically argued philosophical treatise. It is a reading, a sharing of what can be called the wonder and mystery of consciousness. And I have poured out here, for serious consideration, my fairly vast reading and long contemplation on the deeper questions on life and reality. There are no conclusions to be drawn here. Words are deceptive, for they both conceal and reveal. So it's important to stay with the words, to let them unfold and reveal themselves in the context of our living.

To put it differently, this is not an exhaustive work on Indian enlightenment traditions nor on the lives and teachings of sages and saints. The texts I have put together pertain more to non-dual streams of thought or Advaita Vedanta, than on any other tradition or school of thought. For instance, I have considered Adi Shankara and not Ramanujacharya, or the other schools of Vedanta. There are of course many spiritual sects and cults, numerous sages and saints and mystics, voluminous spiritual texts spanning several centuries, but I have considered only those I have felt close to and which I believe are important today.

Hopefully this would whet the appetite of questing beginners; to those already on the path, this could be another opening, another exercise to relook at the texts with a critical eye and let the insights offered here sink in. And then, more importantly, to let go the knowledge, however profound or spiritual. For when we inhale and we don't let go of this breath, we die. So we don't hold on but we let go. It's a continuous process: we breathe, burn, let go and live in the vivid realization of *that* which is always already there!

One

The Word and the Birth
of the Self

What thing I am I do not know.
I wander secluded, burdened by my mind,
When the Firstborn of Truth has come to me,
I receive a share in that selfsame Word.

(Rig Veda Book 1: 164, v. 37)

W e do not know the origin of the universe any more than we do the origin of the human mind. There are, of course, scientific theories and mythical stories of creation of the world. Scientific theories such as the Big Bang and so on offer, in cold logic and clinical language narratives, the origin or the probable cause of origin of the universe and life on earth, while mythical narratives proffer varied origins in rich and lively metaphors.

To know the origin of something is to know its cause. That's the logic on which both science and spirituality proceed and develop. However, while science keeps churning out what it considers better and workable theories, in spirituality, after a point, the question is not so much abandoned as dissolved. This occurs when the mind somehow comes to realize that, given its nature to think in fragments, frames, and pairs of opposites, it can never know the truth. Could this be the reason why the Buddha refused to go into the question of the

3

origin of things, into what he called, 'the tangles of theorizing', and why U.G. Krishnamurti said that stories of the origin of the universe and life on earth, no matter how interesting, were of no importance when dealing with the problems of living?

However, no person, no text, no philosophy and no science can claim to have resolved the mystery behind the origin of things. Scientists, of course, now harbour a growing belief that it will eventually be possible to find and understand the truth about the origin of the universe; indeed to discover a 'theory of everything' that will explain why things are what they are. Perhaps it is possible—if there is such a thing as the origin, the cause or the truth; if not, we are only chasing a mirage! And it shall remain a mystery.

The 'Hymn of Creation' from the tenth book of the *Rig Veda* expresses beautifully that mystery, and also as Max Muller said, 'an eloquent murmur of doubt'. This, as we shall see later, is carried over into the Upanishads for deeper enquiry and contemplation, but always in reverence before that mystery. It is but appropriate that we begin by invoking this enchanting hymn as a prelude to the narrative:

> Then even nothingness was not, nor existence.
> There was no air then, nor the heavens beyond it.
> What covered it? Where was it? In whose keeping?
> The One breathed mindlessly and self-sustaining.
> There was that One then, and there was no other.
> That One which came to be, enclosed in nothing,
> arose at last, born of the power of heat.
> In the beginning desire descended on it—
> that was the primal seed, born of the mind.
> The sages who have searched their hearts with wisdom,
> know that which is, is kin to that which is not.
> But, after all, who knows, and who can say
> whence it all came, and how creation happened?

The gods themselves are later than creation,
so who knows truly whence it has arisen?
Whence all creation had its origin,
he, whether he fashioned it or whether he did not,
he, who surveys it all from highest heaven,
he knows—or maybe even he does not know.

(Rig Veda Book 10: 129)

Clearly this hymn is not a product of mere doubt and discursive thinking but of mystic vision, giving us a taste of that impenetrable mystery of life. There is, however, the description of the primordial state where all is one: *Tadekam*, 'That One', which does not refer necessarily to the conventional Creator or God. Then there is the emergence of desire, the birth of the mind, the self and the seer; the discovery that that which is is related to that which is not.

All of this anticipated the Upanishadic adventure of consciousness that set the direction and tone for the development of several spiritual traditions in India and the world over. And then, finally, the subversive twist in the Hymn of Creation, that keeps the question open-ended: *who knows, and who can say whence it all came, and how creation happened?*

True enough, we cannot say anything for certain. That's the reason why Bahurupi (literally, 'the one with many faces and a teller of stories') says:

Friends, the idea of beginning is an illusion since every beginning is already a second one, a third one, a hundredth one. It is a terrific cycle, never ending, like a story within a story, a circle within a circle. There are only stories, yours, mine and that of the Great Unknown that is everywhere like salt in the sea. (Rao 2010)

We of course need words to tell stories, to pray and perform rituals, to communicate and instruct, and to even teach that which cannot be taught. The Word is called *Vak* in Sanskrit. The Vedas are sometimes referred to as *Vak*; this could also mean revelation, meaning not 'the word of God', but simply the primordial sound, vibration, which is translated or rather abstracted into word(s), of which no God, no human is the author. Hence, in that sense, we could call it *apaurusheya*, or revelation.

The Word or *Vak* marks the dawn of self-reflexive self-consciousness, rather the split in the primordial, unitary consciousness: the coming into being of the world, *nama-roopa*, name and form; in short, samsara. Samsara means 'roaming about' through births and deaths, or, to put it simply, it is the continuity of the self, entangled with *avidya*, ignorance of the non-dual nature of reality. Word is the world, if there is no Word there is no world, and the Word is the mind that disconnects the human from nature and yet sets the human up in search of the self, triggering off the opposite process, that of unification, the return to the ground and source of existence.

Talking about the Word, St. John (1:1) said, 'In the beginning was the Word, and the Word was with God, and the Word was God.' Perhaps we need to put this slightly differently, bring it closer: the Word marked the split in the unitary consciousness and the emergence of the Human, the Word was the Human and the Human was God. Raimundo Panikkar, in his 1983 magnum opus, *The Vedic Experience – Mantramañjari: An Anthology of the Vedas for the Modern Man and Contemporary Celebration*, expressed this enigma beautifully thus:

> The Word is not only speech, though constitutively connected with it; it is also intelligibility, the principle of reason, the power of the intellect, the rational structure of reality ... Word is the embodiment of Man as well as of God. In the Word, whose function is both to conceal and to reveal, God and Man meet.

Now here is the myth of creation from the *Brihadaranyaka Upanishad* that offers a fascinating interpretation of this mystery of the beginning and the emergence of the self-conscious human being:

In the beginning, this universe was the Self (*Viraj*) alone, in the form of a person. He reflected and saw nothing else but His self. He first said: 'I am He.' Therefore He came to be known by the name I (*Aham*). Hence, even now, when a person is addressed, he first says: 'It is I,' and then says whatever other name he may have.

And then He was afraid. Therefore people still are afraid when alone. He thought: 'Since there is nothing else but myself, what am I afraid of?' Thereupon His fear was gone; for what was there to fear? Assuredly, it is from a second entity that fear arises.

But He was not at all happy. Therefore a person even today is not happy when alone. He desired a mate. He became the size of a male and female in close embrace. He divided this body into two. From that division arose male and female. And He united with Her. From that union human beings were born. ... Thus, indeed, they produced everything that exists in pairs, down to the ants—

(*Brihadaranyaka Upanishad* Ch. 1: sec. 4, v. 1–5)

'Beginning' here does not indicate a historical beginning or a temporal origin, but rather an ontological principle. Unlike in the myth of the fall of Adam and Eve—where God is seen as transcendent, where man and God are distinct and separate from the beginning, where the Self is not that of God, nor is it one with the universe— here, in the Prajapathi myth, God and the Human and the universe are not distinct and separate. All is One. The splitting of the One into two, into male and female, life and death, is the beginning of the cosmic play, the *lila* of Brahman. This cosmic play or sport, *lila*, brings in its wake not only joy and wonder but also fear, sorrow, insecurity or lack, which in turn may awaken the deep yearning to return to the state of primordial unity, the state beyond joy and sorrow.

In other words, one can go on with the play and taste the joys and sorrows of life, but one would never know peace. A human being who yearns to be free of sorrow, free of this separation or incompleteness, has to go beyond the play of dualism, beyond the pairs of opposites, of good and evil, of I and thou, and return to the source and become

God again. All major enlightenment traditions in India teach the same: that ignorance of our true nature is the cause of suffering and death, that the human is constitutively immortal, and is always already God.

It is self-consciousness, it is *Vak*, name and form that renders the One into two. With the dissolution of the two, declares the *Mundaka Upanishad*, they become One again, like a river merging with the sea:

> Just as rivers flowing into the ocean
> merge in it, losing their name and form,
> so the wise Human, freed from name and form,
> attains the supreme, divine being.
>
> (*Mundaka Upanishad* Ch. 3: sec. 2, v. 8)

The word 'religion' is derived from the Latin *re-ligio*, which means 'to link back, to bind', to return to the Source. But over the centuries now, religion has come to mean and function as a system of faith that is based on the belief in the existence of God and the rituals and activities that are connected with the worship of God. The Indian notion of 'dharma', derived from the root *dhr*, which means 'to hold up, support or bear, sustain', is generally used to mean religion by some scholars, but it is not the same as religion; rather, the concept of dharma is quite complex, signifying many things. It is in fact the notion of yoga (though a less-understood and much-abused term today), derived from the verb *yuj*, that comes close to the Latin *re-ligio*, meaning 'to yoke, join', or 'to bind together'.

The real task of religion is, therefore, to link, join us back with that which is *without a second*, to enable our return to the source, to become fully human. Otherwise we remain incomplete, half animal, half human, immersed in conflict and sorrow. Sorrow or pain is an undeniable fact of life; in fact, it is constitutive of human existence itself. Our philosophical enquiry and religious search, or yearning for freedom, arise out of this pain, this deep conflict and dissatisfaction with ourselves and ways of living.

Janaka, King of Videha, once approached Yajnavalkya and said:
'Sir, teach me, I pray, about renunciation.'

Yajnavalkya said, 'After completing the life of a student, let a man
become a householder. After completing the life of a householder,
let him become a forest dweller, let him renounce all things. Or
he may renounce all things directly from the student state or from
the householder's state as well as from that of the forest dweller.
Whether one has completed the vows or not, whether one is a
student or not, even if one has not completed the rites, on the very
day when one becomes *indifferent* (to the world), on the same day
should one leave and become an ascetic.'

(*Jabala Upanishad* Ch. 4: v. 1–3)

Renunciation of samsara is only the first step although there is no
guarantee that it would take one very far. For we renounce samsara
in order to know Brahman, to realize peace or to attain life eternal or
freedom. We give up one thing to gain something else. Therefore, it
is still a choice, a desire. It may be considered the desire of all desires,
but it is still caught up in the tension and polarity between action and
contemplation, work and renunciation, engagement and withdrawal.
The Bhagavad Gita, as we shall see later, overcomes this tension with its
philosophy of detachment or total surrender. And sages, too, advise that
we act with detachment, to see every act as an act of sacrifice. But this
detachment is not inaction or non-attachment. A true yogin, therefore,
practises 'holy indifference' and renounces even renouncement, not
because there is 'no-thing' to renounce, but because she understands
that 'no-thing' belongs to you. That is true renunciation, total
surrender; that is the last step in both bhakti and *jnana* marg.

But bhakti or *jnana* or total surrender does not come easily, and
there is one other quality which is absolutely necessary and is of
supreme importance before one even begins this spiritual journey—
honesty or truthfulness. Without it one drifts into the by-lanes of
religious chicanery and deception, and blocks the possibility of coming
into genuine freedom.

Truth cannot be approached without truthfulness and that is the first lesson in spirituality. Honesty is necessary in every walk of life to avoid self-deception and corruption of one's being, but is especially necessary in spirituality which is fraught with a thousand charming deceptions that block and prevent self-realization. You have to be a Satyakama, absolutely transparent, to tread this path of spirituality, which is, as *Katha Upanishad* (Ch. 1: 3, v. 14) warns, 'sharp as the edge of a razor and hard to cross, difficult to tread'. The story of Satyakama is mentioned in *Chandogya Upanishad* (Ch. 4: 4, v. 1–5).

One fine morning, Satyakama approached the rishi Gautama and said: 'Master, I seek the path of the supreme Truth. My name is Satyakama.'

'Blessings be on thy head,' said the master and then asked, 'Of what clan art thou, my child?'

'Master,' answered the boy, 'I know not of what clan I am. I shall go and ask my mother.'

Thus saying, Satyakama went home and asked his mother, Jabala: 'What is the name of my father, mother?'

The woman lowered her eyes, and spoke in a whisper. 'In my youth I was poor and had many masters. Thou didst come to thy mother Jabala's arms, who had no husband.'

The next day, the early rays of the sun glistened on the tree-tops of the forest hermitage. The students, eager to know the lesson of the day, sat under the ancient tree, before the master.

There came Satyakama. He bowed low at the feet of the sage, and said: 'Sir, I know not to what clan I belong to. When I asked the question to my mother, she said that she had many masters in her youth and I was born to her who had no husband.

The students snorted at the insolence of the shameless outcast. But Master Gautama rose from his seat, stretched out his arms, took Satyakama to his bosom, and said, 'Best of all Brahmins art thou, my child. Thou hast the noblest heritage of truth.'

Two
The Upanishads

It is not speech that one should seek to understand; one should know the speaker.

It is not scent that one should seek to understand; one should know the one who smells.

It is not the appearance (of things) that one should seek to understand; one should know the one who sees.

It is not sound that one should seek to understand; one should know the one who hears.

It is not the taste of food that one should seek to understand; one should know the one who tastes the food.

It is not action that one should seek to understand; one should know the one who acts.

It is not joy and suffering that one should seek to understand; one should know the one who experiences joy and suffering.

It is not the mind that one should seek to understand; one should know the one who thinks.

(Kausitaki Upanishad Ch. 3: v. 8)

The above passage from the *Kausitaki Upanishad* signifies a major departure from the Vedas. Brooding on the wonder of the outside world, on the strange baffling elements of the universe and their

terrible and terrific gods and seeking their benediction, has given way
to the meditation on the mystery of the self. The search for reality has
moved away from the objective to the subjective, to the 'space within
the heart'; to delve deep within to know 'that which being known,
everything else becomes known'.

There are about 112 Upanishads in all, their contents ranging from a
few hundred to many thousand words, in verse form, varying in style
and method. The Upanishads are basically compilations of ideas and
insights and revelations of seers who lived over several centuries and
in different places. Though these texts predominantly deal with the
notion of Atman and Brahman they do not present a single, cohesive
or coherent philosophical system. In fact, they are quite inconsistent
and contradictory, sometimes even quite obscure and commonplace,
but nevertheless, a heady mixture of ideas and insights, something like
Copernican, Newtonian and Einsteinian physics all thrown together.
It is important to remember here that they were not composed as
manuals, but went through many hands in the process of being put
together as texts, being edited, revised and probably even re-revised
over several centuries.

Upa-ni-shad means 'sitting nearby' and during this period groups
of students sat with a teacher to learn and receive instruction
about nature and reality, about Atman and Brahman—for centuries
considered esoteric knowledge or secret doctrine fit only for the
tested few. For Sankara, the Upanishads meant brahmavidya or
brahmajnana, the knowledge of Brahman. However, in no single
text can we expect to find the whole truth—rather, between the
thunder of banal observations we find insights and truths that flash
like lightning.

To be fair to the authors of these texts, they were not concerned
with logically building a philosophy, but with recording dialogues and
discourses, and reporting the experiences and insights of the seers.
But let it be said that every utterance we find in the Upanishads is not

Tattoo After Care

1. Keep the bandage on for 5 days or as advised by your artist.

2. Ensure that water doesn't go inside your bandage. If water goes inside or your tattoo begins to get itchy, remove the bandage immediately with the help of lukewarm water and wash your tattoo with a mild soap and drinking water.

3. During the 5 days of keeping the bandage, some plasma/ excess ink will start to deposit on your tattoo but its ok.

4. once the bandage is removed and tattoo is washed, leave it to dry for 5 mins and thereafter begin applying aftercare ointment twice a day for 2 weeks.

5. Avoid swimming/gyming/sunlight exposure for 2 weeks.

6. A very thin scab will form over your tattoo and shed off. Don't scratch or force the scab to come off. It will fall off on it own.

7. Do not wear abrasive material, jewellery or shoes that rub against your tattoo.

8. Listen to your artist, not your friends.

Thank You

TATTOO

Consent Tattoo Studio

Name .... Rani

Tel. .... 9997100061 .... Date. 23/05/2019

Design .... Mandala .... Place. Ankle

6000/—

I acknowledge I am over the age of eighteen and obtaining of tattoo is by my choice alone. I consent to the application of the tattoo and to any actions or conduct of the representatives and employees of the Hawk Tattoo reasonably necessary to perform the tattoo procedure. I also consent to all the terms & conditions told by the Tattoo Artist. Hawk Tattoo is not responsible for any kind of skin problem or any other problem afterwards.

....

Customer's Signature

For Hawk Tattoo

Artist's Signature

HAWK TATTOO F-27 ★

Mh. : 9891009511

E-mail : hawktattoo@gmail.com • Website : www.hawktattoo.in

f ⊙ hawktattoodelhi

Kindly Review us on Google
@hawktattoodelhi

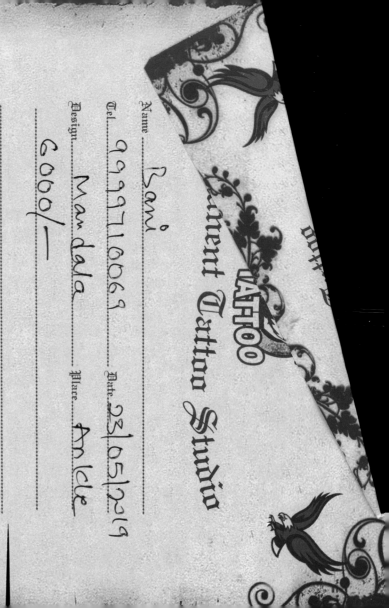

necessarily the insight of a seer or a rishi. This has to be said because it is generally believed that everything you find in these texts is profound and of great spiritual value. That is not true.

Taken as whole, however, at least the thirteen major Upanishads (*Aitareya, Brihadaranyaka, Chandogya, Isha, Katha, Kausitaki, Kena, Maitrdyani, Mandukya, Mundaka, Prashna, Svetasvatara* and *Taittiriya*), notwithstanding the variety of authorship and the long period over which they were put together, display a singularity of purpose and a seriousness that is touching and profoundly inspiring. In the words of S. Radhakrishnan: 'the fever and ardour of seeking the vision of the Real not only enlighten our minds but stretch our souls.'

In these Upanishads, Vedic mantras, rituals and gods are left behind with the realization that 'liberation', if there is such a thing, cannot possibly be attained through mantras and rituals. So it is time to pause, to rethink. What is close at hand and always available is one's own self, one's own mind. That is where one has to begin, with one's self, to delve deep within and search for that by which, and in which, the world exists and moves. It must be pointed out here that the Upanishads portray as seekers not necessarily those Brahmins who chanted mantras and performed sacrifices, but those who were probably rebels—and those non-Brahmins as well, who dared to leave the security of home and hearth, turning away not only from samsara but even its gods and half-gods, to turn within. It is in this sense that the Upanishads mark, not the last part but the end of the Vedas: *vedasya-antah*, Vedanta.

There were of course certain trends in the Vedas that were carried over into the Upanishadic search for truth, but such continuities are true in all forms of cultural and philosophical development; there can never be a complete disjunction between the past and the present. Every significant cultural, philosophical and spiritual movement is at once a continuity and a departure from the past. In other words, over the centuries, a continuous dialectic has operated between and among different cultural and spiritual streams of thought. Therefore, there is nothing in the sphere of Indian culture or spirituality or philosophy that can be said to be exclusively or purely Brahminical, Vedic or non-

Vedic, folk or mainstream. However, our purpose here is not to go into the dynamics of cultural or philosophical processes, but to point out and highlight the continuities, and, more importantly, departures from the past. In the *Chandogya Upanishad*, the confession of Narada—the peripatetic singer and teller of stories from the beginning of time—marks and highlights one such radical departure or shift in consciousness:

> Narada approached Sanatkumara and said to him: 'Sir, I know the *Rig Veda*, the *Yajur Veda*, the *Sama Veda* and the *Atharvanas* as the fourth, the *Itihasa Purana* as the fifth, grammar, the rules for the worship of the ancestors, mathematics, the science of portents, the science of treasures, logic, the science of ethics, etymology, the ancillary knowledge of the Vedas, the physical sciences, the science of war, the science of the stars, the science related to serpents, and the fine arts—all this I know. But I do not know Atman. Indeed I have heard that a knower of Atman goes beyond grief. I am in such a state of grief. I do not know the Atman.'
>
> Sanatkumara said to him, 'Whatsoever you have studied, really, it is only a name.'
>
> Narada asked, 'Sir, is there anything greater than name?'
>
> Sanatkumara said, 'Surely, there is something greater than name'.
>
> 'Sir, please tell me about it.'
>
> 'Speech is greater than name.'
>
> 'Is there anything greater than speech?'
>
> 'Mind is greater than speech.'
>
> 'Is there anything greater than mind?'
>
> (*Chandogya Upanishad* Ch. 8: v. 1–26)

Thus begins the Upanishadic enquiry. These dialogues and teachings attributed for effect and credence to renowned seers and even mythical figures such as Yajnavalkya, Janaka and Narada, for instance, probably took place in spiritual retreats, were committed to memory and then handed down from generation to generation by dedicated spiritual seekers over the centuries. Some of the observations that illuminate the texts, although at times placed between very commonplace statements, stun our minds, yet quicken our imagination. It is in this sense that these utterances are to be understood as spiritual illuminations or revelations, and not as the voice of God or as exclusive insights fixed in time and space. In other words, these striking utterances have to be seen as abstractions of a sage's experience of *that* which cannot be caught in the fishbowl of the mind.

Yajnavalkya and Maitreyi

Centuries before devotion became popular as a way to God, we come across men and women taking to the path of *jnana* and asceticism during the Upanishadic period. We come by women who did not care to marry and live as wives and mothers and also those who gave up the pleasure and security of married life and took to spiritual studies and sadhana, and to a life of asceticism. They were called *brahmavadinis*—the women who spoke about Brahman. Some of the notable *brahmavadinis* during this period (500–400 BCE) were Gargi Vachakanvi, Vadava Pratitheyi, Sulabha, Maitreyi, Romasa and Lopamudra (*Aswalayana Grihya-sutras* Ch. 3: sec. 4, v. 4).

For instance, in the *Brihadaranyaka Upanishad*, we see Gargi, a spiritual seeker in her own right, testing Yajnavalkya's understanding of Brahman in an open court. In the same text we also meet Maitreyi, Yajnavalkya's wife, who declines her share in his property before he renounces samsara and embraces the ascetic life. Instead she asks him to share that *jnana* by which one can attain immortality.

'Maitreyi,' said Yajnavalkya, 'I am going to renounce this life. Let me make a final settlement between you and Katyayani [his other wife].'

Maitreyi said: 'Sir, if indeed the whole earth, full of wealth, belonged to me, would I be immortal through that?'

'No,' replied Yajnavalkya, 'your life would be just like that of people who have plenty. Of Immortality, however, there is no hope through wealth.'

Then Maitreyi said: 'What should I do with that which would not make me immortal? Tell me, venerable Sir, of that alone which you know to be the only means of attaining Immortality.'

Yajnavalkya replied: 'My dear, come, sit down; I will explain it to you. Verily, not for the sake of the husband, my dear, is the husband loved, but he is loved for the sake of the self which, in its true nature, is one with the Supreme Self.

'As a lump of salt dropped into water becomes dissolved in water and cannot be taken out again, but wherever we taste the water it tastes salt, even so, my dear, this great, endless, infinite Reality is Pure Intelligence alone. This self comes out as a separate entity from these elements and with their destruction this separate existence also is destroyed. After attaining oneness it has no more consciousness.'

Then Maitreyi said: 'Just here you have bewildered me, Sir, by saying that after attaining oneness the self has no more consciousness.'

Yajnavalkya replied: 'Certainly I am not saying anything bewildering my dear. For when there is duality, then one smells another, one sees another, one hears another, one knows another. But when everything has become the Self, then what should one smell and through what, what should one see and through what, what should one know and through what? Through what should one know That owing to which all this is known? Through what, my dear, should one know the Knower?'

(*Brihadaranyaka Upanishad* Book 4: v. 1–14)

The Atman and Brahman are the two pillars on which rests almost the whole edifice of a large portion of Upanishadic philosophy. Now, before we go further into dialogues and discourses on Atman and

Brahman, we need to heed the warning of the *Isavasya Upanishad* and offer our salutation to the sun which creates and sustains all life.

> To darkness are they doomed who devote themselves only to life in the world, and to a greater darkness they who devote themselves only to meditation.
>
> Life in the world alone leads to one result, meditation alone leads to another. So have we heard from the wise.
>
> They who devote themselves both to life in the world and to meditation, by life in the world overcome death, and by meditation achieve immortality.
>
> To darkness are they doomed who worship only the body, and to greater darkness they who worship only the spirit.
>
> Worship of the body alone leads to one result, worship of the spirit leads to another. So have we heard from the wise.
>
> They who worship both the body and the spirit, by the body overcome death, and by the spirit achieve immortality.
>
> The face of truth is hidden by thy golden orb, O Sun. That do thou remove, in order that I who am devoted to truth may behold its glory.
>
> O Nourisher, only Seer, Controller of all—O illumining Sun, fountain of life for all creatures—withhold thy light, gather together thy rays. May I behold through thy grace thy most blessed form. The Being that dwells therein even that Being am I. To thee we offer our salutations, again and yet again!
>
> (*Isavasya Upanishad* v. 14–16)

Seer Uddalaka Aruni's son Svetaketu had returned home having completed his education in the Vedas. He was proud of his learning and thought he knew all that needed to be known. But the father doubted that he might not have, after all, learnt from his teacher that which was truly liberating. So he took upon himself the responsibility of instructing the son. And so:

Uddalaka Aruni said to Svetaketu: 'Learn from me, my son. The rivers, my dear, flow from sea to sea and they become the sea. And as these rivers, when they are united with the sea, do not know whether they are this or that river, likewise all creatures, when they have come back from Brahman, know not whence they came.'

'Let me learn even more, sir!'

'Very well, my dear,' he said. 'Put this salt in the water and come to me again tomorrow morning.' Svetaketu did so.

The next day, Uddalaka Aruni said to Svetaketu: 'Bring the salt that you put in the water last evening!'

When Svetaketu searched for it, he could not find it, for it was all dissolved.

'Taste the water on this side! How does it taste?'

'Salty.'

'Taste from the middle; how does it taste?'

'Salty.'

'Taste from that side; how does it taste?'

'Salty.'

'Taste once more and come to me!'

Svetaketu did so and said, 'Sir, it is always the same.'

Then his father said to him: 'In the same way you do not perceive Being here, although it is always present. That is truth; that is the Atman; *that art thou*, Svetaketu!'

(*Chandogya Upanishad* Ch. 6: v. 8–16)

A Dialogue with Death

The fear of death, of coming to an end, of no-thing, void, is the greatest fear. Death is the final frontier, the final passage that we dread but have to cross to come upon that which is *not* the opposite of death; where 'this whole world is bright with light.'

The parable of Nachiketa quite artistically captures what may be called the archetypal spiritual seeker's encounter with Yama, the Lord of Death. Nachiketa does not tremble in fear of death. Rather like one disillusioned with life, like one resolved on knowing what life is all about, he seeks out death. And the Lord of Death turns out be anything but a spectre of terror, rather he sounds like a kind-hearted man and even apologizes to Nachiketa for keeping him waiting for three days.

The story of Nachiketa is moving and poetic, symbolizing man's longing for enlightenment. As Raimundo Panikkar notes, 'Nachiketa is the Man on pilgrimage, the symbol of mankind's itinerant condition. Nachiketa desires to know whether he is or he is not, his thirst for knowledge is not intellectual, not an epistemological curiosity, but gnostic-existential thrust' (Panikkar 1983).

The story goes like this: desirous of reward, Nachiketa's father Vajrasrava (unlike in the story of Uddalaka Aruni and his son, Svetaketu) gives away all his wealth in order to perform a sacrifice, and we see here a reversal of roles of the father and son. Knowing his father's greed for reward, Nachiketa asks in a rather mocking tone, 'Father, I too belong to you, so to whom will you give me?' When his father does not answer, Nachiketa repeats the question, and the father replies in anger: 'I shall give you to Yama.'

Nachiketa thought to himself: 'Of what good am I to the King of Death?' Yet, being determined to keep his father's word, the boy journeyed to the house of Death.

But Yama, the King of Death, was not at home, and for three nights Nachiketa waited. When at length the King of Death returned, he approached Nachiketa and welcomed him with courteous words.

He said, 'I salute you. You are indeed a guest worthy of all reverence. Three nights have you passed in my house and have not received my hospitality; ask of me, therefore, three boons—one for each night.'

'O Death,' replied Nachiketa, 'I gratefully accept your offer. And as the first of these boons I ask that my father be not anxious about me, that his anger be appeased, and that when you send me back to him, he recognize me and welcome me.'

'Granted,' declared Death.

Then said Nachiketa: 'In heaven there is no fear at all. There, free from hunger, from thirst, from sorrow, all rejoice and are glad. You know, O King, the fire sacrifice that leads to heaven. Teach me that sacrifice, for I am full of faith. This is my second wish.'

Whereupon, consenting, Death taught the boy the fire sacrifice, and all the rites and ceremonies attending it. Nachiketa repeated all that he had learned.

And then Nachiketa said: 'When a man dies, there is this doubt: Some say, he is; others say, he is not. What is the actual fact, tell me the truth. This is my third wish.'

'Ah!' Sighed Death. 'Even the gods were once puzzled by this mystery. Subtle indeed is the truth regarding it, not easy to understand. Choose some other boon, O Nachiketa.'

But Nachiketa would not be denied.

'O Death, surely there is no teacher better able to explain it than you—and there is no other boon equal to this.'

To which, trying Nachiketa again, the god replied: 'Ask for sons and grandsons, for cattle, elephants, horses, gold, celestial maidens, beautiful to behold, I will give them all to you, to serve you. But for the secret of death, O Nachiketa, do not ask!'

But Nachiketa stood fast, and said: 'Tell me, O King, the supreme secret regarding which men doubt. No other boon will I ask.'

Whereupon the King of Death, well pleased at heart, began to teach Nachiketa the secret of immortality. He said: 'The goal of worldly desire, the glittering objects for which all men long, the celestial pleasures they hope to gain by religious rites, the most sought-after of miraculous powers—all these were within your grasp. But all these, with firm resolve, you have renounced.

'Now listen. The ancient, effulgent being, the indwelling Spirit, subtle, deep-hidden in the lotus of the heart, is hard to know. But the wise man, following the path of meditation, knows him, and is freed alike from pleasure and from pain.'

Nachiketa said: 'Teach me, O King, whatsoever you know to be beyond right and wrong, beyond cause and effect, beyond past, present, and future.'

The King of Death said: 'It is—OM. This syllable is Brahman. This syllable is indeed supreme. He who knows it obtains his desire.

'The Self, whose symbol is OM, is the omniscient Lord. He is not born. He does not die. He is neither cause nor effect.

'Formless is He, though inhabiting form. In the midst of the fleeting He abides forever. All-pervading and supreme is the Self.

'Brahman is the end of the journey. Brahman is the supreme goal.

'What is within us is also without. What is without is also within.

'This universe is a tree eternally existing, its root aloft, its branches spread below. The pure root of the tree is Brahman, the immortal, in whom the three worlds have their being, whom none can transcend, who is verily the Self.

'The whole universe came forth from Brahman and moves in Brahman.

(*Katha Upanishad* Books I–IV)

Brahman

The word 'Brahman' (not to be confused with Brahma, the Creator God) is derived from the Sanskrit root *brh*, which means 'to grow, to swell, enlarge', suggesting that which expands ceaselessly, that which is eternal.

Brahman is also personified as the One, or as Person, *saguna* Brahman (Brahman with attributes). Sometimes as the sacred utterance and incantation: 'om' or 'aum'; or, as the primordial Word, *Vak*. However, in the Upanishads, it nearly always means *satyasyasatyam* or the Reality of the real, the infinite, immanent yet transcendent Reality; it is *sat* (existence), *chit* (awareness), *ananda* (bliss); in brief, that which is the ground and source of all matter, energy, time, space, being, and everything of and beyond this visible universe.

To know Brahman is to become Brahman and that is the goal
of spiritual journey. The urge to know Brahman is there because
of the presence of Brahman within us. In other words, the human
is constitutively immortal, that is, already always Brahman, and to
realize *that* is the goal of the Upanishads. Moksha, *jivanmukti* and
sahaja sthithi are some of the other terms used to refer to Brahman or
the state of Brahman. Brahman may sometimes be variously described
as this, that and the other, but all these terms telescope into one
another and then merge and explode and evaporate into nothingness.
Ultimately, Brahman is beyond words, indescribable, unknowable, in
the sense it is not in the realm of knowing or knowledge, therefore the
Brihadaranyaka Upanishad describes Brahman negatively as *neti, neti*,
'not this, not this'.

Verily, there are two forms of Brahman: gross and subtle, mortal
and immortal, limited and unlimited, definite and indefinite.

The gross form is that which is other than air and *akasa*. It is
mortal, limited and definite.

Now the subtle: It is air and *akasa*. It is immortal, it is unlimited
and it is indefinite.

Now with reference to the body: The gross form is that which
is other than the air and the *akasa* that is in the body. It is mortal, it
is limited and it is definite.

Now the subtle: It is the air and the *akasa* that is in the body. It
is immortal, it is unlimited and it is indefinite.

The form of that person is like a cloth dyed with turmeric,
or like grey sheep's wool, or like a tongue of fire, or like a flash
of lightning. He who knows this—his splendour is like a flash of
lightning. Now, therefore, the description of Brahman: 'Not this,
not this' (*neti, neti*); for there is no other and more appropriate
description than this: 'Not this.'

(*Brihadaranyaka Upanishad* Ch. 2: sec. 3, v. 1–6)

Atman

The word Atman is derived from the word 'an', which means 'to breathe', the breath of life. Over a period of time the word was inflated to mean soul, self or essential being of the individual. It is also understood as the principle of man's life, that which pervades his being, his breath (*prana*), his intellect (*prajna*), and yet transcends them. It is not the ego, not the self in the sense of the mind, or memories.

According to the Upanishads, our true Self is pure existence, self-aware, unconditioned by the forms of mind and intellect. And that Self, Atman, is Brahman. This identification of the Atman with Brahman is the basic premise of the Upanishads.

This Atman is Brahman

The realization or revelation that Atman is Brahman, *tat tvam asi* or thou art that, and *aham Brahmasmi* or I am Brahman, happens when the experiencer and experience blend into a single whole, when the distinction between subject and object melts away and the two become one. In other words, when the experiencer, the thinker, the self, vanishes then pure consciousness or awareness shines forth like the sun and pervades the whole being.

This moment of illumination is called the attainment of self-knowledge or the realization of the unity of Brahman (the Universal Self) with Atman (the Individual Self). The attainment of this unity or wholeness, this Oneness where there is no other, is moksha, the end of the spiritual journey.

> 'Yajnavalkya,' Ushasta Cakrayana said, 'explain to me that Brahman which is manifest and not concealed, that which is the Atman within everything.'
>
> 'That is your atman, which is within everything.'
>
> 'How is it within everything, Yajnavalkya?'
>
> 'That which breathes with your breath, that is your atman which is within everything. That which exhales with your exhalation, that is your atman which is within everything. That which breathes

diffusedly with your diffused breath, that is your atman which is
within everything. That which breathes up with your up-breath,
that is your atman which is within everything. This, in truth, is
your *atman* which is within everything.'

'How is it within everything, Yajnavalkya?'

'You cannot see the seer of seeing, you cannot hear the hearer
of hearing, you cannot know the knower of knowing. This Atman
which is within everything is your very own atman. Anything else
is the cause of separation and suffering.'

After this Ushasta Cakrayana was silent.

(*Brihadaranyaka Upanishad* Ch 3: sec. 4, v. 1–2)

~

As a mirror covered with dust, when cleaned,
shines with fresh brightness, so the embodied self
is unified on seeing the Atman's true nature,
attains its goal and is released from sorrow.
He who with the truth of the Atman, unified,
perceives the truth of Brahman, as with a lamp,
who knows God, the unborn, the stable, the One free
from all forms of being, is released from all fetters.

(*Svetasvatara Upanishad* Ch. 2: v. 14–15)

~

When there is a dualistic consciousness, the Atman hears,
sees, smells, tastes, and touches all things and is conscious
of it. When there is a non-dualistic consciousness, it
(the Atman) is free from effect, cause, and action;
it is unutterable, unique, indescribable.
It is ineffable!

(*Maitreya Upanishad* Ch. 6: v. 7)

Renunciation, Sadhana and *Jnana*

Renunciation is and is not the way. There is no guarantee that rigorous
study and contemplation will get you there either. Meditation and even

mystical experiences may give one an inkling of the higher state of consciousness, but they do not necessarily lead one to moksha or the state of Brahman. In that state, declares the *Brihadaranyaka Upanishad*:

There a father is no longer a father and a mother no longer a mother; the worlds are no longer worlds, the Gods are no longer Gods, and the Vedas are no longer Vedas. There a thief is no longer a thief, a murderer is no longer a murderer, and an outcaste is no longer an outcaste; a monk is no longer a monk, an ascetic is no longer an ascetic; (for there) he is untouched by merit and untouched by sin; then he will have passed beyond all the sorrows of the heart.

(*Brihadaranyaka Upanishad* Ch. 4: sec. 3, v. 22)

A bit of a caveat is needed here. The expression 'then he will have passed beyond ...' is typical of many Upanishads, indicating the great possibility. You understand or do this, that and the other, then you will have passed beyond, you will know Brahman, you will end sorrow. It is this unmistakable expectant tenor in many Upanishads that makes one wonder if the seer speaking the words is speaking from that state of absolute freedom or has had only a glimpse or intimations of that state; or, should it be seen only as an account of the sage's words put together in an idealistic tone by scribes? But then, these hopeful or promising words such as 'knowing Brahman one attains to freedom and achieves immortality' or, 'then he will have passed beyond' when juxtaposed with affirmations such as 'I am that Brahman without a second', or when you read *Mandukya Upanishad*, you know you are in the presence of an enlightened seer.

Mahavakyas

Pronounce these *mahavakyas* quietly in your mind, and then utter them loudly from the depth of your being.

Prajnanam Brahma—Consciousness is Brahman (*Aitareya Upanishad* Ch. 3: v. 3).

Ayam Atma Brahma—This Atman is Brahman (*Mandukya Upanishad* Ch. 1: v. 2).

Tat Tvam Asi—Thou art That (*Chandogya Upanishad* Ch. 8: v. 7).

Aham Brahmasmi—I am Brahman (*Brihadaranyaka Upanishad* Ch. 1: sec. 4, v. 10).

There is a tremendous sense of certainty in the *mahavakyas*. There has been a lot of debate about the assertive tone of these statements. Would a self-realized person, one who has come into *that* which is indescribable, make such apparently proud statements? How does an individual know that he or she has come into that state of freedom? What gives one that sense of conviction? Is it the sense that the search has come to an end, that there is nothing more to be done, because the ultimate realization has happened?

Adi Shankara would assert that this self-realization, *Aham Brahmasmi* (I am Brahman), was *svamprakasha* (self-evident) and *svasamvedya* (self-revealed). The Buddha, coming into the state of nirvana, declared:

> My mind was liberated from the taint of sensual desire, from the taint of being, and from the taint of ignorance. When it was liberated there came the awareness: 'It is liberated'. I directly knew: 'Birth is destroyed, the holy life has been lived, what had to be done has been done, there is no more coming to any state of being'.
>
> (*Majjhima Nikaya* 36; also see *Samyutta Nikaya* 12: 65, cited in Rao 2018)

In our times, on coming into what he called the 'Natural State', U.G. Krishnamurti said:

How I got into this state I will never be able to tell. I may trace it back to a particular point and beyond that I don't know what happened. There is no story; my autobiography comes to an end on 13 August 1967. It is finished. It is just living. The search has come to an end. The continuity of all kinds has come to an end. The evolution has come to an end. It is finished, complete. Everything is done by itself. It is just a flower giving out its own fragrance. (Rao 2011)

Perhaps, if we could put it in simpler words, when all efforts are surrendered, the search ends with the dissolution of the divided self, then there comes an *awareness* of having arrived and there is no more striving. And there is peace that passeth understanding.

However, we need to humbly concede here that we do not know when that 'quantum leap' takes place. For, when and how the atman reveals itself or nirvana is attained or the natural state is reached, remains something of a mystery. One may do sadhana, or meditate for years and years and yet the door may remain closed. We look for the key to open the door, we study the scriptures, meditate and all that doesn't help. And we realize that there is no key to open the door and we simply surrender and then grace descends and opens the door. Or, perhaps you realize there never was a door!

> This *atman* is not attained by instruction,
> or by intelligence or by learning.
> By him whom he chooses is the *atman* attained.
> To him the *atman* reveals his true being.
>
> (*Katha Upanishad* Ch. 1: sec. 2, v. 23, in Panikkar 1983)

'By him whom he chooses' means grace. Grace of not some benevolent God or an external agency; no external power is implied here. It only means that the illumination, the attainment of Atman-Brahman, or the coming into the natural state or nirvana is not an act of will or sadhana and *tapas*. You may do your study and sadhana for a hundred years and yet may not come anywhere close to attaining the *sahaja sthithi* or the natural state. Sadhana, at best, can be a preparation, but does not necessarily lead to the natural state.

You need to be free of the becoming process, free of the very search which perpetuates the separation, you need something else. Perhaps you need to unconditionally, absolutely surrender, surrender not to an external power but to the power within, the immanent potential, then 'grace' descends upon you, or ascends from within, if you like, and enables you to step out of the river of samsara. This is the paradox, the enigma, the mystery of the spiritual journey—that the search for answers to all questions, the search for *that*, knowing which you know everything is reached, paradoxical as it may sound, happens with the cessation of search.

Turiya Avastha or the State of Pure Consciousness

Mandukya Upanishad, like the *Isavasya Upanishad*, is the shortest of the major Upanishads but is the one on which Gaudapada (considered the *paramaguru* or supreme guru or the guru of gurus of the Vedantic tradition) wrote his *Karika*, commentary. The *Mandukya* is a premier text in which we see the earliest attempt to formulate a 'psychology' or science of the mind. And this text, at least parts of it that deal with *turiya avastha*, the fourth state, could not have been a result of logical or discursive thinking but a tremendous insight and an abstraction of the nature of 'no-mind' by a seer. There is a hint of the fourth state or *turiya avastha*, called 'beyond the unmanifest', in the *Katha Upanishad*:

Beyond the senses are the objects; beyond the objects is the mind; beyond the mind, the intellect; beyond the intellect, the Great Atman; beyond the Great Atman, the Unmanifest; beyond the Unmanifest, the Purusha. Beyond the Purusha there is nothing: this is the end, the Supreme Goal.

(*Katha Upanishad* Ch. 2: sec. 3, v. 7–8, in Panikkar 1983)

However it is the *Mandukya Upanishad* that explicates the state
of *turiya*. The text speaks of (human or the 'universal person's')
consciousness in three stages:

(i)   when the universal person as Vaiswanara (Physical Nature) is
      in the state of wakefulness (*jagrat avastha*);
(ii) when the universal person as Taijasa (Mental Nature) is in the
      dream (*svapna*) state; and,
(iii) when the universal person as Prajna (Intellect) is in a dreamless
      sleep (*susupti*).

The fourth state or *turiya avastha* is the undivided (non-dual) or pure
state of consciousness, which in fact is the state of no-mind. Western
psychology, from the time of Freud, Adler and Jung to the present day,
has no notion of the no-mind or decentred mind, otherwise called
pure consciousness: the ground from which the binary mind emerges
and then collapses into it like waves in a sea.

Freudian notions or categories such as the conscious, subconscious
and unconscious may be useful for understanding and explaining the
functioning of the mind at different levels or for talking about dreams
and behavioural patterns. However, they don't help illuminate the
state of being which is not of the mind, where there is no dreaming,
no images, no self-reflection, no thinking and no operation of will
and experience as we understand within the framework of Western
psychology. Even the religious scholars or authors of New Age
spirituality who took up the subject and tried to make sense of the
varieties of religious experiences, higher states of consciousness and
so on, could do so only within the structure of the mind. For it was
impossible to comprehend *turiya avastha* or the fourth state or pure
consciousness or consciousness without a centre within the framework
of 'cognitive psychology'.

In marked contrast to Western psychology, almost all spiritual
masters of India, specifically from within the Hindu Enlightenment

traditions, speak of the self (mind) and Pure Awareness or the fourth state in the language of the *Mandukya Upanishad* (v. 1–12):

> The first aspect of the Self is the universal person—Vaiswanara, which is awake, and is conscious only of external objects.
>
> The second aspect of the Self is the universal person in his mental nature–Taijasa.
>
> The third aspect of the Self is the universal person in dreamless sleep–Prajna: wise; embodied knowing.
>
> The Fourth, *Turiya*, is not subjective experience, nor objective experience, nor experience intermediate between these two. Beyond the senses, beyond the understanding, beyond all expression, is The Fourth. It is pure unitary consciousness, wherein awareness of the world and of multiplicity is completely obliterated. It is ineffable peace.
>
> (Prabhavananda 1968)

English equivalents, such as 'trance', 'rapture', 'ecstasy', 'oceanic feeling' and so on, do not come anywhere close to describing *turiya*, or to even give an idea as to what it is. As said earlier, the fourth state is not a state of experience at all, rather it is the end of the experiencing structure. Buddhism discusses these levels or different states of consciousness in terms of four *jhanas* (Pali), *dhyana* (Sanskrit), the fourth being a state of consciousness untouched by thought.

To describe this state of being the Hindu sages also used various other terms such as *nirvikalpa* samadhi, *sahaja* samadhi, *bayalu*, open space and so on. U.G. Krishnamurti called it simply 'a state of not-knowing' or 'no-mind', where there is only perception, pure perception without the perceiver. We shall take this up again and discuss it in depth when we come to the modern sages.

Three

The Coming of the Buddha

> Only when men shall roll up space
> as if it were a simple skin,
> only then will there be an end of sorrow
> without acknowledging God.

(Svetasvatara Upanishad Ch. 6: v. 20)

The Vedas (dated between 1500 and 800 BCE) describe the human condition as the wheels of a cart that, well-oiled through the protection of deities or gods, move smoothly towards the destination of *sukha* or happiness. A deep prayer, attended by mantras and yajnas or sacrifices that, at best, gave one hope, solace, *sukha* or happiness, but could not dissolve fear and end *dukkha*, sorrow. It was a gigantic effort, as Raimundo Panikkar says, that tried to explain suffering or sorrow by explaining it away.

The Upanishads, at least some of them, have no use for deities or gods; in fact, the belief in God is found to be part of the problem of the dual nature of the mind, or of separation from reality, identified as the cause of fear and sorrow. And yet, in some Upanishads, as in the *Svetasvatara Upanishad*, the Vedic belief—that without the grace of God there can be no end to sorrow—finds a place. A typical example is the verse quoted above, which means that just as it is impossible to roll up space like a skin, it is impossible to end sorrow without accepting or surrendering to God. It could also be taken as a challenge—if one is really able to transcend time and space, one may succeed in transcending sorrow without having to depend on God.

The Upanishadic seers appear to have questioned and turned their backs on old and already degenerated ways of being and doing. Through their tremendous rigour and honesty, they delved deep within their hearts in search of truth and were able to glimpse 'the beyond', realizing it was *not* the opposite of the here and now. However, the knowledge of the Upanishads (dated roughly from 1000 BCE to 2 BCE) remained sequestered in the eastern Gangetic plains where the seers lived; this knowledge remained secret for centuries, passed on to a select few from generation to generation, until eventually it was committed to writing and brought about a radical shift in human consciousness as it spread.

During this period, in 623 BCE, was born Siddhartha Gautama. Though not a direct inheritor of the Upanishads, Siddhartha Gautama, after emerging as the awakened, as the Buddha, declared the end of sorrow with such unequivocal certainty that it boggles the mind. Unlike the Upanishadic seers, he took the open road and shared his insights with whosoever was ready to listen and enquire, irrespective of caste, creed and gender. He was the first to initiate, in true democratic spirit, what may be called *'jnana yajna'*—offering *jnana* as an act of sacrifice—and he held back nothing.

The Birth of Gautama

The birth of the Buddha is suffused with myth and magical events, as in the case of 'saviours' or messiahs in other cultures of the world. By using the idea of the supernatural or divine intervention, the lives of sages were rendered mystic in order to create a sense of awe, faith and devotion in the minds of the followers, though one might say that the life of the Buddha can do without such devices. The Buddha would have rebelled against such deification as quite unnecessary and even misleading. However, as the idea that the Buddha was not merely human and subject to sorrow and death developed, even his birth was seen as miraculous and immaculate.

The father of Gautama, by name, Suddhodana, who is traditionally referred to as a king of the Shakyas, a scion of the solar race, was probably a small-time king or the head of a tribal republic. His wife, the queen, was called Maya, because of her resemblance, it is said, to the Goddess Maya. Legend has it that as the time of delivery approached, Queen Maya set her heart on going to Lumbini and there, in a glorious grove that resembled the grove of Chitraratha in Indra's Paradise, she gave birth to Gautama. It is said that on the seventh day after his birth, unable to bear the joy which she felt at the sight of her son's majesty, Queen Maya went to heaven to dwell there. And the prince grew up under the care of her sister, Mahaprajapati.

Brahmins, summoned by King Suddhodana, examined the child's body for marks of distinction and predicted that he would either become a Buddha or a *Chakravartin*, a Universal King. King Suddhodana wanted his son to become a *Chakravartin*, not a Spiritual Master. So he made such arrangements that Gautama would never see anything that could perturb his mind enough to take to the path of renunciation. It is said Gautama lived in a palace surrounded by lovely damsels who entertained him with melodious music and sweet laughter. The king also got Gautama married to the chaste and beautiful Yashodhara. In the course of time she bore him a son, who was named Rahula.

Gautama's life of pleasure was so complete that he had no wish to come out into the world outside. But this life of leisure and pleasure could not go on for long. It was time for Gautama to awaken to his higher calling. The one destined to become a Buddha had to taste both pleasure and pain, joy and sorrow, before he embarked upon his spiritual journey. Gautama had experienced only one side of samsara; he was yet to experience sorrow, an inescapable part of the human condition. All that Gautama needed was a little nudge to begin to question the false security of the pleasure and power of samsara and come upon events that triggered 'disgust' with life, to start the process of freeing himself from the shackles of samsara and transcending the human condition.

And so, feeling like an elephant locked inside a barn, he longed to see the world beyond his gates. One day he asked Channa to get his chariot. And they set out and entered the royal street, which, as per Suddhodana's orders, had been cleared of all disturbing sights. Cripples, beggars, the aged and infirm were all driven away so that their presence wouldn't agitate the prince's sensitive mind. The street was lined with healthy and handsome young men and women in colourful clothes and shining jewels.

The story goes that the gods had other strategies and they sent down sundry spirits in the guise of an old man, a sick man and a corpse, each a day for three days, to undo the king's plans, distract the prince and give him that much-needed nudge to begin his search. And so it happened. After being exposed to facets of life that he had never known existed and after sorrow penetrated his being, Gautama returned to his palace and withdrew into himself. Suddenly there was no joy in living and the life he had lived so far seemed an escape from the realities of life. Was there life beyond the triad of old age, illness, and death? If there wasn't, then this life was one long misery, but if anything existed beyond old age, illness, and death, he must find out what it was.

Renunciation

One day, hoping a visit to the countryside might bring him some peace, Gautama rode out on his splendid horse Kanthaka. He rode deep into the countryside and there he saw a field ploughed, the surface soil broken with tracks of furrows that looked like rippling water. Tufts of young grass lay scattered here and there, the field littered with dead organisms, and he was overcome with grief at the sight of death. Legend recounts that it was such an overwhelming yet deep experience that Gautama saw in his mind the origination and passing away of all that lives, he saw the impermanence of things.

This 'near-death experience' was not a vision, not a product of discursive thinking. Rather, without effort, he had somehow penetrated into the nature of things. It was a tremendous insight, an epiphany, and he knew what had to be done.

The next day, Gautama left home stealthily in the small hours, because his father, whose greatest dream was to see him become a *Chakravartin*, would never have consented to his leaving home, not to speak of his wife and son. And so, in the early hours when all were in deep sleep, his mind straight like an arrow, Gautama went out of the palace and roused Channa. 'Quick, Channa, get Kanthaka out. I'm leaving.' And on the beautiful white steed Kanthaka they rode out of the town swiftly and stopped near a grove.

To Channa's question, 'What will I tell your father? And what is to become of me?' the Buddha-to-be said, 'Channa, tell them, and tell my father, there is no reason to grieve for one who has left for the homeless life so as to bring all sorrow to an end. And tell them that one day I shall return and return a Buddha.' Gautama was twenty-nine years old when he renounced his family, his right to be king, and set off on the journey that would make him the Buddha.

The Search and Its End

Buddhist legend says that Gautama, after leaving Kapilavastu as a *sramana* (which means 'to toil or to take on difficulties') donned a yellow robe and tonsured his head. This signified the renunciation of all affiliations to caste, family and native land. He then went in search of a guru. He had to first learn about the different spiritual paths to freedom and verify things out before striking out on his own.

Alara Kalama was his first guru. He claimed to have attained the pure state of the Self (*Purusha*), or what was called the state of 'Nothingness', after several years of sadhana. Gautama however was able to enter the state of 'Nothingness' within a short period of time, only to realize that despite his attainment of the so-called highest state of being he was still not free of desires and conflicts, so he could not claim to have attained freedom from the cause of sorrow.

Once this realization dawned on him, Gautama left Alara Kalama to join a group led by Uddaka Ramaputta, who claimed to have gone beyond the state of 'nothingness' to the 'Real Self', or the state of 'neither-perception-nor-non-perception'. Yet again, in a short period of time, Gautama could enter the state of 'neither-perception-nor-non-perception', only to realize once again that it was not the state of absolute freedom or nirvana. He struck out once again on his own, this time to try out the extreme asceticism practised by yogis and the Jain monks. He believed that rigorous *tapas* could burn up all the negative karma that still lay buried in his being. The severe form of *tapas* was the only means left now to excoriate the last traces of desire, *tanha*, still clinging to him like fine dust. Resolved thus, Gautama plunged into the extreme form of *tapas*.

Living on only a little food at a time and eventually giving up food altogether, his body became extremely emaciated. His limbs became like the jointed segments of bamboo stems, his spine stood out like a string of beads, his scalp shrivelled and withered like a green bitter gourd, and when he urinated or defecated, he fell over on his face right there. He was on the brink of death. Gautama realized that by starving himself he had almost killed the body, not the self and not the negative karma.

So it was not the body that was the problem here, but the mind, which seemed to use every trick under the sun to perpetuate itself. It was the mind that had to be starved of its sustaining power and immobilized. He was ready but his body, now weak and emaciated, was unwilling. He had to start eating to regain strength and begin his journey afresh. Feeding himself with little morsels of food regularly, Gautama recovered his strength and, as the legend recounts, he went to Uruvela and beside the Niranjana River, he found 'an agreeable plot of land, a pleasant grove, a sparkling river with delightful and smooth banks, and nearby, a village whose inhabitants would feed him' (Armstrong 2006), and he decided that 'it was just the place to undertake the final effort that would bring him enlightenment' (Ibid.).

The Fear of Death

Gautama, now thirty-five years old, is believed to have sat down under a Pippala tree with a firm resolution: 'My flesh may wither away and my blood may dry up until only skin, sinews and bones remain, but I will not give up ... until I have found liberation, I will sit here unflinching and utterly still' (Rao 2018).

Buddhist traditions narrate the process of enlightenment as a 'heroic struggle', as a battle against Mara. Mara is variously interpreted as the enemy, the evil one, the tempter and the fear of death. And this Mara was the last frontier Gautama had to cross to reach nirvana. The Buddhist tradition dramatizes this critical moment in the form of a battle against Mara and his forces (daughters) charmingly called Desire, Unrest and Pleasure.

In Buddhism, as in all Indian enlightenment traditions, the self, the ego. is the movement of pleasure which creates separation from all things, it is the chain which binds one to the bondage of pleasure and pain, of death and rebirth, which is an illusion. This is the first and last mystery that has to be penetrated and done with, to come upon enlightenment. It is this overcoming of the fear of death, of void, the legend dramatizes in the form of a fierce battle between Gautama and Mara.

Gautama remains silent and still against the ravings of Mara. Any movement of thought in any direction only adds momentum to the self and strengthens it. You cannot fight and win over the self, because combat is the stuff the self is made of. But when there is no space for the self to move and play around or wage battles, the self crumbles, and burns itself up without a trace. That is the death pang of the self, dissolution of fear, and awakening into a state where the mind is no more the dictator, no more the centripetal and centrifugal force of the individual's consciousness.

With the dissolution of the fear, the self, the Pali Canons say that Gautama looked deeply into the heart of things, reflected upon the conditional nature of life, and then progressively entered into the four levels of samadhi or *jhanas* and gained the insight that forever transformed him and convinced him that he had been freed of the process of becoming.

> When I knew and saw thus, my mind was liberated from the taint of sensual desire, from the taint of being, and from the taint of ignorance. When it was liberated there came the awareness: 'It is liberated.' I directly knew: 'Birth is destroyed, the holy life has been lived, what had to be done has been done, there is no more coming to any state of being.' (*Majjhima Nikaya* 36, in Rao 2018)

Nirvana

The word nirvana means 'blowing out', or 'cooling'. *Blowing out* suggests extinction of the self, and *cooling* suggests not complete annihilation of the self or the mind, but that only the fires of the self, the human passions, are extinguished. The self is rendered toothless, so to say, but it exists in the background as a storehouse of (factual) memory denuded of its emotional content, not as a master but as a servant. It now exists as 'burnt seed', no more capable of reproducing or multiplying itself, and in that sense there is no rebirth to that self, for the becoming has come to an end. Now the five *skandhas* or senses operate fully and purely without interference from the powerless self. This is Perfection, in the sense that the individual freed from 'animal passions' has become fully Human, and lives in communion with the cosmos. In other words, such a Perfect One is the Tathagata, the one who has gone from the world of samsara, and yet arrived as a Buddha, with no self-consciousness because the frontiers have been dissolved. In positive terms, it is a state completely devoid of an ego, but full of peace, calm, bliss, purity and freshness.

Since it is a state that cannot be captured by words which by its very nature fragments reality or frames reality in pairs of opposites, nirvana is often described not in terms of what it is, but in terms of what it is not. Therefore, the Buddhist texts speak of nirvana predominantly in negative terms, such as *achanta* (uninterrupted), *akata* (uncreate), *nirodha* (extinction), *achutta* (deathless), *vimmutti* (liberation) and so on.

> Here, Sariputra, all dharmas, or phenomena, are marked with emptiness, they are neither produced nor stopped, neither deficient nor complete. Therefore, where there is emptiness there is neither form, nor feeling, nor perception, nor impulse, nor consciousness; no form, nor sound, nor smell, nor taste, nor object of mind; there is no ignorance, nor extinction of ignorance; there is no suffering, nor origination, nor stopping, nor path; there is no cognition, no attainment and no non-attainment. (Conze 1976)

The Teaching

The legend says that after his enlightenment, the Buddha passed through Varanasi on his way to the Deer Park in the suburb of Isipatana (modern Sarnath). And there he met with the five bhikkhus, his former companions during the time of his ascetic practice, and to them, according to the canonical texts, the Buddha gave his first sermon.

> There are two extremes, monks, which he who has given up the world ought to avoid. What are these two extremes? A life given to pleasures, devoted to pleasures and lusts—this is degrading, sensual, vulgar, ignoble, and profitless (unskilful). And a life given to mortifications—this is painful, ignoble, and profitless. By avoiding these two extremes, monks, the Tathagata has gained the knowledge of the Middle Way which leads to insight, which leads to wisdom, which conduces to calm, to knowledge, to Supreme Enlightenment, to Nirvana.
> What, monks, is this Middle Way?
> It is the Noble Eightfold Path, namely: right views, right intent, right speech, right conduct, right means of livelihood, right endeavour, right mindfulness, right meditation.

This, monks, is the Middle Way, the knowledge of which the Tathagata has gained, which leads to insight, which leads to wisdom, which conduces to calm, to knowledge, to Nirvana.

The Noble Truth of suffering (*dukkha*) is this: birth is suffering; aging is suffering; sickness is suffering; death is suffering; sorrow and lamentation, pain, grief and despair are suffering; association with the unpleasant is suffering; dissociation from the pleasant is suffering; not to get what one wants is suffering; in brief, the five aggregates of attachment are suffering.

The Noble Truth of the origin of suffering is this: It is this thirst (craving) which produces re-existence and re-becoming, bound up with passionate greed. It finds fresh delight now here and now there, namely, thirst for sense-pleasures; thirst for existence and becoming; and thirst for non-existence (self-annihilation).

The Noble Truth of the Cessation of suffering is this: It is the complete cessation of that very thirst, giving it up, renouncing it, emancipating oneself from it, detaching oneself from it.

The Noble Truth of the Path leading to the Cessation of suffering is this: It is simply the Noble Eightfold Path, namely right view; right thought; right speech; right action; right livelihood; right effort; right mindfulness; right concentration.

(*Samyutta Nikaya* 56:11, in Rao 2018)

The Pali Canons have arranged the first sermon in such a way that the 'essence' of the Buddha's teaching is covered brilliantly in his very first talk to the five bhikkhus. It may not have been the way of the Buddha: to straightaway expound a philosophy of life. However, what is of critical importance here is that the Buddha begins with a *feeling* rather than an *idea*. He does not talk of God, of good and evil, of meaning and purpose of life, or promise salvation. There is suffering, *dukkha*, and there is an end to suffering, because he knows it is possible, because he has found freedom from suffering. There are no good and evil actions, only skilful actions that lead one to the path of liberation, and unskilful actions that bind one to a life of suffering.

With no theology, no metaphysics, no magic, nor any need for rituals or sacraments, this straightforward teaching may appeal to many, but not to everyone, particularly because the Buddha doesn't speak of love and God, but of suffering. So it is assumed that he was a pessimist, a nihilist, and an agnostic. Is there a God, is there a life beyond death, and meaning and purpose to life? Well, once you end suffering, these questions become irrelevant, or you'll know.

The Pali Canons, *Lalita-Vistara* (third century CE), *Nidana Katha* (fifth century CE) and Ashvaghosha's *Buddhacharita* (second century CE) are the main sources for the Buddha's story and his teaching, embellished with supernatural events, with mythical and metaphysical narratives, but which are thankfully interspersed with the more mundane and historically probable events in the Buddha's life.

Three months after the passing away of the Buddha (483 BCE), it is said that his followers gathered in Rajagriha and held a council to recall and collate his words. It is not certain if the Buddha spoke and taught in Pali, a north Indian dialect, close to Magadhi, the language in which most of the Buddha's teaching exists today. However, the story goes that it was during this council that the *Buddhavachana* was composed orally, being written down from memory only in the first century BCE.

These texts written in the form of anthologies were kept in Three Baskets or the *Tripitaka*: the *Sutta Pitaka* (Basket of Discourses), the *Vinaya Pitaka* (Basket of Disciplines), and the *Abhidamma Pitaka* (Basket of Higher Knowledge), containing philosophical and doctrinal analyses of the teaching.

About a hundred years later, serious differences arose within the Buddhist Order over the true interpretation of the Buddha's teachings. Subsequently this led to the formal division of Buddhism into the Hinayana and Mahayana sects. While some sects laid emphasis on faith and devotion to the Buddha and looked upon him as a personal god, some advocated meditation and wisdom as the principal means to nirvana. However, eventually these different schools were brought under one of the three *yanas* or vehicles: the Hinayana, the Mahayana and the Vajrayana, representing, it is believed, three vital stages in the teachings of the Buddha.

The Middle Path

Some degree of preparedness and maturity of mind was deemed absolutely necessary to receive the teaching. Without renunciation, without yoga, it was not possible to comprehend the full import of the Dhamma. A life of samsara was fuelled and strengthened by desire, *tanha*, without giving up which, one could not hope to extinguish the fires of greed, hatred and delusion. For this reason, there were two main lines of the teaching: one for the renunciants or bhikkhus and another for the common people. This clear-cut distinction between renunciant and householder (especially by traditions like Theravada) was later contested by the Mahayanists, for it created the illusion that renunciation, celibacy and sadhana were enough to lead one to nirvana, while a householder had absolutely no chance. After all, the Buddha himself was a family man before he took to the path of a *sramana*.

A life of samsara, with all its joys and sorrows, could give one critical insights into the complexities of living and help develop the maturity of mind required to understand the Four Noble Truths. For all you know, an attentive householder could be nearer the goal of nirvana than a monk who has practised yoga for several years. Also, the Madhyamikas (those who follow the Buddhist doctrine of the Middle Path) argued that it was quite meaningless to talk about these things (monk and householder, cause and effect, samsara and nirvana, etc.) as existing separately. These were all mere conventional truths or true only at the conventional level, for if they were ultimately different then enlightenment would be impossible.

However, the Middle Path makes sense to the extent that both self-mortification and self-indulgence are not the skilful way of sadhana, for both extremities could damage irrevocably the sensitivity of the body-mind, yet strengthen the ego of a person. Philosophically speaking, the Middle Path means we cannot assert that something is such and so, with any certainty.

The Right and Noble Way

Once the Buddha, while wandering through Kosala with a large community of bhikkhus, entered Kesaputta, a town where the Kalama people lived. The Kalamas had heard that Gautama was a fully enlightened person. They went to where the Buddha was, paid homage to him and sat down on one side.

Then one of them asked: 'Venerable sir, monks and brahmins visit Kesaputta and expound and explain only their own doctrines, while the other doctrines they criticise and loathe. We are not sure what to believe and what not to believe.'

The Buddha said, 'Of course, under such circumstances it is only natural to be uncertain and in doubt, Kalamas.'

'But, venerable sir, we want know from you which of these monks and brahmins spoke the truth and which falsehood?'

'What do you think, Kalamas? Do greed and hate and delusion appear in a man for his benefit or harm?' the Buddha asked.

'For his harm, venerable sir,' the Kalamas replied.

'Yes, that is being unskilful, Kalamas, to live in greed, hate and delusion. Now, tell me, Kalamas, does absence of greed, hate and delusion appear in a man for his benefit or harm?'

'For his benefit, venerable sir.'

'Yes, that is being skilful, Kalamas. Such a man does not take life, does not steal, does not tell lies, and such a man prompts another too, to do likewise.'

'Listen, Kalamas. Do not believe something just because it has become a traditional practice, because it is what the scriptures say, or it sounds logical, or it accords with your thought.

'But, Kalamas, when you know for yourselves these things are unskilful, these things when performed and undertaken conduce to ruin and sorrow, then reject them. And when you know for

yourselves these things are skilful, when performed and undertaken
conduce to well-being and happiness then live and act accordingly.'
                    (*Anguttara Nikaya, Tika Nipata, Mahavagga, Sutta*
                                        No. 65, Burtt [Ed.])

Kusala, which means skilful or helpful, and *akusala,* unskilful or
unhelpful, are the key words in Buddha's teaching. Words like 'good',
'bad', 'moral' and 'immoral' could be misleading, for they sound like
commandments and commandments don't work.

We cultivate friendliness, kindness and truthfulness because
they are skilful states, because they are helpful in moving towards
a state of happiness and freedom. And by understanding the nature
of experience and through awareness of things as they are, we free
ourselves from anger, envy, hatred and greed, not because they are
forbidden by the scriptures or some God, or that they are 'sinful', but
because they are unskilful states that drain our energy and conduce to
ruin and suffering.

In other words, all actions that have their roots in greed, hatred
and delusion that spring from self-centredness, from search for
permanence, foster the harmful delusion of selfhood, are *akusala
kamma* and they produce *dukkha.* All those actions which are rooted
in the virtues of generosity, love and wisdom are meritorious, *kusala
kamma,* and they are conducive to health and happiness and wisdom.

But these have to be considered as only suggestions or pointers
which have to be worked out with honesty by us. More importantly,
we need to understand that this ethical path would be of little meaning
and value when considered in isolation from the Buddha's teaching
on the nature of human mind and experience. The ethical path is not
merely directed towards strengthening 'the feeble altruism of human
nature', but more importantly to loosen the grip of the binary mind,
the self, so that the individual opens up to the possibility of freeing
himself or herself from fear and greed, from gods and goals, from the
dualistic mode of living in the world. The intended goal will remain
a dream, at best an ideal, unless the bourgeois mind undergoes a

transformation, unless we attain *prajna*, wisdom, or awareness of the non-dual nature of reality.

Dependent Origination

Pratitya-samutpada (Sanskrit; Pali: *Paticca-samuppada*), variously rendered into English as Conditioned Co-production, Dependent Origination, Interdependent Arising and so on, is central to Buddhist doctrine, especially to the discourse on *anatma*, the doctrine of no-self and nirvana. This is actually common to all schools of Buddhism.

> From Ignorance as condition springs Mental Formations (*samskaras*),
> From Mental Formations spring Consciousness,
> From Consciousness springs Name and Form,
> From Name and Form spring Sense Gates (the six senses, eye, ear, nose, tongue, body or touch and mind),
> From Sense Gates springs Contact,
> From Contact springs Sensation/Feeling,
> From Sensation springs Craving/Thirst,
> From Craving springs Attachment/Clinging,
> From Attachment springs Becoming,
> From Becoming springs Birth,
> From Birth springs old age and death, grief, lamentation, suffering, dejection and despair.
>
> (*Majjhima Nikaya* 89, in Rao 2018)

Although *Pratitya-samutpada* or Dependent Origination may suggest that phenomena arise together in a mutually interdependent web of cause and effect, it is not exactly a theory of causation. For if we take the twelve links literally, we fall under the illusion that things happen one after the other. Things don't happen that way and so it is not possible to say this comes first and that next; rather it is a simultaneous process. The birth of self-consciousness is the beginning of dualism, formations, name and form, 'I' and the 'other'. With the arising of the self, samsara arises, duality arises. And hence desire and fear, joy and suffering, birth and death. This is the Wheel of Life, *bhavachakra*. In actuality, it means the birth and continuity of the self.

Now, as in the Upanishads, in Buddhism too ignorance is declared as the root of sorrow, but with a difference. If, according to the Upanishads, it is the ignorance of the knowledge of Atman and Brahman that is the cause of dualism and suffering, in Buddhism, it is the conditioned knowledge itself and the search for permanence that is the cause of suffering. To put it differently, upon gaining the insight that all knowledge is conditioned, relative, or that all things are conditioned and *anicha*, transient, and have no real independent identity, we give up attachment and transform the energy of desire into awareness and understanding that everything, including the self, is fundamentally insubstantial and *sunya*, empty.

Anatmavada

In the Upanishads and the Advaita texts, the 'self' is generally used for the ego, the mind, the thinking-feeling subject, while the 'Self' refers to what is beyond the ego or the mind. It is the higher self, the Atman, which is said to be essentially the same as Brahman: the source and ground of all existence.

Buddhism deals only with the 'self', the ego, the mind, and does not talk about the higher self. The Buddhist's position is that it is pointless to discuss whether the soul (although the term 'soul' may have different connotations, it is used here to mean the higher self) exists or not, because even if it exists, it cannot be known. It is *avyakta*, inexpressible. For, in the state of being where the binary mind is absent, who can tell what it is and what it is not? Therefore, all assertions or affirmations about the soul or Atman are seen as projections of an unsecured mind, which is still part of the becoming process and hence subject to suffering and rebirth.

In other words, only the material process (of the body) and the mental process that make up the mind exist, but they do not belong to us, for they arise in dependence on conditions over which we have no control. In actuality, however, there is no centre, no self; it is only an illusion.

The self is only a word, a label we attach for the aggregate of certain physical and psychical factors, but they have no independent existence. The self or the mind is made of five elements or *skandhas*: *rupa*, *vijnana*, *vedana*, *samjna* and *samskara*; while the *rupa* stands for the physical, the rest constitute the psychical elements of the self. What we call 'self-consciousness' or 'mental dispositions' are nothing but a combination of these factors or *skandhas* and they are forever in a state of flux. There are only a series of sensations, a play of the biochemical, so to speak, which is put together by the mind into a form, a stream of ideas, and we imagine a common element or character underlying the stream and call it the Self or Atman. This is only a trick of the insecure mind to anchor itself in something it believes to be permanent and immortal.

Philosophers might argue that the very idea of flux anticipates something that is not in a state of flux; therefore it is but right and philosophically valid to ask if there is something, say, an ultimate reality, beyond. This is a classical Hindu position, deriving its authority from the Upanishadic affirmation that there is Brahman, which is beyond the phenomena. The Buddha did not speak about it, refusing to get into 'the shackles of theorizing'. He simply took a position of silence.

The Notion of Rebirth

The belief in rebirth is inconsistent with the Buddha's denial of an enduring self. It damages and defeats the core teaching of the Buddha. Rhys Davids, the noted translator and scholar, observes:

> The position is so absolute. … Yet the position is also original, so fundamentally opposed to what is usually regarded as religious belief, both in India and elsewhere, that there is a great temptation to attempt to find a loophole through which at least a covert or esoteric belief in the soul, and in the future life can be recognized, in

some sort of way, as part of so widely accepted a religious system. There is no loophole, and the efforts to find one have always met with unswerving opposition, both in the Pitakas themselves and in extra-canonical works.

(Excerpt from *Dialogues of the Buddha*, Rhys Davids [Trans.] Vol. 1, 2 and 3, 1971–73)

We may wonder, therefore, how anybody could still justifiably credit the Buddha with a belief in transmigration. Yet, not very surprisingly, several Buddhist texts do reflect this contradiction. There also have been attempts by some scholars to dig into 'primitive' Buddhism to prove that the Buddha did believe in the existence of soul, and that '*anatmavada*', soullessness, was only a later addition. Against such a theory, scholars like T.R.V. Murti would argue that for every textual citation that apparently affirms the Atman, there are ten or twenty which deny it with vehemence.

Indeed, it remains a dilemma within the enlightenment traditions of both Buddhists and Hindus to this day. Within these traditions, there are scholars, gurus and monks to whom the doctrine of rebirth is neither a contradiction nor a dilemma to be resolved. S. Radhakrishnan, for example, reasons that because of karma, people are not alike, and without an explanation to justify things, 'people would feel themselves to be victims of an immense injustice'. If even thinkers like S. Radhakrishnan find it insuperably difficult to conceive of a moral philosophy devoid of all compensatory motives, it is easy to imagine the difficulty experienced in this matter by interpreters of an earlier epoch.

What the Buddha says of the soul, the nature of the mind and experience is so transparently sound and simple that there should be no confusion about his position with regard to the idea of transmigration. He certainly did speak of 'rebirth' but not in the sense of the soul or the self going through the cycle of birth and death until it is liberated. His point was radically different, and its implication should serve as a corrective to the popular understanding of rebirth endorsed by gurus and scholars.

Once, Kutadanta, the head of the Brahmins in the village of Danamati, approached the Blessed One and asked: 'O Master, you say that beings are reborn, that they migrate in the evolution of life and are subject to the law of karma, yet you also teach the non-existence of the soul. I am confused. If I am merely a combination of the mental dispositions, merely a compound of sensations and ideas and desires, then what happens when I die? Do I cease to exist, or something in me survives?'

> The Buddha said: 'O Brahmin, *there is only rebirth of character, but no transmigration of a self.* Your thought-forms reappear, but there is no ego-entity transferred.
>
> 'You are still cleaving to self. You are anxious about heaven but you seek the pleasures of self in heaven. You seek the life that is of the mind. Where self is, truth cannot be; yet when truth comes, self will disappear ... self is death and truth is life. The cleaving to self is a perpetual dying, while moving in the truth is partaking of nirvana, which is life everlasting.'
>
> (Carus [Ed.] 2003)

There is no ambiguity in what the Buddha asserts: there is no soul or self there to transmigrate; it is the 'character' that transmigrates. In effect, what it means is that nothing of our thoughts and deeds disappear without leaving their traces behind, and that the 'good' and 'evil' so resulting recoil, not upon the doer but upon humankind. In other words, there are only thoughts; the self or the 'I' emerges by way of identifying itself (selectively) with thoughts, which in actuality do not solely belong to the individual. It is like an individual getting hooked to a desire, depending upon his disposition, and calling it his own. The self is a continuity of thought and not a unity, and this process of continuity is the wheel of becoming, which is only another name for rebirth or reincarnation.

The Pathless Land

For 500 years after the Buddha's death there were no statues of him nor pictures. Only the Bodhi Tree was depicted in Buddhist temples, symbolizing enlightenment. Siddhartha Gautama, as a karmic self, upon coming into the state of nirvana, had disappeared.

For nearly three centuries after the First Turning of the Wheel of Law, the way of the Buddha had remained predominantly a spiritual cult, with literally hundreds of monasteries, viharas, spread across the Gangetic plain. It was under King Ashoka (c. 268–232 BCE) that the way grew into a full-fledged religion, but at a price. Compromises were made at the cost of it losing its originality, and from the back door, as it were, were brought in all those beliefs and practices that the Buddha had denied of having any spiritual significance.

Joseph Campbell writes, 'The Rock Edicts of Ashoka, which are the earliest Buddhist writings we possess, no mention whatsoever is made of the doctrine of no-self, ignorance, and extinction, but only of heaven, good works, merit, and the soul.' (Campbell 2000) The way began to be interpreted in terms of 'performance' or 'engagement' with society rather than 'cessation' and 'disengagement'. It was this shift, one might say, from an apparently negative approach to a 'liberal' and positive approach and the portrayal of the Buddha as the Compassionate One, Bodhisattva, preaching the Dhamma as a way to end suffering that was instrumental in spreading Buddhism across the world.

The way of the Buddha is neither a historical 'revelation' nor a 'covenant', but a *yana*, a vehicle, a journey to be undertaken by an individual with no external aid to reach the shore of nirvana. There is no God, the Absolute or the Ultimate, no model of perfection, no soul, no paradise or beyond, because they do not exist. These are concepts and are only our converted fears and desires, the inventions of an insecure mind in search of permanence. God is a relief, a solace, security or an anchor we seek against an apparently chaotic world. It is comfortable to believe that there is a supreme power out there that has created us and the universe, and that the power, like a father figure, will take care of us, provided of course we surrender ourselves to it. About such a God, created in our own image, with likes and dislikes similar to our own, writes Karen Armstrong:

> It is all too easy to make 'him' endorse some of our most uncharitable, selfish and lethal hopes, fears and prejudices. This limited God has thus contributed to some of the worst religious atrocities in history. The Buddha would have described belief in a deity who gives a seal of sacred approval to our own selves as 'unskilful': it could only embed the believer in the damaging and dangerous egotism that he or she was supposed to transcend. (Armstrong 2006)

The Buddha was merciless. He did not bring the dead back to life but taught us to reckon with it as a fact of life and not escape into beliefs which have no basis in reality. He refused to offer false promises, prop or sugar-coated pills to comfort us, or allow us any childish desires. He would not allow us to cling to any lie, howsoever consoling, for a lie is a lie and it can only produce false consciousness and thereby conflict and sorrow.

The truth has to be brought to us, no matter how hard and unpalatable it is. In effect, the Buddha offered the possibility of freedom from the tyranny of gods, from the authority of the Word, from illusory goals. And once we are courageous enough to see the truth of it all, we realize that there is compassion in such a teaching; it is a benediction.

Four

One Source, Two Streams

With the exception of Tantra Yoga which remains rather esoteric and sequestered to this day, we could, broadly speaking, say that there are principally two streams of spiritualities, namely, Buddhist and Hindu. All other Indian spiritualities (we are not considering here spiritualities inspired by Judaism, Christianity and Islam, since they don't come under the scope of this narrative), which are many and varied, speak in the idiom of one of the two, but some may use both in varied and complex ways. For instance, the Shiva *saranas* (devotees) of the twelfth-century Karnataka spoke of *bayalu* ('empty space' or 'field' in Kannada) or *sunya*, a Buddhist concept for emptiness, and Shiva (which may not necessarily refer to the Puranic Shiva or Shankara, but to the notion of the Absolute Infinite Principle or Transcendent Creative Force) in their *vachanas*, prose poems, and the term nirvana too was used interchangeably as a term for liberation.

The fact that Hinduism and Buddhism have shared the same culture and a common language (Sanskrit) for the last 2,600 years, has led many to think that Buddhist and Hindu doctrines are essentially the same. This is not entirely true, although there may be an appreciable overlap of theories and practices. Sometimes both traditions may even speak the same language or use the same concepts but with different meanings and consequences.

For instance, both Advaita Vedanta and Buddhism see ignorance or *avidya* as the root cause of sorrow. However, Advaita Vedanta defines *avidya* as the ignorance of the knowledge of the unity of Atman and Brahman, and identifies that as the cause of duality and suffering; while Buddhism defines *avidya* as conditioned knowledge (conceptual construction) itself and states the search for permanence is the cause of attachment and suffering.

Both Advaita Vedanta and Buddhism may assert that the Truth, the Real or the Absolute is indescribable, inexpressible, and no category of thought applies to it. And they both may concur that it is *avidya* that invests the Absolute with *nama-roopa*, name and form, conceptualizes what cannot be expressed, what is *paramartha satya* or beyond phenomena. However, although Brahman is not considered as an object of knowledge in Advaita Vedanta, there is this stubborn insistence that it is knowable, realizable, for It or the Real is *svamprakasha*, and self-evident, *svasamvedya*, self-revealed.

The Madhyamikas maintain that there simply is no two or *advaya*. There is nothing outside of the conditioned physical and mental elements that constitute our being. There is no Higher or Ultimate Reality, it is only a view which can neither be affirmed nor denied, neither true nor false, it is just that these concepts are not to be found. There is no two or *advaya*, but to say there is *one* would imply there is two or more. Therefore, to avoid such an ambiguity or epistemological traps, the Madhyamikas declare that Reality, like nirvana, is empty, *sunya*, void, which is not the opposite of something else. That is to say, the Real or *tatva* is neither one nor many, neither permanent nor momentary, neither subject nor object; rather, It (*tatva*) is the indeterminate, the mystery, the unknown and the unknowable. Any attempt to conceptualize It as 'this' or 'not this' is a case of *vikalpa*, imagination, it is unproductive, a futile exercise, a *viparyasa*, a cognitive distortion or futility.

Nagarjuna

Asanga, Vasubandhu, Nagarjuna, Chandrakirti, Shantideva and Atisha are some of the most distinguished and widely read Buddhist masters in history. Among them, Nagarjuna stands out as a great mystic philosopher, who has had a tremendous impact on not only Buddhist philosophy but also on Hindu thought over centuries, and now, on modern Western thinkers. During his time and even later, however, many devout Buddhists considered him to be the second Buddha who, in the words of K. Satchidananda Murty:

> once again set in motion the wheel of Dhamma. There was a fresh flowering of Buddhism: certain old and basic ideas were reaffirmed, others reinterpreted, clarified and amplified, and some new concepts evolved ... and in course of time disseminated all over India and deep into Central Asia, China, Korea, Japan and Tibet. (Satchidananda Murty 1971)

We know very little of Nagarjuna's actual life. The Chinese and Tibetan biographies, composed many centuries after his death, are the only records but they tend to be hagiographical, suffused with myth and metaphor. According to some Tibetan accounts, Nagarjuna was born in 482 CE, Chinese tradition believed it was in 212 CE, and Mahayana texts simply state that he was born 1,200 years after the Buddha's death. These sources are not unanimous as to where Nagarjuna was born, either. The ancient kingdoms of Vidarbha and Videha, and areas in the modern Indian states of Andhra Pradesh, Tamil Nadu and even Karnataka have been identified as where his birthplace might have possibly been. However, from legends, combined with the texts reasonably attributed to him, we may yet gain a fairly balanced portrait of Nagarjuna's incredible life and his remarkable contribution to the philosophical traditions.

Nagarjuna was born a 'Hindu', probably into a Brahmin family in an area that is now part of the Indian state of Andhra Pradesh. At birth it was predicted that he would die an early death, so his parents are said to have admitted the sickly boy to a Buddhist order. As fate would have it, his health improved and he went on to live a long and great life.

By the time Nagarjuna grew to be a sharp, intelligent young man, many competing schools of thought and exciting philosophical debates had spread throughout north India, especially between Hindu and Buddhist thinkers. Buddhism was probably a dominant and influential philosophy by then, alongside competing schools of thought such as Sankhya, Yoga, Vaisesika and Nyaya. Nagarjuna deeply engaged with not only these different schools of thought, but also with sects within the Buddhist stream.

Going by the available records we could safely state that he was the author of many philosophical works. His seminal work *Mulamadhyamakakarika* (Fundamental Verses on the Middle Way) was followed by *Sunyatasaptati* (Seventy Verses on Emptiness), *Yuktisastika* (Sixty Verses on Reasoning), *Vyavaharasiddhi* (Proof of Convention) and a few more works addressing and challenging many a philosophical issue of his time. More importantly, his work carried forward the Buddha's revolutionary insights into the human condition.

We cannot, however, say with any certainty from which aspect of the Buddha's teaching Nagarjuna would have drawn inspiration for his *sunyavada*. Could it be from the Buddha's dialogue with Ananda about 'emptiness'? To the question, 'It is said that the world is empty, the world is empty, lord. In what respect is it said that the world is empty?' the Buddha responds thus: 'The eye, ear, nose, tongue, the body (all sense experiences) and ideas, or intellect consciousness are empty of a self or of anything pertaining to a self. Thus it is said that the world is empty.' (*Samyutta Nikaya* 35–85; *Sunna Satta*, Bhikku, Olendzki and Buddharakkhita [Trans.])

In effect, the Buddha was trying to underline the fact that all experiences are sense experiences, an interpretation of the world. Formations. With no formations taking place the 'mind' is empty, not in the sense that there is no world, but in the sense there is no thinker, no interpreter, therefore no formations, no experience at all.

But then, it is quite likely that Nagarjuna's notion of 'emptiness' and his contestation of all theories Brahminical and contemporary Buddhist thought was inspired and informed by his own inward understanding—that is, the understanding of the binary nature of the mind and the fragmentary nature of all experiences, which enabled him to have the perception of 'emptiness' and thereby develop his 'four-corner' negation of all the metaphysical schools of philosophy that were at the time flourishing around him.

It's important to note here that Nagarjuna's philosophy—rather, his anti-philosophy, armed with notions of *sunyata* or emptiness—worked like a double-edged sword to deconstruct all systems of thought and helped construct the vocabulary and character of many philosophies and spiritualities that came after him in India.

Nagarjuna also offered two views of reality as a sort of corollary to his *sunyavada*. He distinguished between propositions that have the truth of ultimate meaning (*paramarthasatta*), and those that are employed for a practical purpose, namely, conventional truth (*samvritisatta*).

Paramarthasatta, or supreme truth, is the truth of the void or emptiness, the truth that all our views, our very perception or experience of reality, are shaped by the knowledge we have acquired, that they are mere constructs without any basis. Understanding this truth would enable us to free ourselves from attachments and let go all views. *Samvritisatta*, conventional truth, is the truth we use to transact in our social interactions. We need to accept the conventions of the logocentric world view to live in the world but with the awareness that they don't have a permanent basis.

Selected verses from *Mulamadhyamkakarika*

I bow down to the most sublime of speakers, the completely awakened one who taught contingency (no cessation, no birth, no

annihilation, no permanence, no coming, no going, no difference,
no identity) to ease fixations.

Like a dream, like a magician's illusion, like a city of *gandharvas*,
likewise birth and likewise remaining, likewise perishing are taught.

When nirvana is not born and samsara not eliminated, then
what is samsara? And what is considered as nirvana?

It is said that 'there is a self,' but 'non-self' too is taught. The
Buddhas also teach there is nothing which is 'neither self nor non-
self.' Fixations are stopped by emptiness.

Do not say 'empty,' or 'not empty,' or 'both,' or 'neither': these
are mentioned for the sake of conventional understanding.

                                                      (Batchelor 2000)

Reading the above selected verses, you'll remember the Buddha's
refusal to go into the metaphysical question about the origin of things,
into what he called 'the shackles of theorizing' and upon which
maintained a position of silence, simply because these questions could
not be answered. And he compared a person convinced he could find
the answers to such ultimate questions to a mortally wounded person
dying from arrow-delivered poison, demanding to know everything
about the whys and the wherefores of the situation. This refusal to
answer metaphysical questions in pursuit of nirvana eventually came
to be known as *chatuskoti* or 'four error' denial.

So it appears that Nagarjuna only revived and refined the 'four error'
method into a sort of logic machine to 'deconstruct' metaphysical
constructs, which had been growing in influence both in the Buddhist
and Hindu schools of thought. He deployed this technique of four-
corner negation to expose the limits of epistemology, and demonstrate
the futility of all attempts to know what cannot be known. In effect, his
question was: when there is no thought, no self, who is to say reality is
this or that, is or is not?

The negation of positions was no position just as the criticism of
theories was not another theory, but an awareness of the conditioned
nature of all positions and views. It was not a philosophical treatise
aimed at challenging and destroying other views, but to exhaust and

reject all views as obstacles on the path to nirvana, which is no path at all. In other words, Nagarjuna's main concern was to demonstrate the fallacy of clinging to views, however profound, or apparently valid, and to let go all our concepts and ideas, including the concept of *sunyata* and nirvana. In his *Mulamadhyamakakarika* in particular, Nagarjuna shows a masterly approach to the problematics of *sunyata* and nirvana.

But, Nagarjuna warns: do not say 'empty', or 'not empty', or both, or neither: these are mentioned for the sake of (conventional) understanding. For, 'Like a snake when it is not properly grasped, or a magical spell when it is not properly executed, voidness when it is not properly apprehended can be the ruin of a person of weak intelligence' (Ibid.).

Thought brings in the thinker and creates the world. Thought, thinker and world are not different. Thought is sound, word, matter, and the word is the world. Without the word there is no world. It does not mean that the world, with its mountains and seas, flora and fauna and millions of living creatures, does not exist; rather, it is filtered through our binary mind, our divided consciousness—'world' is an interpretation. For all experiences are sense experiences, an interpretation of the world. Formations! But when no formations are taking place the 'mind' remains empty, in the sense the thinker, the interpreter, is absent, therefore there is no formation, no experience at all. All reference points have disappeared; in short, the binary mind has ceased to be. *Sunyata!* Emptiness!

Gaudapada

Gaudapada (c. sixth century CE) is considered to be the *paramaguru* in the tradition of the Advaita Vedanta school of Hindu philosophy. He was the teacher of Govinda, who in turn was the teacher of Shankara.

In some of his texts, Shankara himself affirms this and quotes and refers to Gaudapada as the teacher of the Advaita Vedanta *sampradaya* or tradition.

Gaudapada's *Mandukya Karika*, also known as the *Agama Shastra*, is the earliest available systematic treatise on Advaita Vedanta. Actually it is a treatise in verse form on the *Mandukya Upanishad*, consisting of thirteen verses, wherein Gaudapada goes on to establish the non-dual nature of reality.

The excerpts from the *Karika* given below should give the readers a sense of his style which is quite distinct from the Mahayana Buddhist style of dialectic. Interestingly he mentions the Buddha with reverence, advances arguments similar to Vasubandhu and Nagarjuna in the course of his exposition to point out and explain the illusory nature of our phenomenal experience, but only to ultimately establish Atman-Brahman as the only reality.

The following translated, edited verses from *Mandukya Karika* have been sourced from different texts to give a feel of Gaudapada's philosophy.

Visva is all-pervading and experiences the gross. *Taijasa* experiences the subtle. *Prajna* is a mass of awareness. It is one who is known in all three states. *Visva* and *Taijasa* are conditioned by both cause and effect, *prajna* by cause alone. Neither exists in *turiya*. Non-cognition of duality is common to the *prajna* and *turiya*. But *prajna* is associated with the causal state of sleep, and that does not exist in *turiya*.

~

The mind should be absorbed in OM. OM is Brahman, the fearless. One who is absorbed in OM is totally devoid of fear. OM is truly the beginning, the middle and the end of all. Knowing OM in this way, one attains immediately.

The mystic syllable 'om' is linked to three states of consciousness: the state of waking consciousness (*jagrat*), where we experience externally through our mind and sense organs; the state of dreaming (*svapna*), where inward experiences are available; and dreamless sleep (*susupti*), where consciousness seems to gather in upon itself and lie quiet. In all three states the self or ego remains very much active and is the basis of all the experiences. That is to say, divided consciousness or the self is the constant factor in all the three states.

Turiya or *turiya avastha* is the fourth state, the substratum of the other three states, and yet it is a state devoid of fear, beyond the state of sleep or dream. It is self-luminous, pure consciousness. It is the state of Brahman.

Self-luminous Atman, by the power of its own *Maya* imagines itself in itself. He alone is aware of the objects. This is the conclusion of the Vedanta.

Just as in the dark a rope whose nature has not been fully ascertained is imagined to be various different things such as a snake, in exactly the same way the Self is imagined in various different ways.

When the rope is realized to be a rope, all illusions about it cease, and only the rope remains. Realization of the Self is just the same.

What does not exist in the beginning and does not exist at the end certainly does not exist in the middle! In other words, the world is imagined and unreal. It does not mean there is no world or existence; rather, the meaning or reading we put on the world and life is mind-made, *kalpita*, imagined, in that sense an illusion.

Later, Shankara was to pick on these verses and declare that the material world, its distinctness, the individuality of the living creatures, and even Ishvara (the Supreme Lord) itself, were all untrue, maya, a mere dream, a grand illusion. We could understand this in two ways:

(i)   in the light of the ultimate experience, the Brahman, where
       the binary mind goes quiet and so the interpretation of the
       world and life ceases, the world is seen as an illusion; and,

(ii)   as *maya*, which means 'to measure'. Now, to measure anything
       there has to be a space, and a point of reference. The self takes
       its birth in that space, and that is the *point*, and with reference
       to it we create another point and try to measure. Anything
       we measure or experience from that point is only relative, not
       absolute, but to think of it in absolute, permanent terms is
       an illusion. In simpler terms, the world is what it is, forever
       in flux and we can never experience or understand it in the
       fishbowl of our mind; rather, what we see and experience
       is only a 'construct' put together by the knowledge we have
       devised over thousands of years, but has no basis in reality.

So, it is in that sense, almost in the style of Nagarjuna, Gaudapada
concludes, 'There is no dissolution, no origination, none in bondage,
none possessed of the means of liberation, none desirous of liberation,
and none liberated. This is the ultimate truth.'

Nothing comes into existence, though it may well seem to come
into existence.

   The Self is spoken of as existing in individual souls just as space
exists encompassed by a pot. Its existence in composite things is
like the space in pots.

   When the pot is smashed, the pot-space merges totally with
space—in the same way souls merge in the Self.

   On realization that the Self is the Real, thinking ceases: it
becomes non-mind; in the absence of anything to perceive there
is no perception.

~

   It is totally ineffable and utterly inconceivable, completely
peaceful, eternally radiant, ecstatic, immutable, fearless.

Gaudapada uses the analogy of space and pots to explain the relationship, rather the essential unity between the *jiva* or the individual self and Brahman or the Cosmic Self. The Cosmic Self is like the sky or space which is all-pervasive, formless, and the *jiva* or individual self is like the space in jars or pots. Just as space is enclosed in a pot, so is the Cosmic Self manifested as the individual self. When the pot is broken, the space inside the broken pot automatically merges with the space outside. Similarly, when ignorance is destroyed by *jnana*, *jiva*s merge into the Cosmic Self or Brahman. That is to say, when the individual self transcends the superimposed separateness and realizes its essential unity with the Cosmic Self, it becomes one with *It*.

Spaces in pots may differ in form, function and name, but still there's no difference in space. Likewise, though the *jiva* may differ in form, function and name, still there's no difference in Atman. Just as space undergoes no change, no modification, there's no change nor modification as regards the *jiva*, for both the *jiva* and the Atman by their very nature are calm from the beginning, unborn and merged with Brahman.

The Awareness is without frontiers, unborn, immortal and omniscient. Gaudapada calls it Contactless Awareness or *Asparsha* Yoga. It is a transcendental state in which the mind is stripped of all desires and affliction. Contact with sense organs results in the identification of the Self with the non-Self, causing bondage. We perceive and experience life and the world through our senses; rather, the binary mind, by way of interpreting sense experiences, constructs the world in which we live. That's how maya or conditioning sets in and we begin to see, smell, touch, hear and feel the world through the mind. Thereafter, there is no pure sense experience but only interpretations of sense experience in terms of likes and dislikes, in terms of pairs of opposites, in terms of knowledge we have gathered. This mechanism is nullified in the state of Pure Consciousness or the state of *turiya*; once the mind is put in its place and goes quiet, stops interpreting the senses, there is *turiya*.

In other words, through *Asparsha* Yoga or the yoga of non-contact of the mind with any object, through *viveka* (discrimination), *vairagya* (spirit of renunciation) and *abhyasa* (repeated efforts), you are able to see through the world of constructs and its falsity and in so doing you transcend the make-believe world. The fire dies out when there is no fuel; similarly through *viveka* and *jnana* the mind goes quiet and you step into the state of pure consciousness, *turiya*. In (*turiya avastha*), Gaudapada says:

> All the multiple objects, comprising the movable and the immovable, are perceived by the mind alone. But when duality is never perceived, the mind ceases to act, it ceases to be the mind.

Alatashanti Prakarana—Quenching the Firebrand

If the cause is produced from the effect, it can never be established. How can a cause, itself not established, give birth to an effect?

If the cause is dependent on the effect and the effect is dependent on the cause, then which comes first for the other to come from it?

~

As a moving firebrand appears as a curve, consciousness when set in motion appears as the knower and the known.

As the firebrand when not in motion is free from appearances and from becoming, so too consciousness when not in motion is free of appearances and becoming.

When the firebrand is in motion, the appearances do not come from somewhere else; when it is motionless, the appearances do not go somewhere else, nor do they go into it.

For so long as there is attachment to cause-and-effect there is samsara; once the attachment ends, there is no attachment to samsara.

Gaudapada refutes Sankhya's theory of causality. There is no cause per se, nor effect, as such. Cause itself is born as effect; rather, cause-effect is a continuum. And he proposes the theory of *Ajativada* or non–

origination to explain this conundrum. Gaudapada's position is built on the premise that nothing is ever born, nothing is created whatsoever and there is no transactional reality either. The argument is simple: when the Self is the only reality and is eternal, then, whatever it is that seems to exist apart from the non-dual Self must be unreal, maya, and hence non-existent.

Consciousness is the only reality but appears as objects, like a rotating burning stick—*alatachakra*—by the power of maya. Buddhists used the metaphor of *alatachakra*—a burning firebrand that is waved in a circle—to insist that the impression of a continuous circle is an illusion. It is plainly an error to see the burning circle as having any *svabhava* or nature of its own.

Gaudapada overturns this Buddhist metaphor to assert that the burning brand is itself the *substratum* of its momentary spatial positions and the illusion of a burning circle caused by waving the brand. Hence, according to him, even if the burning circle is an illusion, its *svabhava* is nothing other than that of the burning brand. He uses Buddhist metaphor and terminology to come to Vedantic conclusions regarding the ultimate presence of Atman-Brahman as the substratum (*adhishthana*) of all experience—and thereby asserting that Atman-Brahman is the only reality, unborn, omniscient, eternal, and it is our attachment to unreality that brings in the duality that causes bondage, fear and sorrow.

Five

Songs in Dualism and Non-Dualism

Bhagavad Gita

The Bhagavad Gita, probably composed between 200 BCE–100 CE, is a 700-verse text introduced in the *Bhishma Parva* of the Mahabharata. It is set in the form of a dialogue between Pandava prince Arjuna and his guide and charioteer Krishna. It is a stupendous attempt to integrate some of the most influential schools of thought, such as Sankhya and the Upanishads, and concepts such as yoga, dharma, karma, and moksha through the *jnana*, bhakti and karma marg. It is not out of place here to state that the Gita marks a period of consolidation in the development of Hinduism in its interaction and debates with Buddhism, Jainism, Ajivika and other schools of thought. That such a profound integral philosophy should be set in the middle of a battlefield remains something of an enigma, although many commentators have tried to resolve this riddle by interpreting it as an allegory for the 'war within', or as an allegory for the philosophical and ethical struggles of human life.

However, the Gita is certainly a grand, sealing synthesis of Hindu spiritualities and it is so rich and complex and multilayered that, over the centuries, numerous thinkers, gurus and writers have written commentaries on it with widely differing views on the central message of the text. While the Advaita Vedantins see the non-dualism of Atman and Brahman as its essence, the Vishishtadvaitins see Atman and Brahman as both different and non-different, and the Dvaitins see both as different and distinct.

On the whole, the Bhagavad Gita is a vital contribution to the Hindu way of life and has received the status of a scripture, rather a *sruti* (revelation, or 'what is heard'), among the Hindus. The text brilliantly combines many different elements from Sankhya and Vedanta philosophy and yet its emphasis on bhakti as a way to God and liberation is often seen as a central path in Hinduism. Theism and the transcendentalism of the Upanishads converge, and a God of personal characteristics is identified with the Brahman of the Vedic tradition. In other words, the Gita, while occasionally hinting at the impersonal Brahman as the ultimate goal, revolves around the relationship between the Self and a personal God or *saguna* Brahman. It is an inspiring synthesis of *jnana*, bhakti, and desireless or selfless action as an antidote to Arjuna's despair, and a clear way to freedom.

The following selection of edited verses is based on Ramesh Menon's (2016) translation of *Srimad Bhagavad Gita*.

I. The Despair of Arjuna

After the failure of Lord Krishna's peace mission, the Pandavas were left with no alternative other than to fight for their rightful share of the Kuru Kingdom. And so the great Mahabharata war between the Pandavas and the Kauravas took place on the holy plains of Kurukshetra. All the famous warriors from both sides assembled on the battlefield.

Arjuna, along with Krishna, as his charioteer, arrived on the scene in a magnificent chariot yoked by white horses. Conches blared forth, announcing the commencement of the battle. Arjuna requested Krishna to place his chariot between the two armies so that he could survey the battlefield and his opponents. As they moved into the middle of the field, Arjuna beheld fathers and grandfathers, teachers and uncles, fathers-in-law, grandsons, relatives and friends on both sides and was suddenly struck by despair.

Should he participate in this terrible carnage? Was it dharma to destroy one's kith and kin for the sake of kingdom and power? Would it not be much better to surrender everything in favour of his enemies and retire in peace? As these thoughts swirled through his mind, he turned to Krishna seeking guidance and enlightenment.

Arjuna said:
I see my kinsmen, Krishna, gathered avid for war.
My limbs turn weak, my mouth is parched;
and my body trembles, and my hair stands on end.

The Gandiva slips from my hands and my skin burns;
and my anxiety I cannot control and the fierce whirling of my mind;

I do not want victory, Krishna, neither kingdom nor happiness;
for what a kingdom, Govinda, what for pleasures or even life?

I do not want to kill them even if they kill me, Madhusudana:
not for lordship over the three worlds, what then of this earth?

Killing Dhritarashtra's sons, what joy will we get, Janardana?
We will only find sin ourselves if we slay these sinners.

Even if these, their hearts ruined by greed, see no

atrocity in destroying the clan and no crime in harming friends,
why don't we realise that we must desist from this sin—

With the destruction of the clan, ancient family traditions are lost
forever;
when dharma is no more, evil takes all that race.

When adharma rules, Krishna, the women of the clan become loose;
when the women are depraved, the varnas (castes) become mixed.

Crossbreeding only casts into hell those that ruin the clan, and the
clan, itself;
their manes surely fall, for the ritual of the offering of rice-balls and
holy water having disappeared.

Through the sins of these clan-destroyers, defilers of the varnas,
lost are sacred traditions of caste and family, forever.

Ah, what a great sin we have decided to commit:
that from greed for the pleasures of kingdom, we are ready to kill
our kinsmen.

While I am unarmed and unresisting,
let Dhritarashtra's sons kill me on the field of war—that I could
still bear.

Saying this, Arjuna sat down in the back of that chariot, in war; he
cast aside his
arrows and bow, his heart plunged in profound anguish.

There are two kinds of despair here. One, the despair over the
prospect of killing kith and kin for the sake of the kingdom, which
suddenly seems a terrible sin; two, despair over the possible deaths of

tens of thousands of men on both sides, which would lead to destruction of families, corruption of women, of religious rites, confusion of castes, and intermingling of castes—*varnasankara*. This second cause of despair, about the fear of the destruction of *varnashrama* dharma, is hardly mentioned, let alone discussed by most commentators.

No text or narrative, including the spiritual and philosophical, is free of (the dominant) social and political interests and anxieties of the age when it was composed. The last few verses (39–44) clearly betray the 'Brahminical' ideology with regard to the preservation of the caste system. Possibly, elements supporting *varnashrama* dharma were interpolated at some stage by Brahminical hands, which spoils the otherwise profound philosophy of the Gita. Though we do not go to the Gita to understand the social reality of the times, nor to seek a social philosophy, we cannot escape the fact that the insertion of the then prevalent caste rules and the Brahminical injunction about *varnashrama* dharma would have alienated huge sections of society.

It is when you come across such verses even in profoundly non-dual philosophical texts that go against the rights and dignity of communities and peoples that you are persuaded to think that perhaps we need to clean these texts of verses (interpolations) that are patently against human rights and social justice.

II. Sankhya Yoga

Krishna rebukes Arjuna for his dejection and exhorts him to get over his mental conflict and fight. And then he goes on to explain the immortal nature of the Atman and expounds the importance of the performance of action without expectation of the fruit of action. From here on, the dialogue moves beyond the battlefield of Kurukshetra and turns philosophical and deeply spiritual.

Arjuna said:
We do not know which of these would be better for us:

that we conquer them or that they vanquish us!

The weakness of pity besieges my nature;
my mind confounded about what dharma is, I ask you –
tell me what is unquestionably best for me. I am your disciple;
teach me, I submit to you.

The Gracious Lord said:
You grieve for those not worth grieving over,
and argue as if you were a wise man discoursing;
not for the dead or for the living do the wise grieve.

Surely, at no time ever did I not exist, or you, or all these kings;
and for sure, not in any future to come will any of us cease to exist.

Just as the indweller passes, in the body, through childhood, youth
and old age,
the soul also assumes new bodies; the wise are not perplexed by
this—
Never does the unreal exist, and the real never ceases to be;
of both these, surely, the end has been seen by seers of truth.

But, know, what pervades all this is immortal;
that everlasting Being no one can destroy.

Mortal these bodies; eternal, it is said, the embodied soul;
It is immortal, ineffable—so, fight Arjuna!

He that thinks of it as being a killer and he who thinks This is slain:
both do not know—it neither kills nor is slain.

This is not born nor ever dies, not in the past, present or future;

un-born, changeless, eternal it is, primeval; it is not killed when the
body is slain.

Knowing this is indestructible, constant, un-born, immutable,
how does a man kill anyone, Partha, whom does he kill?

Even as a man abandons old, tattered clothes and puts on other
fresh ones, the
indweller leaves old, worn bodies and enters other new ones.

Weapons cannot pierce *it*; fire cannot burn it;
water does not wet it, nor dry it, the wind.

Not pierceable, not burnable, not wettable, and also not dryable –
permanent, ubiquitous, abiding, invariable, eternal.

So, knowing it is such, you must not despair.
and if you think that it is constantly being born and continually
dying,
even then, mighty-armed, you ought not to despair.

For him who is born death is certain, and birth is certain for who
dies;
so, over what you believe to be ineluctable, you should not despair.

These are some of the oft-quoted and celebrated verses from the
text, which speak about the immortal nature of the Atman: 'This Self
cannot be cut, burnt, wetted nor dried up. It is eternal, all-pervading,
stable, ancient and immovable.'

Unfortunately, spiritual discourses often indulge in privileging
Atman over the body and the body is regarded as an enemy or obstacle
to be overcome in the spiritual quest, while enlightenment or nirvana
is viewed as separate from the body or unrelated to the body. This is

not true. This dichotomy must end. We need to transcend this division and see the body and the self together as a unitary phenomenon. We need to revise this view and overcome the duality implied in it in the light of our new understanding. That is, the body, too, is immortal. There are some cases where this is brought out, for instance, in a Vedic chant recited during funerals which suggests the enduring nature of the body:

'May your eye go to the sun, your life's breath to the wind. Go to the sky or to earth as is your nature; or to the waters, if that is your fate. Take root in the plants with your limbs' (in Dharwadker [Ed.] 2001).

Taking cue from this Vedic hymn, as it were, and giving a scientific view of the immortality of life, of the body, in his popular book *The Origin of Life*, Paul Davies (2003), writes:

Since the Earth formed, its material has not remained inert. Carbon, hydrogen, nitrogen and oxygen are continually recycled. When an organism dies, its atoms are released back into the environment. Some of them eventually become part of other organisms. Simple statistics reveal that your body contains about one atom of carbon from every milligram of dead material more than 1000 years old. This simple fact has amazing implications. You are, for example, host to a billion or so atoms that once belonged to Jesus Christ, or Julius Caesar, or the Buddha, or the tree that the Buddha once sat beneath.

Here is Sri Aurobindo's line of reasoning with regard to the body-mind problematic:

In the past the spiritual seekers regarded the body as an obstacle, as something to be overcome and discarded than as an instrument of spiritual perfection and a field of the spiritual change—

If our seeking is for a perfection of the being, the physical part of it cannot be left aside. The body is the material basis, the

instrument which we have to use. *Sariramkhalu dharma-
sadhanam*—the body is the means of fulfilment of dharma. A total
perfection is the ultimate aim which we set before us, for our ideal
is the Divine Life ... in the condition of the material universe.
(Aurobindo 1971b)

In fact, we shall see that within the Gita, Chapter XI, 'The
Yoga of the Vision of the Cosmic Form' or '*Vishwaroopadarshana*',
establishes the immortal nature of the body. But we shall come to
this aspect later. We return to the discussion on the battlefield as
Krishna continues to remind Arjuna that the performance of action,
without expectation or attachment to its fruits, is the path that leads
to 'evenness of mind'.

Lord Krishna said:
You surely have the right to do your karma, not to its fruit, at
any time;
the fruit of karma should not become your motive, nor be attached
to sloth.

Steadfast in yoga, do your duty, renouncing attachment, Arjuna;
success and failure becoming the same: that equanimity is
called yoga.

Performing karma, mind devoted, but its fruit renouncing,
wise men,
from the bondage of birth entirely freed, come to the place of
no sickness.

When beyond this chaos of illusions your mind passes,
then you will arrive at indifference to what you have heard and
what you will hear.

Arjuna said:

How can you tell a man of resolution, who is founded in samadhi,
Kesava?
How does a realized one speak? How does he sit, how walk?

The Gracious Lord said:
When a man abandons all desires, Partha, which spring in
the mind,
and gratifies himself in just his soul,
a man of steady wisdom, a *sthithaprajna* is said to be.

Unaffected by adversity, whose mind, in fortune unmoved to desire;
free of passion, fear and anger, a true muni is called.

Who everywhere is without affection; who, upon finding fortune
or misfortune,
neither exults nor feels aversion, his wisdom is founded.

And when, like a tortoise completely retracts all its limbs, a man
does his senses from their objects of desire, his wisdom is founded.

Of even, son of Kunti, a restrained man,
his turbid senses forcibly ravish his mind.

All the senses restraining, the sage sits intent on me;
for, one whose senses are tamed, his wisdom is established.

Dwelling on the objects of desire, a man becomes attached to
these;
from attachment is born desire; from desire anger arises.

From rage comes upheaval; from turmoil, the wavering memory;
after the loss of memory, destruction of the mind;
when the mind is destroyed, he dies.

Emancipated from attraction and revulsion,
but going among the objects of the senses,
tamed and ruled by the Atman, he attains grace.

So, he, Partha, who withdraws completely
the senses from the objects of sensuality, his wisdom is profound.

When night comes for all creatures, is when the *sthithaprajna*
awakes; what is waking for the rest, that is night for the visionary.

Always still, the ocean, though being filled by water entering into it;
equally, he who contains all desires entering him,
acquires peace, not he who submits to desire.

The above verses describe the state of being of a *sthithaprajna*,
one who is of steady wisdom. It is the state of being of a sage who
has stepped away from samsara, from all kinds of attachments, and
lives in a state of unitary consciousness. Krishna tells Arjuna that
a *sthithaprajna* will not be affected by adversity and will have no fear or
anger. He will take things as they come, and will not have any likes and
dislikes. He will neither hug the world nor hate it.

Like a tortoise withdrawing itself into its shell, it is said, a sage
withdraws his senses and remains stable-minded. Perhaps 'stable-
minded' is not the right description, since the mind, by its very nature,
is never stable. We need to relook at the concept in the light of what
the sages themselves have said of their state of being.

The senses are involved in looking, touching, smelling, tasting and
hearing, and the binary mind is all the time involved in translating these
sense perceptions in terms of the experiencing structure, in terms of
likes and dislikes. This interpretation of the senses in terms of likes and
dislikes has come to an end for a sage, because the binary or divided
mind has dissolved in the unitary consciousness. So a sage is not
affected or ruffled by emotions. That is not to say the sage would not
respond to situations; rather, the sage would respond spontaneously

to a particular situation, and it is a total and complete action with no residue left behind. It is not as if a sage never gets angry, he does, but within a given situation and not carried over. As Nisargadatta Maharaj has said:

> Normally people suppose that a *jnani* should suppress all the emotional outbursts. That is not correct. With your standpoint in the Absolute, you are not concerned with the feelings and instinctive outbursts of the apparatus. A *jnani* does not volitionally participate, it is spontaneously happening; while an ignorant person is deeply involved in that, he assumes everything is real. (Dunn [Ed.] 1980)

In fact, a sage is affected by everything, responds to every situation in his own unique way, but is never swayed by circumstances. In U.G. Krishnamurti's words:

> *Affection* means that you are affected by everything, not that some emotion flows from you towards something. The natural state is a state of great sensitivity—but this is a physical sensitivity of the senses, not some kind of emotional compassion or tenderness for others. There is compassion only in the sense that there are no 'others' for me, and so there is no separation. (Rao [Ed.] 2010)

In effect, what is being said here is that a *sthithaprajna* is not one who is in control of the senses, rather, his sense perceptions are different, not based on likes and dislikes, or on ideas, because, the mind, the interpreter, is absent. *Sthithaprajna* simply means a sage, his *prajna* or awareness, rooted in the non-dual condition, responds as per the situation and it is always a complete, right action, and he lives in a state of tranquillity.

III. Karma Yoga: The Way of Action

Arjuna said:

If you think knowledge superior to action, Janardana,
then why to this ghastly deed do you commit me, Kesava?

With your seemingly ambiguous words, you only confuse
my mind;
say one thing, decidedly, by which I can attain felicity.

The Gracious Lord said:
In this world, two kinds of devotion were of old ordained by me,
O sinless –
the yoga of knowledge for samkhyas, the way of deeds for yogis.

By not doing his duty a man does not achieve freedom from karma;
nor by mere abstention is transcendent perfection attained.

Nor, certainly, can anyone even momentarily ever stay inactive;
because all are helplessly made to act by the Prakriti-born gunas.

He who, restraining the senses with the mind, Arjuna, engages
the organs
of action in karma yoga, dispassionately—he excels.

Thus, without attachment, always do your duty immaculately;
for, by performing karma without attachment man attains
the Supreme.

    The idea of selfless action is an inspiring one. Karma, which means
'to act' or 'action' is natural to human life. We cannot but act and we
act or work without attachment to the fruits of our actions, for we
understand we have no control over them; they are not in our hands.
This attitude helps us accept the result of our action, whatever that
may be, and move on.

    Yoga is skill in action, skill to act mindfully, with the awareness
that we are moved by forces over which we have no control, so we

act without attachment, and let go the fruits of our actions. Acting thus, we go with the flow of life and are able to live without conflict and suffering.

IV. Jnana Yoga: The Way of Wisdom

The Gracious Lord said:
Myriad births of mine are past, and yours, Arjuna;
these I know, every one; you do not know, Parantapa.

Though un-born, my soul immortal, the Lord of creatures though being,
abiding in my own nature, I incarnate through my soul's maya.

Whenever there is a decline of dharma, Bhaarata,
an ascendancy of adharma, then myself I manifest.

For the deliverance of the good and for the destruction of sinners;
in order to establish dharma, I come from age to age.

Herein lies the polemical notion of an avatar. But what is an avatar? Is he really the one born for the protection of the good, for the destruction of the wicked and for the establishment of righteousness? This is one of the most finely manipulated notions across the world today. Heroes of movies, gurus in the marketplace, even political leaders are portrayed as avatars born especially for the protection of the good, for the destruction of the wicked and for the establishment of righteousness.

Avatar, in Sanskrit, means 'to come down', or the descent of the Divine, whenever dharma decays and *adharma* is in ascendancy. Similar concepts of avatar—especially with regard to the coming of Kalki Avatar in Kali Yuga, modern times—can be found in the *Srimad Bhagavath Purana* and the *Vishnu Purana*. According to many commentators of the Gita and spiritual gurus, Lord Krishna is an avatar of Lord Vishnu. A *purna* avatar or the complete incarnation of God in flesh comes down for the protection of the good and to establish dharma firmly.

Now, from within the framework of the Mahabharata, we may ask these questions: What is this dharma that Lord Krishna establishes, and what *adharma* does he destroy? What does the story of the Mahabharata really reveal? Lord Krishna's role in the life and times of the Kuru dynasty doesn't exactly fit the image of the idealized, popular notion of an avatar; nor does he fit the picture of an angry, vengeful god or messiah, eager to establish a new order. Rather, Lord Krishna comes through as a shrewd, charming and enigmatic god who suffers and participates in the trials and tribulations, triumphs and defeats of the Pandavas and the Kauravas. He seldom directly involves himself in the bloody war between the cousins, although he plays a pivotal role in influencing the course of events that unfold. He is 'omniscient' and knows the Kauravas are not an incarnation of 'evil' any more than the Pandavas are the agents of 'good', yet he takes positions and favours the Pandavas, well aware of the consequences.

There is vaulting ambition, irrepressible passion, irreconcilable conflict, revolting violence, endless intrigue and relentless suffering, and in this inexorable human drama, Lord Krishna offers delightful but also disturbing insights into the human condition. Being an inevitable part of the maya of human existence and the *lila* of Brahman, Lord Krishna succeeds only in presiding over an age coming to an end.

There is destruction all round, yet with a smile of supreme understanding of sorrow and death, and of *That* which is not bound by sorrow and death, he, too, at the end of the great tale, quietly passes away. A close examination of the narrative reveals that nothing gets established, and everything is allowed to manifest and play out to its end.

Every concept and every value is questioned, contested and shown to be relative, ultimately, maya. There is no clear distinction between the dharma and *adharma* in black-and-white terms; they take on layered and complex meanings: '*adharma*' may be shown, in the long run, to be not that bad at all. We are given to understand that dharma is born from the womb of *adharma*, or is it vice versa? In any case, one cannot exist without the other.

There is no escape from karma, from actions and the consequences of actions, even for the gods. There are simply no absolutes, and that, in short, seems to be the burden and the message that Lord Krishna, the avatar, embodies on the one hand; on the other, through the Bhagavad Gita, which may be read independently of the Mahabharata, Lord Krishna speaks of a state of being where the human drama of desire, conflict, pleasure and pain has come to an end, and where the mind—the source of opposing emotions—has been transcended. This is the state of supreme understanding or *jnana*, which is moksha, Brahman.

From such a reading of the Mahabharata and the notion of an avatar, we could argue that when there is real and great danger to the living beings on earth, Lord Vishnu descends in different animal and human forms—if we are to include the earlier incarnations of Lord Vishnu as well—to avert a crisis or to prevent the destruction of humanity. In other words, Lord Vishnu comes down as an avatar to prevent total destruction; yet, at the same time, he oversees the end of an age, and thus marks the beginning of a new one.

But this 'new' age is not an entirely new beginning, for there is no such thing. It is only a revaluation and modification of the old, for the past never dies or goes away completely. To put it differently, the avatar may work as a catalyst for the emergence or development of a new consciousness in the world which, over a period of time, may degenerate into rigid or dogmatic ways of being and doing, thereby creating the need for yet another intervention, another fresh revaluation of old values, another avatar (Rao 2014).

Here, Sri Aurobindo's view on avatars could add to what we have said. According to him, avatars do not mark the culmination of life; rather, they may be seen as turning points in the evolutionary history of the human beings. In his words: 'Avatarhood would have little meaning if it were not connected with evolution. The Hindu procession of the ten Avatars is itself a parable of evolution. ... If we admit that the object of Avatarhood is to lead the evolution, this is quite reasonable' (Sri Aurobindo 1998).

In the light of the lives and teachings of Ramana Maharshi, Anandamayi Ma and U.G. Krishnamurti, we could say that a sage is one within whom the search and seeking is over, and within whom sorrow has come to an end. A sage is one who lives and moves in a state of unitary consciousness. Such sages are indeed the 'messengers of God', or what you call 'saviours', or 'avatars', not in the orthodox religious and exclusive sense of the term, but in the sense that they bring home the wonder and mystery of life, indicating the possibility of ending sorrow, transcending the thought-structure, the self, which is the cause of sorrow. They come with the wonder of life, not with a blueprint of life (Rao 2010).

V. Sannyasa Yoga: The Way of Renunciation

Arjuna said:
Renunciation of karma, Krishna, then again, yoga you extol;
which one of the two is better for me, say for certain.

The Gracious Lord said:
Sannyasa and karma yoga effect liberation, both;
but of the two, doing karma is superior to inaction.

Know him as a constant renunciate, who neither dislikes nor desires;
for, detached from duality, Partha, he is easily freed from bondage.

Krishna redefines *sannyasa* (renunciation) here, perhaps it was the need of the times to distinguish between false and genuine sannyasis (renunciants). Sitting under a tree, wearing an ochre robe and chanting the name of God doesn't make one a renunciant or sannyasi. Physical renunciation of objects is no renunciation at all. In other words, a sannyasi is one who renounces desires and egoism. A true sannyasi practises 'holy indifference', neither attachment nor aversion to anything and renounces even renouncing. Such an individual, free from passions, free from pairs of opposites such as good and evil, birth and death and so on, is a true sannyasi, a sage, who lives in the state of freedom.

VII. The Yoga of Wisdom and Realization

In this chapter and the one following this (VIII. The Yoga of the Immortal Brahman), Krishna explains the enigma of his being and non-being, manifest and unborn, unmanifest form. In the manifested or incarnated form he is Krishna, he is also the Absolute Infinite Principle, the ground and source of all creation: the lower and higher *prakritis*. The lower *prakriti* is made up of the five elements and the mind, ego and intellect. The higher *prakriti* is the life-element which upholds the universe, activates it and causes its appearance and final dissolution. The three acharyas, namely, Shankara, Ramanuja and Madhva, drew inspiration from such descriptions to develop their Advaita, Vishishtadvaita and Dvaita philosophies respectively.

Also, these verses mark and articulate bhakti as a mode of liberation from bondage.

The Gracious Lord said:
To me the mind cleaving, Partha, devoted in yoga, taking refuge in me,
without doubt, you will know me in full—listen how.

This knowledge to you, I, together with wisdom, will tell in full,
which knowing, nothing else here will remain to be known.

Among thousands of men scarcely one strives for perfection;
among these seekers, even among sages, hardly one knows me in truth.

Earth, water, fire, air, ether, mind, intellect and also
ego—this my differentiated nature, eightfold.

This is my lower nature; know my other transcendent nature—
the *Living Spirit*, Arjuna, which supports this world.

These two are the womb of all beings, know;
I am all the world's source and its dissolution, as well.

Than me higher nothing else at all exists, Dhananjaya;
in me all this is strung like so many jewels on a thread.

Taste am I in water, Kaunteya; light I am in moon and sun;
Aum in all the Vedas, sound in ether, manliness in men.

The pure fragrance in the earth I am, and brilliance in fire;
life in all beings am I, and austerity in ascetics.

The seed am I of all creatures, know, Partha—eternal;
the intelligence of the intelligent I am; the splendour of
the splendid, I.

And I am the strength of the strong; of lust, passion devoid;
in beings, legitimate desire am I, Bharatarishabha.

And whatever sattvik existences, of rajas and tamas there are:
from me alone they are, know—I am not in them; they are in me.

By all these, the three gunas' manifestations, this whole world,
deluded, does not know me, transcendent, supreme, immutable.

For, this divine, guna-comprised maya of mine is impenetrable;
only who in me refuge, they cross over this maya.

XI. The Yoga of the Vision of the Cosmic Form

Krishna bestows the divine eye on Arjuna, by means of which he
beholds the Lord in His cosmic form. The vision is at once all-
comprehensive and simultaneous. All the created worlds, gods,
beings, creatures and things stand revealed in the measureless Body
of the Lord. Soon Arjuna is unable to bear the tremendous pressure
building up due to the never-ending expansion of consciousness
and is filled with fear. He begs the Lord to assume once more His
usual form.

It is interesting to note here that Krishna reiterates that this
divine vision cannot be had through austerities, study, sacrifices or
philanthropic acts, but only by means of supreme devotion and grace.

Arjuna said:
To bless me, the supreme, secret, Adhyatmam, you revealed;
with these words that you spoke, my bewilderment has gone.

Indeed, of the appearance and passing of beings, I have heard
extensively
from you, Lotus-eyed; and also your greatness, imperishable.

It is just so: what you have said about yourself, Parameswara—
I want to see your Form Divine, Purushottama!

The Gracious Lord said:
Behold, Partha, my forms, hundreds and thousands,
of many kinds, divine, vari-coloured and -shaped.

Behold the Adityas, Vasus, Rudras, the two Asvins, also the Maruts;
many previously unseen wonders, behold, Bharata.

Here, as one, the Universe, whole, see now, moving and immobile,
in my body, Gudakesa; and whatever else you wish to see.

But you cannot see me with just these your eyes;
I give you divine sight—behold my Sovereign Yoga.

Sanjaya said:
So saying, then, the Great Lord of yoga,
showed Partha his supreme Form Divine.

Countless mouths, eyes; countless amazing visions;
countless divine ornaments; countless divine weapons raised;
divine garlands, raiment, wearing; with divine perfumes anointed;
of all wonders, refulgent; infinite faces everywhere.

In the sky, if a thousand suns were together risen,
light like that might perhaps compare with the splendour of that
Great Being.

Arjuna said:
I see the Devas, O God, in your *body*, also all the myriad hosts of
beings,
Brahma, the Lord upon lotus-throne seated, and all the Rishis and
Uragas divine.

With countless arms, bellies, mouths, eyes: I see your infinite form
everywhere;
neither your end nor middle, nor again your beginning, do I see,
O Lord of the Universe.

With crowns, maces, and chakras, a mass of light, everywhere
shining,
I see you, hard to look at, on all sides with irradiance of fire, blazing
sun—immeasurable.

Without beginning, middle, end; of infinite power; endless armed;
the Sun, Moon, your eyes,

I see you, burning fire your faces, with your refulgence this universe searing.

Your great *form*, many-mouthed, -eyed, of many arms, thighs, feet,
many bellies, many fangs, horrible, seeing, the worlds tremble, as also I.

Sky-touching, ablaze, countless-hued, mouth agape, huge blazing eyes:
seeing only you, my inmost soul quails; no stability do I find, nor peace,
O Vishnu.

As many rivers' swift waters just towards the ocean flow,
even so, those heroes of the world of men enter your fiery mouths.

You lick, devouring on all sides the worlds, entirely, with mouths aflame;
your brilliance covers all the universe, you lustre terrible, searing,
O Vishnu.

Tell me who you are, of dreadful form; salutations to you, best of gods!
I want to know you, the first, for I do not understand what you do.

This is the most powerful and enigmatic of all chapters. Arjuna beholds this terrific kaleidoscope of life with the 'divine eye' bestowed on him. And what does he see? He beholds the whole cosmos reflected in the *Body* of Krishna with multitudinous arms, stomachs, mouths and eyes. It is boundless, with neither end nor middle nor beginning. Everything, all the innumerable forms of life are there, and in the centre of it all is Lord Brahma resting on a lotus, surrounded by all the sages and the heavenly serpents.

The sun, the moon and the heavenly planets blaze along, worlds radiate within worlds in a never-ending series, torrents of rivers flow relentlessly into thunderous seas, and behold, the flaming mouth licking up, devouring all worlds, all creatures; it is the *Body*, with no beginning, middle or end, swallowing, burning itself up in an endless maya of creation and destruction.

There couldn't have been a better metaphor for the Body. Many scholars and commentators on the Bhagavad Gita might find it difficult to accept the following interpretation. However, the text reveals that truly, within the body is the cosmic dance of life. Rather, the cosmos itself is the Body, and the different, immeasurable life forms, like bacteria in the bloodstream, like fish in the ocean, rising and dissolving continually, floating, moving back and forth, up and down, with no beginning and no end. That this Body is the microcosm of the cosmos—that within the Body all the manifold forms of the universe unite—only reveals that the body, too, is immortal.

The Self is not the opposite of the Body, nor antithetical to it. The Body is the manifested form of the Self. The body is not the prison of the Self, rather, it is the face of the Self. It, Body and Self, is a continuum. The Body of course has a form and limitation, but within this Body is also the whole cosmos, the great intelligence and energy that destroys, sustains and maintains the universe.

After its so-called death, the Body disintegrates into its constituent elements and that becomes the basis for another form of life: the ashes enrich the soil and aid germination, the worms live on the buried body. If you throw it into the river, it becomes food for the fishes; in short, the body is only recycled and so gives continuity to life. Life is immortal; the Body which is its form is also immortal.

XII. Bhakti Yoga: The Way of Devotion

Bhakti as a way of invoking, appeasing and seeking the blessing of god(s) may be traced to the Vedic culture. However, it was the devotional narratives on Lord Vishnu and Lord Shiva, such as *Vishnu Purana*, *Linga Purana* and *Bhagavata*, that laid the foundation for the emergence of bhakti as a way to God. And in the Bhagavad Gita, bhakti as a mode of worshipping, surrendering and reaching God gained prominence, even though the bhakti culture spread across India on a mass scale among Hindus of various sects only in the sixth and seventh century CE.

In this chapter, Krishna advocates the path of devotion as simpler than the path of knowledge. Even people who may not possess the intellectual ability to enquire and cogitate over spiritual matters could take to this path. This has had a tremendous appeal to people, so much so that bhakti as a mode of worship and surrender to God developed into a dominant form of religious quest. And over the years, bhakti took on different forms: *sravana* or hearing; *kirtana* or hymns in praise of God or Goddess; *smaran* or remembering; *padasevanam* or tending the feet of the Divine; *archana* or worship; *vandanam* or adoration, veneration; *dasya* or service; *sakhya* or friendship, and *atmanivedanam* or surrender to the Divine.

Arjuna said:
Thus, always yoked, those devotees who worship you,
and, again, those who do the Imperishable, the Unmanifest—
of these, which of them are better versed in yoga?

The Gracious Lord said:
On me fixing the mind, who, ever absorbed, worship me,
with devotion supreme endowed, them, I the best yogis consider.

And who all karma to me renounce, on me intent,
with singular yoga, me, through meditation, worship:
of them, I, the deliverer from death, samsara's sea.

On me alone your heart set; in me let your mind dwell:
you will live in me, surely, thereafter, beyond doubt.

But who this immortal dharma, as told, follow,
with faith, me the goal, those devotees are very dear to me.

After offering bhakti as an easier and direct way to freedom and
happiness, Krishna now offers illuminating insights into the nature
of consciousness. In many ways, the discourse in Chapter XIII is an
extension and amplification of the Upanishadic discourses on the
nature of Atman and Brahman.

The liberating knowledge or *jnana* that Krishna speaks of here is
not an intellectual understanding of reality but something radically
different. It is *jnana* that blossoms when the discursive, divisive mind
goes silent, *jnana* that is not a product of dialectical thinking, not
knowledge, rather the end of knowledge, which is *darshana* (seeing
and experiencing), the oneness of reality.

XV. Purushottama Yoga: The Way of the Supreme Person

Here Krishna gives the metaphor of an inverted tree whose roots are
in *Para Brahman*, the highest, the Absolute. This brings to mind the
description of the Asvattha tree in the *Katha Upanishad*: 'This is that
eternal Asvattha tree with its root above and branches below. That
root, indeed, is called the Bright; That is Brahman and That alone
is the Immortal. In That all worlds are contained and none can pass
beyond. This, verily, is That' (*Katha Upanishad* Ch. 2: sec. 3, v. 1, in
Swami Krishnananda [Trans.]).

In a similar vein, Krishna explains the mysterious tree as being a
creation of His inscrutable power of maya and why it is difficult to
understand. Only the one who penetrates this mystery transcends the
samsara that is embroiled in conflict and sorrow.

The Gracious Lord said:
Root above, branches below, the Aswattha, they tell of,
imperishable,

of which the chhandas are the leaves; who knows this, he is a Veda
knower.

Below and above, extend its branches, guna-nourished,
sense-objects for twigs; and below its roots stretch,
binding in karma the world of men.

Not its form, either, is here perceived, not its end, nor beginning,
and neither its foundation.

This aswattha, deep-rooted, with the mighty sword detachment
severing,
then, let that condition be sought, going where, there is no
returning again;
only to that original Purusha surrender, from whom this ancient
world came.

Without pride, delusion; quelled, the sin attachment; spiritual
always;
rid of desire; liberated from the dualities, called pleasure, pain—
the undeluded go to that state eternal.

We shall end the discourse here with the wise and dispassionate view
on this astoundingly layered spiritual text by Sri Aurobindo. He states that
the central message of the Gita is not pure monism, nor is it qualified
Monism. It is not Sankhya, either, or, 'Vaishnava Theism, although it
presents to us Krishna, who is the Avatar of Vishnu as the supreme Deity'.
In effect, he argues that like the Upanishads, the Gita, at once spiritual and
intellectual, avoids, naturally, every such rigid determination as would
injure its universal comprehensiveness. Its aim and message, in fact, is the
opposite to that of the acharyas (Shankara, Ramanuja and Madhva) who
attempted to turn the text into a weapon of offence and defence against
other schools and systems. As Sri Aurobindo (2003) noted:

The Gita is not a weapon for dialectical warfare; it is a gate opening on the whole world of spiritual truth and experience and the view it gives us embraces all the provinces of that supreme region. It maps out, but it does not cut up or build walls or hedges to confine our vision.

Ashtavakra Gita

The *Ashtavakra Gita*, sometimes also called the *Ashtavakra Samhita,* is an extraordinary spiritual text in many ways. It starts as a dialogue between Ashtavakra and King Janaka and soon, after the very first salvo of wisdom from Ashtavakra the teacher, the ready and already matured disciple Janaka directly realizes his true Self:

Dualism is the root of suffering. And this suffering would melt away with the realization that all this that we see is unreal, and that I am pure awareness ... There is neither bondage nor liberation. The illusion has lost its basis and ceased.

After this life-altering, mutating, self-realization, it is no more a dialogue but what may be called an enchanting Advaitic *jugalbandi*—a musical duet!

The legend of Ashtavakra appears in the *Vana Parva* of the Mahabharata. The story goes like this: while Ashtavakra was in his mother's womb, he listened to his father, Kahor, reading aloud the sacred Vedas late into the nights. One night, the unborn child suddenly cried out to his father thus: 'Father, it's through your grace that I have already learnt all the Vedas. However, I'm sorry to tell you that you often make mistakes in your recitation.'

Enraged, the father cursed his son and the child was, therefore, born deformed with eight curves in his anatomy. Hence he was called 'Ashtavakra', the one with eight deformities in his body.

Pressed down by poverty, we are told, Kahor goes to King Janaka's court to seek help. In order to be eligible for any sort of help, Janaka tells him that he must first prove his scholarship by defeating the court philosopher, Vandin, in a debate. Not surprisingly and as fate would have it, Kahor is defeated and as a consequence is employed in the service of Vandin and therefore cannot return home.

Years roll by and Ashtavakra, now grown up, goes in search of his father, Kahor, determined to bring him back home. He meets with King Janaka, defeats Vandin in debate and wins his father's freedom. Highly impressed and inspired, King Janaka begs Ashtavakara to teach him the way to liberation.

According to scholars the *Ashtavakra Gita* was probably composed sometime after the Bhagavad Gita, but before Gaudapada's *Mandukya Karika*. However, in content, tone and style, it comes much closer to the *Mandukya Upanishad*. Here is an edited version of the *Samhita*:

Janaka said:
Reverend Sir, tell me, how is one to acquire the jnana that leads to liberation?

Ashtavakra said:
Avoid the objects of the senses like poison and cultivate sincerity, compassion, and truthfulness as the antidote.

You do not belong to any particular caste, you are not at any stage of varnashramadharma, nor are you anything that the eye can see. You are unattached and formless, the witness of everything.

Pain and pleasure, ideas of right and wrong, all these feelings and thoughts are purely of the mind and are no concern of yours. You are neither the doer nor the reaper of the consequences, so you are always free.

If you think of yourself as free, you are free, and if you think of yourself as bound, you are bound. It is because of ignorance that you seem to be involved in samsara. You have long been trapped in the snare of identification with the body and the world; sever it with the knife of jnana.

Your real nature is pure consciousness, the all-pervading witness—unattached to anything, desireless and at peace.

The teaching starts with a bang! No steps to approach that which cannot be grasped by the divided mind; rather, the first step is the last step that could open the door to Infinity. To meet and listen to Ashtavakra is like meeting with Allama Prabhu, the twelfth-century sage, or the U.G. Krishnamurti of our times, who exploded all concepts to give us a taste of the ineffable. If you are seeking liberation you need to straightaway see through the complex, deeply entrenched structure of thought and be free of it. Seeing is ending.

Seeing has to take place not in stages, but here and now. Blessed Janaka sees what has to be seen through, and as a result, with the separation gone, he finds himself in the non-dual state. And the musical duet emptying all forms of duality begins!

Janaka said:
I am spotless and at peace, the awareness beyond natural causality. The whole world is my-self, or alternatively nothing is.

The known, and the knower do not exist in reality. I am the spotless reality in which they appear because of ignorance.

Truly dualism is the root of suffering. I am beyond all forms of duality. I am pure awareness though through ignorance I have imagined myself to have additional attributes.

There is neither bondage nor liberation. The illusion has lost its basis and ceased.

Ashtavakra said:

Knowing oneself as pure consciousness, how could a wise man possessing this jnana feel any pleasure in acquiring wealth? Only when one does not know oneself, one takes pleasure in the objects of mistaken perception.

Seeing this world as pure illusion, is it possible for a self-realized person to feel fear, even at the approach of death?

He who has known That is untouched by good deeds or bad, just as space is not touched by smoke, however much it may appear to be.

Knowing all categories of beings, from Brahma down to the last clump of grass, only a jnani is capable of eliminating desire and aversion.

To a jnani there is neither renunciation, acceptance nor cessation of it for he knows he is infinite like space.

Janaka said:

It is in the infinite ocean of myself that the mind-creation called the world takes place, yet my true nature is not contained in objects, nor does any object exist in it, for it is infinite and spotless. So it is unattached, desireless and at peace.

Ashtavakra said:

Bondage is when the mind longs, grieves, and holds on to something. Bondage is when the mind is tangled in one of the senses, and so trapped in the circle of pain and pleasure.

Liberation is when the mind does not long, grieve, or hold on to anything, and is not tangled in any of the senses.

The mind, by its very nature, is binary, divisive; it divides up life into black and white, good and bad, birth and death and so on. It uses the senses to perceive and experience the world through ideation. When the senses are untangled from the mind, from ideation, when the mind, the 'me' or the ego ceases to manipulate the senses, the individual is freed from the tangle of binary perception of reality and that is the liberation.

Janaka said:
Both, the performance of actions and their abandonment, are due to ignorance. By fully recognizing this truth, I live as I please, abandoning both renunciation and acquisition.

Recognizing that in reality no action is ever committed, I live as I please, just doing what presents itself to be done.

I live as I please, abandoning success and failure, the pleasant and unpleasant. With my desire dissolved, I have lost attachments to wealth, friends, senses, or knowledge.

Realizing my supreme self-nature as the Witness, I feel no inclination for liberation, either.

Ashtavakra said:
You are not the body, nor are you the doer of actions or the reaper of their consequences. Your nature is pure consciousness, in which the whole world wells up, like waves in the sea.

It is through your ignorance that all this exists. There is only you, the witness, there is no one else within or beyond samsara.

You have no bondage or liberation. You are pure consciousness, so do not disturb your mind with thoughts of for and against.

Give up meditation, let not the mind hold on to anything. You are free by nature, so what will you achieve by forcing the mind?

When the mind is freed from pairs of opposites, you become indifferent to merit, wealth, sensuality, and even liberation.

Meditation creates expectations, hope, and strengthens duality which has no basis. So give up, says Ashtavakra, don't hold on to anything, whether sacred or secular. It's the mind, through its likes and dislikes and ideations, that creates attachment, and thereby pain, conflict and fear. Once the mind is freed from pairs of opposites—

the stuff of our grand narratives—the division disappears, duality
ceases, and there is the realization that there is neither bondage nor
liberation.

Ashtavakra said:
If even Shiva, Vishnu, or the lotus-born Brahma were your teacher,
until you let go everything, or you have forgotten everything, you
cannot be established within.

All teaching is problematic, even if it is from Shiva himself.
A teaching implies a method or a system, a technique or a new way
of thinking to be applied in order to bring about a transformation
in one's way of life. What Ashtavakra is saying is outside the field of
teachability. The oneness, the tranquillity is not the result of following
a teaching; rather, when one is cleansed of all teaching, all methods,
hopes and aspiration, then what is there is something that is neither
bondage nor liberation. It is pure consciousness, stripped of the
machinations of thought and its several binding traps. You have to just
let everything go, sacred and profane, spiritual and material, bondage
and liberation.

Ashtavakra said:
The liberated man is resplendent, free from all desires: His seeing,
hearing, feeling, smelling, tasting, speaking, and walking about, is
freed from trying to achieve or avoid anything.
    There is no distinction between pleasure and pain, man and
woman, success and failure; no aggression nor compassion, no
pride nor humility, no wonder nor confusion, for his days of
samsara are over.
    There is no delusion, no meditation, or liberation, for these
things are just in the realm of imagination. Even the thought 'I
am Brahma' doesn't occur, for what is he to think who is without
thought, and who sees no duality?

In the state of being where thought, the (binary) mind, is absent, who can tell what it is and what it is not? Therefore, all assertions or affirmations about the Higher Self or Brahman are seen as projections of an insecure mind, which is still part of the becoming process and hence subject to suffering and rebirth. Pride and pleasure and suffering, the whole gamut of emotions are in the realm of imagination. The samsara, world, is *kalpita*, imagined; once imagination is knocked off, the duality ceases.

Ashtavakra said:
The wise man goes on doing what presents itself for him to do. For him there is no sense of individuality, no samsara, no goal, neither darkness nor light nor destruction; he is neither happy nor unhappy, neither detached nor attached, neither seeking liberation nor liberated, he is neither something nor nothing.

Janaka said:
Established in my own glory, freed from all opinions, there are no religious obligations; no self or non-self, no good or evil, no thought or even absence of thought, no dreaming or deep sleep, no waking nor fourth state beyond them.

For me, established in my own glory, there is nothing within or without; there is no life or death; there are no elements, no body, and no mind.

There is no being or non-being, no unity or dualism, either. I remain in my own pristine state. What more is there to say?

This is absolute, candid, uncompromising, unapologetic non-dualism. All thoughts are burned to ashes. There is nothing there, not even void. Ashtavakra and his scorching words bring to mind U.G. Krishnamurti, who talked about the 'Natural State', a term he preferred over terms like enlightenment, moksha and so on. He warned:

You would not touch it with a ten-foot barge pole. This is going to liquidate what you call 'you', all of you—higher self, lower self, soul, Atman, conscious, subconscious—all of that.

When the 'you' is not there, when the question is not there, what is, is understanding. You are finished. You'll walk out. (Arms 1982)

When U.G. Krishnamurti said, 'no self to realize, no psyche to purify, no soul to liberate, no enlightenment' or, when Allama Prabhu said, 'there is nothing to achieve, no yonder shore to reach ... there is only *bayalu* ... emptiness emptying itself turning into emptiness,' they were both echoing the absolute non-dual position that Ashtavakra and Janaka expressed several centuries ago:

There is no illusion, no samsara, no attachment or detachment, no liberation and no bondage, no being or non-being, no unity or dualism, no initiation or scripture, no disciple or teacher, and no goal of human life—

'You are only a witness, in need of nothing,' adds Ashtavakra; rather, you are a witnessing consciousness, for, 'He by whom the Supreme Brahman is seen may think, "I am Brahman", but what is he to think who is without thought, and who sees no duality?'

This teaching is not for a *sadhaka* who has just started on the search for *that*, knowing which you realize there is nothing to know or understand, for you have become one with everything and nothing. In other words, you are everything that is there, for the separateness has gone. You understand this supreme truth only if you have covered some distance on this journey and realized the absurdity of the question and the questioner.

The *Ashtavakra Gita* has the power to break the 'chain', the 'bondage', and enable the listener with a silent mind to achieve that 'quantum leap' to be able to see that it's in the very nature of the mind to perceive and experience reality always in pairs of opposites—joy and sorrow, good and evil, life and death and so on. And so you give up, let go.

Avadhuta Gita

The *Avadhuta Gita* is yet another text that is similar to the *Ashtavakra Gita* in content and style. The text, probably composed, or orally transmitted over several centuries and committed to writing, in the ninth or tenth century CE, is attributed to Sage Dattatreya. Dattatreya is mentioned in the Mahabharata, in the *Jabala Upanishad* and Puranas, and is revered as an incarnation of God. He is usually depicted with four dogs by his side, representing, it is said, the four Vedas, a cow behind him representing Lord Vishnu, a trident in his hand representing Lord Shiva, and three heads representing Lord Brahma.

As a boy, the story goes, Dattatreya left home, naked as he was born, declaring, 'I will live just as I have come.' And he spent his whole life as an *avadhuta*—one who has 'passed away from' or 'shaken off' all worldly attachments and cares and has attained liberation. Though the word 'avadhuta' naturally implies renunciation, it includes an additional and yet higher state which is neither attachment nor detachment but beyond both. An *avadhuta* has no guru, no disciples, seeks nothing, avoids nothing. Having realized that he is the Infinite Self, he lives in that vivid realization. Dattatreya, an *avadhuta*, spent his life wandering, teaching those who sought his guidance, without any discrimination of sect, caste, sex or conduct.

Here is my edited version of the translated verses from *Avadhuta Gita*, interspersed with my commentary.

The universe is like water in a mirage. All is verily the absolute Self—Atman/Brahman. Distinction and non-distinction do not exist. I am filled with wonder!

In the state of *turiya*, all distinctions or differentiations disappear and there is only a sense of wonder—what U.G. Krishnamurti called a state of 'not knowing' or 'declutched state'. Knowledge, which is memory, is held in the background, unless there is a question or demand. Otherwise the 'mind' remains in a state of wonder, which is the state of pure consciousness. There is no thinking, no self-talking, no 'formations'.

The whole of Vedanta is this supreme *Jnana*: that I am by nature the formless, all-pervasive Self. I am that God who is the Self, pure, indivisible, like the sky, naturally stainless.

'I am that God' is an apparently arrogant statement. But, actually, what it means is that the 'outside' and 'inside' have disappeared, everything is a seamless whole. In other words, it implies the human is constitutively immortal, and that s/he is always already God/Brahman. The human is God/Brahman, in the sense the energy or power, or whatever one wishes to call it, that created the world is the same energy that is operating in the human and in all creation.

Reality is one only, and through renunciation of attachment, the mind, which is one and many, ceases to exist.

If I am the Supreme One, the highest Truth, how then shall I speak of Him and worship Him?

When the pot is broken, the space within it is absorbed in the infinite space, similarly when the mind becomes pure, any difference between the mind and the Supreme Being ceases.

Actually there is no pot, no within and without; neither is there an individual soul nor the form of an individual soul.

Never doubt That Self is everything, everywhere, it is eternal, steady.

Know that there are no Vedas, no gods, no sacrifices; no caste, no stages in life, no family, no birth. There is only the highest Truth, the Brahman.

In the state of non-duality, the so-called sacred Vedas, along with gods and the imagined or conceptualized world, are thrown out of the window. There is no caste, no birth, no death, for everything has turned into one bright light that permeates the beingness.

This almost sounds like the Buddhist position, which is that it is pointless to discuss whether Atman or Higher Self exists or not, because, even if it exists, it cannot be known, it cannot be spoken about, it is *avyakrta*, inexpressible. For, in the state of being where the (binary) mind is absent, who can tell what it is and it is not? Therefore, all assertions or affirmations about the Higher Self or Soul are seen as projections of an insecure mind.

The only difference here is that in the Hindu enlightenment traditions there seems to be a persistent need, as it were, to conclude the series of negation with the assertion that 'There is only the highest Truth, the Brahman'.

How can there be illusion and non-illusion, duality and non-duality? All this is one Truth, of the nature of space and without taint.

I am free in the beginning, in the middle, and in the end. Never bound, naturally spotless and pure.

~

The Self is neither eunuch, man, nor woman, neither idea nor imagination. There is no body nor mind, nor the three states and the fourth.

I am not bound, not liberated. Being neither doer nor enjoyer, devoid of the distinctions of the pervaded and the pervader, I am not different from Brahman.

~

The *avadhuta*, alone, abides in an empty dwelling place. Having renounced all, he moves about naked, perceiving the Absolute, the All, within himself.

There exists neither void nor fullness, neither truth nor untruth, the *avadhuta*, having realized the truths, has uttered this spontaneously from his own nature.

~

Free from past, present and future, eternal, space-like transcendental Truth am I.

I have no birth and death, no father nor mother, neither wife nor child. Eternal, space-like transcendental Peace am I.

Devas and Gods, Paradise nor Heaven exist in Atman. The one taintless transcendental Truth am I.

This Supreme Truth cannot be invoked or worshipped with flowers and leaves. Meditations and mantras cannot reach It. In It there are neither distinctions nor unity, so how could It be worshipped as Shiva?

~

The *Avadhuta* who has realized this mystery of all mysteries, moves about among people unconcerned, radiating bliss and highest knowledge.

Clothed in a habit of old and worn, free from all taints and modifications of *maya*, he walks in a path that is free from religious merit or sin.

The *Avadhuta* lives in the temple of absolute emptiness; he has cast off the worn-out garments of purity, righteousness, and all ideals. Having lost his identity in Atman, he is far above the clouds of *maya* and ignorance.

He is like the immeasurable space. He is eternity. In him is neither purity nor impurity, no bondage nor absence of bondage. Alone and secondless, is Shiva and that is the *Avadhuta*.

Let alone the pundits and yogis, even the Vedas cannot speak of
him perfectly. Radiating bliss absolute and the highest knowledge
is the *Avadhuta*.

The *Avadhuta Gita* is more akin to the *Ashtavakra Gita* in its
uncompromising position with regard to the oneness of reality.
Avadhuta, as mentioned earlier, is one who has literally 'shaken off'
everything, all systems of belief and practice, and walks sky-clad, with
no destination or goal, no purpose of meaning, he lives and moves
in the bright and lucid non-dual state. He is Shiva Himself, beyond
conceptualization; even the Vedas cannot claim to understand this
supreme truth.

It is interesting to note here that there is what may be called
an *Avadhuta parampara* or tradition, not in the sense of a fixed,
institutionalized tradition, passed on from generation to generation,
or from gurus to disciples, but in the sense of a vital, cleansing stream
within the enlightenment traditions. Sometimes the term *avadhuta* is
used as a generic term for all those homeless ascetics and yogis who
lived the life of total renunciation, indifferent to the 'civilized' world, to
its conventions or social norms, living as per the dictates of their heart,
adrift in spells of trance. They did not offer any teaching or accept
disciples. Sometimes they even drove people away, flinging abuse or
even stones at them and acted like 'mad' men. There must have been
innumerable such *avadhuta*s in the past and they do exist even today,
but remain invisible and unknown.

Allama Prabhu was a wandering sage, an *avadhuta*, who had no
permanent abode, no guru, no tradition and no teaching; nevertheless,
offering his blazing yet cleansing insights on life and living. So was
Kabir, as also Nisargadatta Maharaj, though, he decided to stay put
at his little tenement in the back lanes of Mumbai and meet there

with seekers who came from all over the world. He belonged to the
Avadhuta tradition, what is called the *Navanath Sampradaya*, which is
supposed to have originated with the teachings of Dattatreya.

Being the genuine *avadhuta* that he was, Nisargadatta Maharaj
did not attach much importance to sects, cults and creeds. He often
reiterated that belonging to a *sampradaya* was a matter of one's
feeling and conviction. However, he emphasized that it was of crucial
importance to understand that 'After all it is verbal and formal. In
reality there is neither Guru nor disciple, neither theory nor practice,
neither ignorance nor realization. It all depends upon what you take
yourself to be. Know yourself correctly. There is no substitute for self-
knowledge' (Frydman 1987).

Six

Jnana Yajna

Adi Shankara

Adi Shankara's life story is surrounded by too many myths for one to be able to get a clear picture of the man. But there is absolutely no doubt that he was one of the great acharyas of Hinduism and remains one of the most significant voices of Advaita Vedanta. However it would be incorrect to claim that, at the time of his arrival, utter chaos pervaded all through India in the matter of religion and philosophy, and that he single-handedly overpowered it all and restored Vedic Dharma and Advaita Vedanta to its pristine purity. For, as a matter of fact, hundreds of years before Adi Shankara was even born there were already many different spiritual paths and many gurus.

There were different schools of thought such as the Charvaka, Kapalika, Shakta, Sankhya, Jain, and Buddhist schools, not to speak of the Upanishadic tradition, engaged in serious and penetrating discussions and debates on the nature of the world and the self, the distinction of the soul, mind and body, if there is a beyond, a life after death and so on. The real story of Adi Shankara, therefore, is not that he defeated Buddhism or other philosophies but that he creatively engaged himself in discussions and debates with some of them, that he absorbed and integrated the core ideas and insights from some of these philosophies, especially Buddhism, to formulate his philosophy of Advaita Vedanta as a *direct* interpretation of the Upanishads, although, strictly speaking, there are many passages in the Upanishads which are clearly of a theistic and dualistic consequence.

Adi Shankara was born in 788 CE, to a Namboodiri Brahmin couple, Sri Sivaguru and Aryamba, in a village then known as Sasalam. The legend relates that Shankara was born after his parents prayed to Lord Shiva, as they had been childless for many years. Sivaguru died when Shankara was hardly seven years old.

He was a precocious child and the story goes that at quite a young age he had mastered the four Vedas. On reaching his sixteenth year, it is said, mother Aryamba wanted to get him married. But Shankara, who had resolved to renounce the world and become a sannyasi, refused. Widowed Aryamba lamented that she would be left all alone and there would be no one to perform her funeral rites after her death. Moved by his mother's plight, Shankara promised her that he would be there to serve her at her deathbed and perform the necessary rites. He then left her under the care of his relatives and proceeded to find a guru who would formally initiate him into the sacred order of *sannyasa*.

Legend has it that Shankara met Swami Govindapada at Badrinath and became his disciple. And it was Swami Govindapada who initiated and invested him with the robe of a sannyasi and taught him the philosophy of Advaita, as taught to him by his guru, Gaudapada. Later, Shankara is believed to have visited Kashi, the holy city, stayed there for a considerable period of time to write his now famous commentaries on the *Brahma Sutras* and the Bhagavad Gita.

Madhava-Vidyaranya's *Shankara Digvijaya* on Shankara's life makes for an interesting and revealing title. *Digvijaya* means 'tour of conquest or victory'. It is interesting to note here that epithets used for kings and emperors and their victorious battles should be used for spiritual masters and their spiritual triumphs. Indeed the spiritual masters were seen and celebrated as the ones higher than the 'earthly' masters.

A *jnani*, one who knows, has transcended duality and lives in a state of tranquillity, and he imparts his state of knowing and being to the world. His path, unlike a king's path, is not one of power, but renunciation of power. His teaching is an offering, an act of sacrifice— *jnana yajna*. Shankara, like the Buddha who took an open road centuries before him, initiated a *jnana yajna* in public space and set in motion a great spiritual fervour across the length and breadth of India.

Later, Allama Prabhu, Kabir and J. Krishnamurti were some other notable sages who, in many ways, followed in the footsteps of the Buddha and Shankara, by going into the world to engage, challenge and even provoke people to enquire, reflect, quest for answers to the deeper questions on life and reality and come upon the unfettered truth.

Among the many philosophical battles that Shankara won in favour of his Advaita Vedanta, the one against Mandana Misra, an authority on Vedic rituals or what is called *karmakanda*, is noteworthy. The great debate took place in Mandana Misra's house and his wife, Ubhaya Bharati, known for her learning, was the referee.

The arguments and counterarguments went on for several days and in the end Shankara came through victorious, thus establishing the supremacy of Vedantic Knowledge. Ubhaya Bharati gave her verdict; Mandana Misra accepted defeat and willingly became Shankara's disciple.

Flushed with success, Shankara now desired to defeat Ubhaya Bharati the judge, too, and proclaim his absolute superiority. Ubhaya Bharati accepted the challenge and the debate went on for 'seventeen days' and she finally silenced Shankara by opening the subject of sex. She said: 'Discuss the science and the art of love between the sexes. Enumerate its forms and expressions. What is its nature and what are its centres?' (Tapasyananda 1980).

Shankara was obviously stumped. But he was not a master of logic and philosophy for nothing! He asked for a month's time to answer her questions and then left with his disciples. Thereafter, it is said he used his yogic powers to leave his 'gross body' behind in a cave (to be taken care of by his disciples), while his 'subtle body' (invoking *parakayapraveshavidya*) entered the (about-to-be-cremated) dead body of a king named Amaruka. The ministers and the many wives of the king were overjoyed to see him return to life.

Now in the body of King Amaruka, Shankara went about his task of acquiring knowledge and experience of sex; in short, to know himself in the body. Eventually, his disciples, disguised as dancers, came into the royal court to remind him of his incomplete debate, and Shankara withdrew from the king's body. In his subtle form he left the court and re-entered his own body resting in the cave. From there he went to meet with Ubhaya Bharati and won the debate with his newly acquired knowledge of sexuality.

There are two ways we could interpret this episode, which is considered by traditional Shankarites to be only a metaphysical drama played out in the world of maya. One, the narrative could be implicitly saying that the experience and knowledge of samsara, of sexual desire and fulfilment, which Shankara lacked, is obligatory in one's quest for truth. Two, despite all his sadhana and learning, all his intelligence and attainment of mystical states, Shankara still had to deal with, or purge the remnants of sexuality in himself before coming into the highest state. And so, Ubhaya Bharati, supposedly an incarnation of Goddess Saraswati, had to nudge him into it.

In his *Shankara Digvijaya*, Madhava-Vidyaranya writes most poetically about Shankara's encounter with a *chandala*—a child born of a Brahmin woman and an 'untouchable' man. According to Brahminical tradition, sexual relations, or marriage, between a Brahmin woman and an 'untouchable' man was the most sacrilegious of all possible inter-caste unions. A child born of such a couple was condemned to remain a *chandala* (outcaste), *anamika* (nameless), and unfit to live in society. Manu, the lawgiver, decreed that a *chandala* dare not even look at a Brahmin. A *chandala* was not allowed to live in any town or village. Clad in the garments of the dead, alone he roamed, but only on the periphery of the civilized world, with dogs and donkeys as his only permitted companions.

One day in Varanasi, while Shankara was returning from his ablutions in the Ganges, he ran into a *chandala* with his pack of four dogs. Annoyed, he ordered the *chandala* to step aside and give him way. The *chandala* did not move away, instead he challenged Shankara:

> You are always going about preaching that the Vedas teach the non-dual Brahman to be the only reality and that He is immutable and unpollutable. If this is so, how has this sense of difference overtaken you? ... You asked me to move aside and give you way. To whom were your words addressed? To the body which comes from the same source and performs the same functions in the case of both a Brahmin and an outcaste? Or to the Atman, the witnessing Consciousness, which too is the same in all unaffected by anything that is of the body?'(Ibid.)

The reference to the 'body' in the passage is most revealing. It establishes the equality between 'bodies' of all caste the same way it asserts the oneness of Atman in all creatures. Shankara promptly recognized his folly. His eyes were opened and he realized that even in the so-called lowliest of the lowly, the *chandala*, the same Atman-Brahman exists, and then and there he composed five verses called the *Maneesha Panchakam*, in praise of the truth:

> The idea 'this is a Brahmin and this is an outcaste' is only something conjured up by me because of *avidya*, (ignorance). One who has attained this definite realization about Brahman which is bliss itself, eternal, supreme and pure, is my Guru, whether he is an outcaste or a Brahmin.

> The Self, which is Brahman, is the eternal ocean of supreme bliss. By meditating on the Self with a perfectly calm mind, the

sage experiences fulfilment. The person whose mind has become identified with this Self is not a mere knower of Brahman, but Brahman itself. (*Central Chinmaya Mission Trust* 1978)

Advaita Vedanta

Vedanta philosophy is generally equated or associated with Shankara although Shankara's Vedanta is only one among several other Vedanta philosophies, such as that of Ramanuja, Madhva, Nimbarka and Vallabha. The Upanishads, along with the *Brahma Sutras* and the Bhagavad Gita, have been the primal source and inspiration for these different Vedantas propounded by the acharyas.

Unlike the Vedantas of other acharyas, based as they are on the qualified or otherwise dualistic notions of reality, Shankara propounded what we call Advaita Vedanta, a complete non-dual philosophy. However, Shankara was not the first one to offer or propound the non-dualistic understanding of reality; indeed as Shankara himself submits he derived the philosophy of oneness from the Upanishads and from his guru Govindapada, a disciple of Gaudapada, who propounded the oneness of all reality, or non-dualism, in his *Central Chinmaya Mission Trust*, which is considered a seminal work on Advaita Vedanta.

Shankara harmonized Gaudapada's non-dual philosophy with that of the Upanishadic texts and built a systemized foundation for Advaita Vedanta. He argued that there exists a Reality (*sat*) that is unborn, eternal and is the source and ground of all existence, or the primordial reality that creates, maintains and withdraws within it the universe. While Atman is the perceptible personal particular, Brahman is the unlimited universal, but essentially both Atman and Brahman are identical.

In contrast to the Buddhist notion of *advaya*—according to which there is nothing outside of the conditioned physical and mental elements that constitute our being, and no Higher or Ultimate Reality, no two (*advaya*), which is 'empty, *sunya*, undescribable'—Shankara asserted that Brahman, although *It* is not considered as an object of

knowledge, is knowable, realizable, and that this profound knowing is
svasamvedya—self-revealed.

He laid a strong emphasis on *pramanas*, or valid (epistemological)
means by which one could obtain *jnana* of Brahman and Atman
and their essential unity. Accepting the Vedas and the Upanishads as
a source of knowledge, Shankara reasoned that through practice,
sravana (hearing), *manana* (reflecting) and *nididhyasana* (meditation) a
sincere seeker can gain self-knowledge and self-realization that lead
to the complete understanding of one's real nature as Brahman. This
supreme realization of the identity or unity of Atman and Brahman is
moksha, liberation.

> I am other than name, form and action.
> My nature is ever free!
> I am the Supreme Self,
> the Supreme Unconditioned Brahman.
> I am pure Awareness.

This supreme realization or liberation or *jivanmukti* can be achieved
while living and the one who has achieved this state of being is a
jivanmukta, one who has been freed from cycles of birth and death.
Emphasizing the importance of study and reflection on spiritual texts,
Shankara wrote *bhasyas*, commentaries, on the *Brahma Sutras* and
the Bhagavad Gita, and also composed a few substantial texts such
as *Viveka Chudamani*, *Atma Bodha*, *Aparoksha Anubhuti*, *Ananda Lahari*,
Atma-Anatma Viveka, *Drik-Drishya Viveka* and *Upadesa Sahasri*; yet, it
needs to be pointed out that he never rested his case on these texts;
rather, quite rightly, he insisted that ultimately, the state variously
denoted as Brahman, *Sat-Chit-Ananda*, Pure Being, Consciousness and
Bliss is something to be experienced, to be lived through.

The Notion of *Maya*

According to Shankara, maya is the empirical reality that entangles
human consciousness. It is the power of maya that creates a bondage

to the empirical world, preventing the unveiling of the true, unitary Self, the Brahman. Maya operates as ignorance, *avidya*, due to which Brahman is perceived as the material world, although, in reality, Brahman is attributeless and formless. It is ignorance that has made us forget our identity with Brahman.

Brahma Satyam Jagat Mithya,
Jeevo Brahmaiva Na Aparah

Brahman alone is real,
this world is unreal;
the *Jiva* is identical with Brahman.

Talking of *sunya*, emptiness, Nagarjuna proposed two notions of truth, in order to draw a distinction between limited truth and absolute truth. He introduced the notions of *samvritisatta*, truth as veiled by ignorance and depending on the common-sense perception of reality, and *paramarthasatta*, the ultimate, unqualified truth. In a similar vein, probably borrowing the idea from Nagarjuna, Shankara also proposed two kinds of truth: *vyvaharikasatya*, phenomenal reality, and *paramarthikasatya*, ultimate reality, to explain maya. Brahman is the absolute, ultimate reality. It is the Infinite Being, Infinite Consciousness and Infinite Bliss, without form, qualities, or attributes. It is the Ultimate Truth: beyond the senses, beyond the mind, beyond imagination. From the point of view of the experience of this Ultimate Truth, Brahman, Shankara asserted, the material world, its distinctness, the individuality of the living creatures, and even *Ishvara* (the Supreme Lord) itself, are all untrue, maya, a mere fantasy, a dream, an illusion.

This needs some explanation, since maya as illusion has posed many problems even to scholars, not to speak of lay people. Actually, maya means 'to measure'. Now, to measure anything there has to be a space, and a point of reference. The sages state that the self or ego takes its birth in that space, and that is the *point*, and with reference to it we create another point and try to measure. Anything we measure or experience from that point, which is the 'I' or ego, is only relative, not absolute, and to think of it in absolute terms is an illusion.

The world is not maya, an illusion; rather, the world is what it is, but our perception or experience of it in absolute, static and eternal terms is an illusion. So when a mad elephant comes charging at us, we run or step aside to protect ourselves as Shankara wisely did when a mad elephant rushed at him on the streets of Varanasi. It doesn't mean that the elephant or the world or the act of stepping aside is an illusion, or imaginary. To reiterate, maya means measurement and all measurements are relative and arbitrary, and therefore, to believe in it as absolute and unconditional is an error, and in that sense, an illusion.

Aphorisms

Knowledge, *jnana*, is the only direct means to liberation.

~

The phenomenal world seems to be real, but ... only until Brahman is realized.

~

One should understand the self to be the witness of the organism's activities.

~

The self is absolute consciousness as distinguished from *buddhi*, individual consciousness.

~

By mistaking the Self to be the individual self, one only imagines that the individual self knows, does and sees everything well. The Self illumines the consciousness.

~

I am other than the senses. I am not the mind. The Self is neither the senses nor mind, but is unconditioned.

~

I am that reality or knowledge that is ever unconditioned and ever free.

~

Sitting in a lonely place one should contemplate the one self, one-
pointedly.

~

Meditate on that whose nature is reality, bliss, and knowledge and
which is the witness of consciousness, as yourself.

~

All creatures are born of Brahman, the Supreme Self.

Allama Prabhu

The main sources for the biographical information on Allama Prabhu
are hagiographical texts such as Harihara's *Prabhudevara Ragale* (1220
CE), Bhimakavi's *Basava Purana* (1369 CE), fifteenth-century texts such
as Chamarasa's *Prabhulinga Lile* and four different versions of *Sunya
Sampadane*. Nonetheless, by creatively negotiating the mythical
elements in these stories and from the study of his *vachanas*, we should
be able to draw a fairly credible picture of Allama Prabhu, though it
would be difficult to fit that picture into a particular spiritual framework.
Was he a mystic and poet, an *avadhuta*, a *jangama* (a wandering monk),
a poet maverick or a sage? Perhaps he was all these rolled into one, if
such a thing were possible. To use a line from one of his *vachanas*, he
was like a butterfly with 'no memory of the caterpillar'. His life was
like the flight of an eagle in untrammelled air.

Legend recounts that Allama Prabhu was born to Sujnani and
Nirashankara in Shivamoga district in the present-day Indian state of
Karnataka. We do not know the exact year he was born, but since he
was a contemporary of Basavanna and Akka Mahadevi, we presume
it was sometime in the early part of the twelfth century. According
to Harihara's *Prabhudevara Ragale*, Allama's father Nirashankara
was a dance teacher and as a young man, Allama worked as a

temple drummer. Legend has it that he fell madly in love with one Kamalathe, a temple dancer, and married her. But as fate would have it, she caught a fever and died soon after. Devastated by the loss and heartbroken, Allama drifted from place to place, suffering, unable to forget her. One day, while sitting on a grassy mound, he happened to see the golden tip or pinnacle of a *gopuram* (pyramidal tower) jutting forth from the earth, as he describes in one of his *vachanas*, like 'the nipple-peak on the breast of the goddess of freedom'. When the site was excavated, he noticed a door to what appeared to be a shrine.

He kicked open the door and came upon a yogi, Animisayya (the one without eyelids, or, the open-eyed one), sitting in trance in the heart of the temple. The narrative takes on a supernatural turn here to tell us that Animisayya handed over a sacred lingam to a stunned Allama and vanished into thin air. It was an explosive moment that burnt away his suffering and Allama found himself totally transformed. From then on, it is said, Allama turned into an *avadhuta*, the one who has no place, no guru, no tradition and teaching, nevertheless offering his blazing yet cleansing insights into life and living, tendering a glimpse of *bayalu*, emptiness, to those interested in his words. His *vachanas* end with his signature line, 'Guheshvara' or 'Lord of Caves', signifying light and darkness, that *which is* and *is not*, and that which cannot be comprehended by the binary mind.

Allama is believed to have visited Kalyana and even presided over *Sunya-Shimasana*, the Throne of The Void, at the Anubhava Mantapa, the Hall of Experience, and engaged himself in conversations with the Shiva *saranas* (devotees). It is said that he rejected Vedic tradition, questioned and ridiculed image worship, the caste system, customs and rituals. Most *vachanakaras*, composers of *vachanas*, including Basavanna, Akka Mahadevi, Siddarama and others, spoke of him in their *vachanas* worshipfully and in glowing terms. They always referred to him as *prabhu*, master, indeed, as the guru of gurus, yet one who had no wish to offer a teaching, found a sect or have disciples.

His *vachanas* are littered with explosive images and bewildering metaphors that break and leap over and against the limitation of language. The mind is stunned reading about a 'black *koil* eating up the sun', or 'the toad that swallowed the sky', and the eye turns within itself, as it were, seeing a 'blind man catch a snake'. Both hunter and hunted die and the seeker realizes there is nothing to seek or to know; the truth is neither here nor there, and the one who knows 'gets no results'.

About one thousand three hundred *vachanas* are attributed to Allama. But he was not a bhakti poet in the conventional sense of the term. As the noted scholar and critic, the late D.R. Nagaraj said, 'Allama's insistence on opaque and mysterious modes of metaphor is in stark contrast with the emotionally transparent model of bhakti' (Nagaraj 1999). While his early *vachanas* seem to emphasize the importance of moral values and devotional worship of, and surrender to, Shiva, his later *vachanas*, which are mystical and cryptic, rich in paradoxes and inversions, are critical of rituals and social conventions and are persistently against any form of symbolism. More akin to the method of four-corner negation used by Nagarjuna in the second century, and the 'anti-teaching' of U.G. Krishnamurti, Allama's made him the ultimate negater of everything that can be expressed. No wonder he was called Allama, Allayya, Alla, which (in Kannada) means 'no', 'not it'.

In Allama's *vachanas* we don't so much look for the meaning of words and metaphors and images (for all meanings get subverted and then ultimately negated), as see or sense an inner crisis that explodes, causing a seismic shift and transformation of consciousness. In other words, we realize there is nothing to achieve, no yonder shore to reach. There is only *jnana* (knowledge), *arivu* (understanding or awareness)' a fire that burns up not only what is false but also the illusion of gods and goddesses, heaven and earth, boundaries and borders, and what is left is only *bayalu*, open space, emptiness, the void that has no beginning and no end. In Allama's words: '*Bayalu bayalali bithi bayalu bayalali beladu bayalu bayalaagi bayalayithaiah'*: Emptiness sown in emptiness, growing in emptiness, emptiness emptying itself turns into emptiness.

Fifteenth-century works such as Harihara's *Prabhudevara Ragale*, Chamarasa's *Prabhulinga Lile*, *Sunya Sampadane* by Gummalapurada Siddalingadevaru, and *Halageyaryana Sunya Sampadane*, give a vivid account, in the form of dialogues, of Allama's interaction with contemporary saints and poets such as Basavanna, Chenna Basava, Akka Mahadevi, Siddarama and others.

Here is an edited account of one such set of dialogues adapted from the fifteenth-century works and from a modern narrative, *In Search of Shiva* (Rao 2010) These profound yet fiery dialogues should give us a feel of the mystic power and revolutionary character of Allama and his uncompromising non-duality, akin to Ashtavakra and U.G. Krishnamurti.

Basavanna invited Allama Prabhu to Anubhava Mantapa, The Hall of Experience, to speak with the Shiva *saranas*. The hall was built like an indoor theatre. At one end was a raised platform and around it, in horseshoe fashion, were seats built of bricks and mortar. And there were six entrances, representing the six phases of the Virashaiva faith. In the middle of the platform, was a large seat called the *Sunya Simhasana* or Throne of Void. Inlaid with gold, it looked majestic like a king's throne and was flanked by four smaller seats, two on either side. Clad in a white top and cotton dhoti, imposing with his long, grizzled shaggy beard, Allama sat on the *Sunya Simhasana*, unsmiling, looking grave, even severe. On the four smaller seats, two each on either side of the throne, sat Basavanna, Chenna Basava, Chowdayya, and Siddarama. Down below on the floor sat men and women, Shiva *saranas*, eagerly waiting for Allama to speak.

The first round of discussion centred on Allama. The *saranas* were very curious about Allama's background: his parents, his guru, his *sadhana* and experiences. They wanted to know if he was really married, if so, what happened to his wife. They wanted to know if it was true that he accidentally discovered a cave and that inside the cave he met a yogi and received *diksha* from him. And then they were keen to know of his understanding of *kayaka* (work), *linga*, and *anubhaava*.

Allama refused to answer questions about his life. Reacting to his indifference and curt refusal to answer, Siddarama said, 'Prabhu, be kind enough to answer the questions. The *saranas* are very eager and anxious to hear your story from your own lips.'

Allama said, 'There is nothing extraordinary about my birth and growing up. It is like anybody else's. Don't attribute any divine purpose to my birth. Better still to believe that every birth is divine, even the birth of a buffalo, dog, or bedbug.

'There is no special story to tell here. Like everyone else I was born of a woman. And like a fool I too went in search of God, struggled through all kinds of *sadhana*. There is nothing I did not try, including sleeping with a corpse, eating from a skull and doing *tapas* standing on one leg. And then came a point when I felt totally disgusted with myself and my search for things that existed only in my imagination. The very will to search, to do anything, even the urge to quench my thirst and hunger, broke down. Everything came to a standstill, to a nought, and I found myself free. I don't know how it happened and therefore, I have no way of talking about it.'

A daring *sarana* stood up and asked rather bluntly, 'Prabhu, were you married?'

Caressing his beard, grinning mischievously, Allama replied, 'Yes, I was married. And my wife died of illness after three months of our marriage. It was good she died early, otherwise, married to one like me, she would have died of misery, or who knows, she might even have committed suicide.'

The *saranas* were stunned by Allama's apparently insensitive answer. However, another *sarana* got up and asked, 'Prabhu, in one of your early *vachanas*, you mention Animisayya, the one without eyelids. Was he the yogi you met inside a cave?'

'I didn't meet any yogi without eyelids or without eyes, either inside the cave or outside,' grinned Allama. 'I don't know who gave you that *vachana* or where you heard it. It must surely be a product of someone's imagination.'

'It *is* in your *vachana*,' insisted the *sarana*, 'and you do mention Animisayya.'

'Then it could be my imagination. There is nothing more to it so forget it, it has no significance whatsoever.'

Chenna Basava attired in a long gown, stood and respectfully joining his palms asked, 'Prabhu, what does *Animisayya* mean?'

'Open-eyed one.'

'What does it mean?'

'When there is no thought, then your eyes don't blink, they stay open, that's what it means.'

'I don't understand.'

'When *you* are not there, you'll know.'

'Prabhu, I have another question,' said Chenna Basava, 'almost all your *vachanas* end with a reference to Lord Guhesvara. What or who is Guhesvara?'

'Good question,' chuckled Allama. 'It's not what you think—Lord of Caves—like Lord of Rivers, Lord of the Sky, Lord of the Heart or what have you. It only means the hidden one, the mystery, the unknown.'

'You mean the Supreme Reality, the Infinite Absolute, is hidden, unknown?'

'Mere words.'

'But don't words work as signs, guiding symbols?'

Allama shouted in irritation, 'When there is no outside or inside, when there is no I or other, where is the sign, where is the need for any sign or symbol?'

'Yes, Prabhu,' Chenna Basava agreed hastily. 'But, we can approach or understand that only through symbols, is it not?'

'Ah! You are clever!' Allama sighed. 'This talk is not going to help. Language only distorts what is there.'

'You mean language destroys meaning?'

'It only means language fragments and distorts reality and thereby falsifies your understanding.'

'What is true understanding then?' demanded Chenna Basava.
Allama replied:

> 'The one who knows joy is not the happy one,
> the one who knows sorrow is not the unhappy one,
> the one who knows both joy and sorrow
> is not the *jnani*.
> Only the one who grasps
> the sign of the dead,
> and of the one who was never born,
> knows Lord Guhesvara.'

Chenna Basava flushed. The little crowd of *saranas* came alive.
Bahurupi Chowdayya slowly stood up from among them and after
adjusting his orange turban, he put his palms together in reverence
and said, 'Prabhu, you are the story that has no beginning, no
middle and no end.'

'So are you, friend,' bellowed Allama, 'so is everyone.'

'I do not know about that,' said Bahurupi, 'But, Prabhu, what
I know is that all of us start our lives with stories. We come to
know and begin to understand the world around us and ourselves
through stories—stories of life and death, of joy and sorrow;
stories of love, hatred, jealousy, pride, devotion and all that. There
simply is no end. Or, perhaps one could say that the end is in the
beginning, and beginning in the end. But, still, it's a mystery. It
remains a mystery. What is this mystery, Prabhu?'

'You are that mystery, Bahurupi,' replied Allama.

'If I'm that mystery,' asked Bahurupi, 'does it mean that if I
know myself, I'll understand that mystery?'

'If you can really know yourself, if your eyes can really see
themselves, you may.'

'Prabhu, I can see myself in the mirror; my eyes can see
themselves in the mirror!'

'Can you, really?' asked Allama. 'Do you see yourself or do you see only the idea of yourself? If you can see yourself without the idea, without the image of what or who you are, you'll be fortunate. Try it.'

This did not go down well with some *saranas* and Nageya Marithande stood up angrily saying, 'Prabhu, you don't seem to approve of anything. You find fault with everything, reject everything. Why then do you travel so much and why do you speak at all? More importantly, why are you here?'

Allama smiled. 'I travel and speak because I have nothing better to do and because I can't help it. You think you are very smart, eh? Would you ask a bird why it sings and why it keeps flying about from place to place? Would you?'

Chenna Basava stood up again, offered obeisance to Allama and said with renewed vigour, 'Prabhu, I do not understand why you reject the need for bhakti. Don't you think without bhakti we'll be lost in the hustle and bustle of samsara? Bhakti is certainly not the end but a means to an end. Bhakti is the boat in which we cross the sea of dualism to reach the shore of oneness. And *linga* is what gives bhakti the needed focus and direction. Again, *linga* is not the end but a means to go beyond, to reach *nirakara*, the formless, Supreme Reality. Without bhakti, and *linga* worship, I believe, we will keep going round and round, lost in a desert, reaching nowhere.'

Allama smiled and caressed his beard. 'When the whole universe is the temple of Shiva, and the sky the *linga*, where is the need for yet another symbol, Chenna Basava?'

Chenna Basava challenged, 'Doesn't the *linga* represent more simply and effectively what you are saying? Or, do you think all external forms are meaningless?'

'I didn't say meaningless. But, yes, quite unnecessary.'

'On the contrary,' said Chenna Basava with great vehemence, 'I think they are absolutely necessary. Just as a ritual when performed

with a sincere and pure heart is a stepping stone, a symbol is a
springboard to that which is beyond. Just as through rituals you
connect with the unknown,' he argued, 'through form you connect
with the formless. A pot is not without space, though you might say
that that space is constricted and limited by the pot. But actually, it
is a matter of realization through devotion, discipline, rigour and
experience. And with that realization, form becomes the formless.
So I would argue and maintain that form is formlessness.'

His fingers picking at his beard, eyebrows raised, Allama
remarked, 'Brilliant play of words!'

'Prabhudeva, why do you deny the obvious?' asked Marayya, a
senior *sarana*, his voice cracking in pain. 'Why do you doubt the
indisputable? A kite that plays about freely in the untrammelled air
needs an anchor, doesn't it? Similarly, can a cartwheel move without
solid ground under it? Likewise, can there be bhakti without *linga*?
And without *linga*, can one come upon emptiness? O, Prabhudeva,
why do you ridicule *linga* worship?'

'Don't be silly,' snapped Allama, 'I'm not against *linga* worship.
Did *I* ask you to stop worshipping the *linga*? What does it matter to
me whether you worship the *linga* or a tree or some boulder? It is
your life, your fate.'

Chenna Basava leapt to his feet, he had never been so frustrated
and annoyed. 'Prabhu, this is unfair. We know that before coming
upon this supreme realization and understanding, you too
went through rigorous *sadhana*. One time you too had a guru,
worshipped the *linga*, and performed *tapas*. Why then do you deny
the same to others? Every master in the past, as it has been the case
with you as well, has gone through a process, a method, a path. It is
natural, inescapable; I would even say absolutely necessary.'

'Shut up,' shouted Allama. Then he stood up, an imposing
figure with a long, flowing beard, and said stridently: 'There is no
guru, no *linga*, no *jangama*, no *padodaka*, no *prasada*, no *vibhuti*,
no *rudraksha* and no mantra. No method, no process whatsoever.
If your *elders*, whom you call masters, either of the past or of the

present have talked of a process, a method, a path, then, they were
and are all misguided fools. Just forget about them. Don't ever
mention them to me again. They are all no match for the little toe
of my left foot.'

Chenna Basava stood speechless as though struck by lightning,
his face ashen. The *saranas* couldn't believe their ears. Allama had
not only silenced their invincible Chenna Basava, but had even
called him a fool. At last, getting up, Basava took a step forward,
folded his palms in greeting, and then turned and slightly bent his
head in a show of respect to Allama. Then straightening up, he
spoke: 'Why this long debate about form and formless? Does a
lover need proof of love before he begins to love?'

He paused, and surveying the *saranas* asked, 'Tell me, can *prana*
exist without a body? Can the face see itself without a mirror? Of
what significance or worth is inward knowing, if it can't express
itself in the outer world?' He paused again to huge murmurs of
approval from the *saranas*, and then continued in a voice charged
with emotion. '*Linga* is that body, *linga* is that mirror, *linga* is that
inner vision assuming a form in the external world.'

'Yes, true, true, very true ...' chanted the *saranas*. 'Why all this
long debate, O, Kudalasangamadeva!'

Basava continued, 'You may sing passionately profound lines,
you may listen to the great Puranas and you may speak eloquently
the philosophy of Vedanta, but, with no bhakti in your heart, it'll
be like washing a toddy-pot only from the outside.'

Now no more harsh, but in a voice that was loud yet grave,
Allama responded:

> 'Born to earth as rock,
> shaped by a sculptor,
> turned into an idol in guru's hand,
> as what do I worship, the bastard,
> born of these three?'

There was a huge groan of extreme shock and strong disapproval. Siddarama saw several *saranas* put their hands over their ears and wince. Enraged though Chenna Basava was, he had not the courage to stand up to Allama. A great, almost palpable silence pervaded the hall. Then Basava smiled, adjusted his turban and stood up again. His palms folded together, the smile still playing on his lips, he chanted:

> 'Lord, your sacred feet
> cover the earth and sky,
> extend to the underworld and beyond.
> The crown of your head
> touches the boundaries of boundless space.
> O, Kudalasangamadeva,
> both visible and invisible,
> mysterious is your form,
> now come alive as *linga* in my palm.'

Allama arose again from the Throne of Void and thundered:

> 'He is not the three-eyed one
> reigning over the three worlds;
> not the one in rags,
> wearing garlands of skulls and roaming the forests.
> He is not Isvara, nor Maheshvara;
> Guheshvara Linga is beyond thought.'

Basava bowed his head thrice to Allama. Then he replied:

> 'Without *anubhaava* bhakti is empty;
> Without *anubhaava* linga is unattainable;
> Without *anubhaava* one understands nothing.
> When such is the truth, why call

anubhaava an invention of thought,
O, Prabhudeva?'

Allama smiled:

'If there is no desire,
there is no imagination;
if there is no imagination,
there is no thinking;
if there is no thinking,
there is no Guheshvara;
if there is no Guheshvara,
there is no truth,
no void, either.'

Quickly, Basava countered:

'You exist,
like light hidden in the horizon,
like a frame in a picture,
like meaning in a word,
O Kudalasangamadeva!'

Allama smiled and replied:

'Escaping the claws of the cat
waiting for it in the loft, the rat
hid itself in its eye.
With the separation gone,
nobody ever saw Lord Guhesvara.'

The *saranas* were stunned by the mind-boggling analogy. What was Allama saying? But Basava, finally getting Allama's point, put his palms together and closed his eyes for a while in deep thought. Then, opening them, he raised his voice and chanted:

> 'I saw a lion come,
> devour another
> and itself die.
> I saw inwardness
> without an interior,
> outwardness without refuge.
> I saw in a field
> flowers without petals, and
> beheld a magnificent form
> take shape,
> and the whole world
> become a wonder.
> O Allama Prabhu,
> salutations to you.'

Taking the cue from their master, the *saranas* immediately rose to their feet and chanted: 'Allama Prabhu, *namo-namo.*' There was no stopping Allama Prabhu, there was no stopping the roar of silence.

It is quite possible that Allama may impress upon a few as an argumentative or quarrelsome mystic. If so, then, it is not entirely incorrect. However, we need to see this aspect in the context of his 'individuality' and background. He was probably, unlike the gentle Ramana, the kind of person who wouldn't put up with falsehood. Ramana may have just smiled away the stupidities of the seekers who went to him, or politely pointed out their mistakes. But Allama, given his explosive character, had to blast and take to pieces the 'false' perceptions and pretensions.

The Buddha did it in his own way and overturned many a conventional and established views and practices. So did Kabir by chiding and reprimanding the religious priests and gurus who he thought exploited the gullible and misled the people, and so did J. Krishnamurti and U.G. Krishnamurti in our times. Allama was, like U.G. Krishnamurti, the fiercest among the sages, who would not allow the seekers to anchor themselves and find comfort in false ideas and practices. The truth had to be brought home, howsoever hard and unpalatable.

Allama Prabhu: Selected Vachanas

I saw the toad swallow the sky,
the blind man catch the snake.
I saw the heart conceive,
the hand grow big with a child,
the ear drink up the smell of camphor,
the nose eat up the dazzle of pearls, and
hungry eyes devour diamonds.

~

I saw the corpse of samsara
alive with swarming worms.
I saw dogs come to devour
the reeking body, start a fight.
But I didn't see you anywhere there,
O Lord Guheshvara.

~

Whence this great tree,
whence the koel bird?
Whence and what kind of relationship?
Gooseberry from the mountain,
salt from the sea,
whence and what kind of relationship?
O, Lord of the caves,
between you and I,
whence and what kind of relationship?

~

Your Vedas are mere words,
Your *Shastras* and Puranas a gossip,
Your bhakti so much noise—

No one may trace
the footstep on the water;
nor the sound of the word…
Guhesvara
is neither here
nor there.

Kabir

The images are all lifeless, they cannot speak:
I know, for I have cried aloud to them.
The Purana and the Koran are mere words:
lifting up the curtain, I have seen.

Legend has it that after Kabir's death a dispute arose between groups of Hindus and Muslims with regard to the funeral. The Hindu party, led by Raja Bir Singh, and the Muslims by Bejli Khan Pathan, laid claim to the body. Just when heated arguments between the two parties threatened to turn violent, an old man appeared at the spot, appealed for calm and told the disputants to go and look for Kabir's body that lay covered with a sheet of cloth. They removed the shroud only to find a heap of flowers in place of the corpse. The two parties divided the flowers—one portion was buried in Maghar and the other portion cremated in Kashi.

Where did Kabir's body disappear to? Are such miracles possible? It's an enigma and indeed many such enigmas surround Kabir's life.

For we do not know with certainty where and when and into which caste or religion he was born, whether he had a guru and received initiation, whether he was married and had children and so on. But what we can be certain of is that he did not give importance to caste and religion, customs and rituals and traditions, that he was a spiritual maverick, an *avadhuta*, who spent a large part of his life in the holy city of Kashi, composed *bijaks* or poems and spoke to those who cared to listen to him and died at Maghar.

There are of course enough indicators to believe that he was brought up in the family of a Muslim weaver, although the question of his parentage remains shrouded in mystery. Kabir himself does not help us in this matter; in one of his profoundly philosophical *bijaks*, he says:

I did not take birth,
nor did I dwell in a womb.
A child appeared. At Kashi
I made my abode in the forest,
there a weaver found me.
… I am beyond all body,
the Infinite and Perfect One.

However, scholars more or less agree that from all the circumstantial evidence available, we could fairly say that Kabir was born around 1398 CE and breathed his last around 1448 CE or 1455 CE. He was born to or adopted into a family of weavers, *julaha* (Farsi), or *kori* (Sanskrit), which may have converted to Islam a few decades earlier, which is why he was probably not that well acquainted with Islamic beliefs and practices. But, going by his poetry it appears that he had an intimate knowledge and understanding of Hindu thought and mythology.

A better and creative way to understand Kabir would be to not give much importance to his social background, or to the probable influences he might have come under; instead, to see him as a sage who trod a path all his own. Take the example of Sri Ramana. At the age of seventeen he underwent a 'near-death experience', went to Arunachalam where he went through a series of 'death' experiences that put him in *sahaja sthithi*. Later, Sri Ramana made use of the available Hindu thought and vocabulary to make sense of the non-dual state he had come into and to communicate with others.

Similarly, it's quite possible that Kabir underwent a life-altering experience that opened him up to come into the *sahaja sthithi*, or the natural state. And since he had been exposed to the Hindu religion, he employed its language and mythological stories to communicate the burning oneness of reality.

The experience of oneness of reality happens with the breaking down of the experiencing-structure, namely the 'I', the self that divides up life into this and that and is the cause of conflict, fear and sorrow. It is this explosive experience or transformation of the body-mind that shapes a sage's life and his teaching. This aspect is crucial to our understanding of a sage, otherwise we might end up trying to trace the possible influences on him and then fit him into a particular background or school of thought.

Even as a young man, it is said, Kabir offended Hindus and Muslims alike. To Muslims who accused him of becoming a Kaffir, an unbeliever, he responded: 'He who uses wicked violence or robs the world by deceit, who eats or drinks intoxicants, or seizes the goods of others, he is the *kafir*'. To Brahmins who considered him a Muslim and thus an untouchable *mlechcha* who posed as a Vaishnavite by applying the tilak on his forehead, Kabir replied: 'On my tongue Vishnu, in my eyes Narayan, and in my heart Gobind dwells.'

Kabir's *bijaks* are like a finely woven tapestry of queries, wonderment and assertion of the oneness of reality; or like a continuous text that sees the world as it is and deconstructs the illusion that surrounds human existence. Indeed, human life, rather all creation, is like a finely woven fabric by the Master Weaver:

You haven't puzzled out
any of the Weaver's secrets:

it took Him
a mere moment
to stretch out the whole universe
on His loom.

While you were there,
listening
to the Vedas and Puranas,
I was here,
spreading out
the threads for my warp.

He fashioned His loom
out of earth and sky:
He plied the sun and moon
simultaneously
as His twin shuttles.

When He worked the pair
of treadles in the pit below
in tandem,
I acknowledged Him
in my mind
as a master weaver.

I found His signs,
the signs of a weaver,
inside my house:
in a flash
I recognized Him
as Rama.

Kabir says, I've smashed
my loom:

only the Weaver
can mesh
thread with thread.

> (*Shabda* 36, in Dharwadker 2003)

Kabir's Rama was not the mythological Sita Rama, or Dasharatha
Rama, but God without attributes, *Nirguna* Brahman, the formless
Eternal Presence. He still had to use religious terms and mythological
figures to drive home what he wanted to, which was to show that the
hardened religious identities and mechanical adherence to customs
and rituals were in fact antithetical to the true religious spirit, which
brooked no barriers, no borders and boundaries. Spirituality, which is
the core of any and every religion, is the way out of religious chicanery
and bigotry, and religion's divisive character. There simply is no two.

Brother, whence came two divine masters of the world?
Who has led you astray?
Allah, Rama, Karim, Keshava, Hari, Hazrat, are but names given.
Jewels and jewels are made of one gold bar; but in it is one nature
only—
One reads the Vedas, another Khutbas; one is Maulvi, another is
Pande.
Kabir says, both alike have gone astray; none has found Rama.

> (*Shabda* 30, in Tagore 1915)

~

If Allah resides
inside a mosque, then whose is the rest of the land?
Hindus claim His Name
inhabits an idol:
but God can't be found
in either place.

The southern country

is Hari's home,
the west is Allah's camping ground.
Search your heart,
your heart of hearts:
that's His abode,
that's His camp.

Kabir says, listen,
O men and women:
seek shelter with the One and Only.
Repeat His singular Name,
you creatures: for only then
will you be able
to cross life's ocean.

(*Goindval Pothi, Raga Prabhati*, in Dharwadker 2003)

~

Why look for Me anywhere else, my friend,
when I'm here, in your possession?

Not in temples, not in mosques—
not in the Ka'aba, not on Kailash.

Not in rites, not in rituals—
not in yoga or renunciation.

Look for Me and you'll find Me quickly—
all it takes is a moment's search.

Kabir says, listen, O brothers—
He's the very Breath of our breaths.

(*Kabir Vani: Pada* 1, in Dharwadker 2003)

The main thrust of the Bhakti Movement (which was of course not a monolithic or homogenous movement) was a call for a return to the original of all temples, namely, the spirit within—whether we call it God or Khuda or Rama or Shiva, or the Absolute Infinite Principle—all-pervasive, pulsating and revealing itself in every form of life.

Over the centuries, saints, mystics and sages have pointed out again and again the absurdity of our clinging to customs and rituals, the dangers of spiritual authority and power, of the institutionalization of God's grace and the sacred. And Kabir was one of the severest yet most cleansing voices against such religionisms and their politics of power.

To Kabir, reading of the scriptures, *yajnas* and mantras, tantras and yantras, temples and pilgrimages, mosques, mullahs, prayer and fasting—all of these beliefs and practices are flawed and misleading, in the sense that these beliefs and practices have become substitutes or proxies for the real thing. They take you away from God, that great vibrant presence which is all-pervasive and beyond name and form. True bhakti needs no mediation, for all the mediating agents—scriptures, temples and priests, mosques and mullahs—block your spiritual growth and put you on the wrong path. In short, Kabir's was at once a critique of organized religions and their tyranny and a call to return to the unmediated vision or experience of *That* which has no attributes.

But the world being what it is, the reality on the ground appears to have remained the same, thanks to the religious authority of priests and mullahs and the political patronage; the walls of separation remain intact and the belief systems that produce conflict and anxiety, fear and sorrow, continue to thrive. It's a saddening thought. In such a world, Kabir laments, talking of oneness of reality is like 'selling mirrors in the city of the blind'.

But then, Kabir also knows this is the work of maya: the enchanting and mesmerizing power that holds the credulous in its web of illusion. *Maya*, like a great robber, wanders the world mesmerizing the common man as much as the kings and ascetics, and it's an intriguing yet an 'ineffable' tale. Unless we get out of this web of maya in which we are trapped, we'd forever live in conflict, fear and sorrow.

His poems on maya directly link him with the teachings of Advaita
Vedanta as propounded by the likes of Gaudapada and Shankara.
According to Advaita Vedanta, the entire phenomenal world is simply
a dream or fantasy, and is ultimately unreal. It is the power of maya
that creates a bondage to the empirical world, preventing the unveiling
of the true, unitary Self. So, as a castle in the air is seen to be an
illusion, maya, so is this whole manifested world seen by those who
have realized Brahman.

O yogi,
the world of *Maya*
is hard to renounce.

When I renounced my home,
I was trapped in my clothes;
when I renounced my clothes,
I was stuck with my mendicant's rounds.

When I renounced desire,
anger wouldn't leave me;
when I renounced anger,
I was stuck with greed.

When I renounced greed,
my ego wouldn't leave me;
my self-regard, my boastfulness,
my attachment to appearances.

When my mind was finally detached,
I renounced the world of *Maya*:
my concentration, my ancient memory
then fused with my words.

Kabir says, listen,
my good brothers—
one in a million
has solved this mystery

(*Kabir Vani: Pada* 12, in Dharwadker 2003)

Kabir overcame the make-believe world of maya. He penetrated the mystery of maya and knew why we cling to customs and rituals, scriptures and gurus, and fall into the delusion that with these aids we can reach the shore of tranquillity. Why we constantly suffer anxiety, doubt, fear and pain, why we fail to come to terms with reality as it is and fail to come into intelligence with compassion in our hearts— he knew, but could not say how he actually solved this mystery for himself. It just happened, and he could not say either why it didn't happen to many others but to only one in a million.

This is the great enigma: millions tread the path of spirituality, seeking liberation, but the blessed lightning strikes only one in a million. There is no guarantee that the seeking or search will end in fulfilment. You meditate, do sadhana for years and still the goal eludes you. Allama Prabhu, Akka Mahadevi, Lalleshwari and Kabir, however, by some luck as it were, were thrown off the river of samsara and found themselves on the shore, in a state of being where the seeking had ended. It was the instance of bhakti, which is, to borrow a phrase from Ramana Maharshi, 'like the stick used for stirring the burning pyre', in that 'it will itself in the end get destroyed'.

Perhaps it worked when there was total surrender, surrender not to an external agency, but surrender in the sense of giving up, letting go all efforts with the piercing realization that the very effort is the impediment to the realization of *that* which cannot be willed.

Kabir has been variously described as a philosopher and a poet, a fearless speaker and a penetrating social critic, a great musician and a poet of extraordinary depth and understanding, a gifted mystic and a sage, one who had ended conflict and sorrow and come into the non-dual state of being or *sahaja sthithi*. We use terms like *sahaja sthithi* or samadhi, nirvana, moksha and so on, to describe that state of being, but in actuality, it is impossible to describe, it is inexpressible. It is a state that cannot be captured in words, which by their very nature either fragment reality, or frame reality in pairs of opposites. So, like the Buddhists, Kabir speaks of himself in negative terms, to give us a sense of that enigmatic state of being.

> I'm neither pious nor impious—
> I'm neither an ascetic nor a hedonist.
> I don't dictate and I don't listen—
> I'm neither a master nor a servant.
> I'm neither a captive nor a free man—
> I'm neither involved nor indifferent.
> I haven't been estranged from anyone—
> and I'm no one's close companion.
> I'm the agent of all my actions—
> yet I'm indifferent to my deeds.
> A few in a million can grasp this notion—
> they sit with poise, ensconced in immortality.
> Such is the creed of Kabir—
> some things it builds, some it destroys.
>
> (*Kabir Vani: Pada* 79, in Dharwadker 2003)

For the past six centuries now, Kabir's poems have been translated and circulated in several languages and he remains probably the most widely read and sung and quoted mystic-poet across India today. His poems and aphorisms have a vital presence in the *Adi Granth*, the holy book of Sikhs.

Today there are several branches of Kabir Panths, each one claiming to be true to Kabir's teaching. Kabir's *Bijak* is their sacred book. Some of these groups, which have been instrumental in popularizing Kabir's songs, are like any other religious sects, like Vaishanvites, for instance.

Members of some of these groups, ironical as it may sound today, worship the idol of Kabir, and even wear the sacred thread and sandal paste, practices against which Kabir taught all his life.

'He nevertheless remains an enigma,' writes Vinay Dharwadker, 'a shadowy presence eluding our grasp', who, 'disappeared into his songs: he has ceased to be a "person", and has become a "whole climate of opinion" instead' (Dharwardker 2003). However, we may still assert with confidence that through his songs he remains a fearless voice against the organized or institutionalized forms of religions and their narrow, contentious discourses that have become a source of conflict, fear and violence; his remains a voice, bold and cleansing, celebrating the Oneness of life.

A Selection of Kabir's Songs

As the seed is in the plant, as the shade is in the tree,
as the void is in the sky, as infinite forms are in the void—
so from beyond the Infinite, the Infinite comes; and from the
Infinite the finite extends.

~

He makes the inner and the outer worlds to be indivisibly one;
the conscious and the unconscious, both are His footstools.
He is neither manifest nor hidden,
He is neither revealed nor unrevealed:
There are no words to tell that which He is.

~

I have found the key of the mystery,
I have reached the root of union.
Travelling by no track, I have come to the sorrowless land.

~

I have known in my body the sport of the universe:
I have escaped from the error of this world.
The inward and the outward are become as one sky,
I am drunken with the sight of this Infinitude.
This Light of Thine fills the universe: the lamp of love that

burns on the salver of knowledge.

Kabir says: 'There error cannot enter, and the conflict of life
and death is felt no more.'

~

In the beginning was He alone, sufficient unto Himself:
The formless, colourless, and unconditioned Being.

Then was there neither beginning, middle, nor end;
then were no eyes, no darkness, no light;
then were no ground, air, nor sky; no fire, water, nor earth;
no rivers like the Ganges and the Jumna, no seas, oceans, and
waves.

Then was neither vice nor virtue; scriptures there were not, as
the Vedas and Puranas, nor as the Koran.

Kabir ponders in his mind and says, 'Then was there no activity:
the Supreme Being remained merged
in the unknown depths of His own Self.'

(Tagore 1915)

Seven

Beyond Gender

Akka Mahadevi

Akka Mahadevi (*c.* 1130–60 CE) the poet saint, like others of her time, did not keep any record of her work. The main sources of her *vachanas*, as well as biographical information on her and on the other *saranas* (devotees) that we have today, come from hagiographies composed later—such as *Mahadeviyakkagala Ragale* and *Prabhudevara Ragale* by Harihara in the twelfth century CE, *Basava Purana* by Bhimakavi in 1369 CE; fifteenth-century texts such as Chamarasa's *Prabhulinga Lile* and four different versions of *Sunya Sampadane*. All the same, Harihara's *Prabhudevara Ragale* and *Mahadeviyakkagala Ragale* are considered by many scholars as relatively reliable sources of information on both Allama Prabhu and Akka Mahadevi.

Wading through these different texts where 'traditional forces' were already at work, fitting Akka Mahadevi and other *saranas* into a traditional framework, it is difficult to pinpoint and assert that this is exactly how Akka Mahadevi lived, moved and composed her *vachanas*. However, reading between the lines of these texts, and in light of her *vachana*s and the observations made by the likes of Allama and Basavanna and other *sarana*s on Mahadevi, we should yet be able to arrive at a fairly balanced and credible view of this extraordinary, awe-inspiring being who walked this land more than eight hundred years ago.

Mahadevi was born in Uduthadi, in Shivamoga district in Karnataka. Her parents, Nirmala Shetty and Sumati, were ardent devotees of Lord Shiva. Legend recounts that at quite an early age Mahadevi took to worshipping the Shivalinga and displayed strong religious proclivities. By the time she reached sixteen or seventeen years of age she had, in all probability, attained a high degree of spiritual maturity. Possibly, she had even had a deep life-altering mystical experience that set her up on the spiritual journey which took her to Kalyana, and then eventually to Srisailam, her final resting place, where she is believed to have attained *aikya*, or the unitary experience.

At the early stage of her calling, Mahadevi must have had a guru, for she does acknowledge the help she derived from her guru in one of her early *vachana*s. However, going by her *vachana*s as a whole, it appears she was largely steered by her own inner experiences. There is no doubt she was a highly determined person, who responded unswervingly and fearlessly to her spiritual calling. While we acknowledge her strong will there was perhaps something more than will power, some inscrutable power that guided her towards her destiny.

Mahadevi was initiated into *Sri Aurobindo Centre for Arts and Communication* worship, possibly by her guru, at the age of ten and from then on she considered herself betrothed to Lord Shiva. She spent her adolescence in His worship and composed *vachana*s that spilt over with fervent longing for her Beloved, whom she called 'Chennamallikarjuna', the name of Shiva, it is said, in her home-town temple. Mahadevi considered herself wedded to Chennamallikarjuna, the Shiva of the Peaks, who, at this stage does have a name and form. He is *saguna*, one with attributes. And so her *vachana*s are intensely

iconic, relational; there is rasa or aesthetic emotion: love and the sense
of being lovelorn, hope and despair, ecstasy and agony.

> Listen, sister, listen,
> I had a dream.
> I saw rice, betel, palm leaf
> and coconut.
> I saw an ascetic
> come to beg,
> white teeth and small matted curls.
> I followed on his heels
> and held his hand,
> he who goes breaking
> all bounds and beyond,
> I saw the lord Chennamallikarjuna.

(Ramanujan 1973)

~

> I am in love with the one
> who knows no death, no evil, no form.
> I am in love with the one
> who knows no place, no space,
> no beginning, no end.
> I am in love with the one
> who knows no fears nor the snares
> of this world.
> He is my husband
> Lord Chennamallikarjuna.
> Take these husbands who die and decay,
> feed them to your kitchen fires.

(Author's translation)

We find several such stories of 'bridal mysticism' in the bhakti
tradition. In most, the women remain unmarried or if married, their
earthly husbands, who are 'second' husbands so to say, are of no great

consequence. Mahadevi feels complete and whole only as the bride of Chennamallikarjuna. And, like Mira, she too is forced to marry an earthly husband, though she leaves him eventually. The Lord of the Peaks is her real husband, the very meaning and purpose of her existence. Everything else is mere maya, an illusion.

Marriage with Kaushika

It is said that Mahadevi was very beautiful and fit to be married to a king. With her stunning beauty and unusually long curly hair that trailed down to almost her knees, she is believed to have stood out like a goddess in a crowd. As Mahadevi approached the age of sixteen, she was thrown into a world not to her liking. One morning, when the family had set out to a nearby Shiva temple, King Kaushika happened to be on his way to the next town. Mahadevi and her family had to wait for the royal cavalcade to pass before proceeding to the temple. Legend recounts that Kaushika saw Mahadevi in the crowd, was smitten and decided to marry her.

He sent a marriage proposal the very next day. Mahadevi's father Nirmala Shetty was perplexed and did not know what to say. It was all too sudden; moreover, there was no way he could give his consent, since Kaushika was a Jain, a *bhavi*, a non-Shaivite. Trembling with fear at the possibly dangerous consequences of giving the king an unwelcome answer, he rejected the offer, saying, 'We are Shiva *saranas*. And we do not marry outside our community.' And Mahadevi, her face flushed in rage, is said to have declared, 'Brother, go tell your king that I'm already married. Lord Chennamallikarjuna is my husband.'

Kaushika had not expected Nirmala Shetty to jump at the offer, or Mahadevi to accept his proposal without demur. He knew the *saranas* were too proud a lot and so he had presumed some initial resistance. But Shetty's blatant rejection, without fear of possible dire consequences, was least expected. Enraged, and desperate to have Mahadevi as his wife, the king brought pressure to bear on the parents. He sent word that he would shower riches on them and accept all their demands and conditions. If they still refused, he instructed his minister to tell them that they could be thrown into prison for disobedience or even put to death.

The threats were effective and the reluctant parents gave in. Not so, Mahadevi. Though heartbroken, because she had not expected her parents to yield, she remained entirely devoted to her Lord Chennamallikarjuna and stubbornly refused to submit to pressure. Only the realization that Kaushika would put her parents to the sword led her to agree to the marriage. She married Kaushika for the sake of her parents. But she first set him three conditions.

'You will not come in the way of my devotion to Lord Shiva and my sadhana.'

'Never,' Kaushika agreed, too readily. 'You can go on with your *pujas* and rituals and your sadhana. I have no objection.'

'I am not to be prevented from meeting my guru and any *maheshwaras* who visit.'

'By all means meet your guru and the visiting *maheshwaras*,' said Kaushika.

'I shall live the way I like.'

'Rest assured, Mahadevi,' Kaushika swore, 'I give you my word as King.'

Finally, Mahadevi warned: 'I shall forgive only three violations of these conditions, and then I'm gone.'

Kaushika had no objection, for he had not expected things would work out so soon; that Mahadevi would willingly wed him and come to the palace. Her conditions did not matter much. In fact, he did not take them seriously at all, for he believed it was just a matter of time before Mahadevi herself ran into his arms.

That did not happen. After marriage Mahadevi spent her days immersed in prayer, or with wandering monks who came and went like flocks of birds. She refused to wear royal attire and donned the simple cottons she had brought from home. She ate frugal meals from plantain leaves and lived in the palace like an ascetic. Kaushika bore it all patiently, telling himself she couldn't possibly go on this way too long. Her ascetic garb and dignified deportment only enhanced his

sexual appetite and his will to overpower her. And come evening, he
would send for her. Darkness would descend upon her world and she
would go numb. But there was no escape, she was his wife and had
voluntarily agreed to the sacrifice. Most unwillingly she would enter
the bridal chamber, and let him take her.

It is quite probable that the following *vachanas* were composed in
the throes of her agony over her inescapable wifely duty while she was
in her deepest longing for her Lord Chennamallikarjuna.

> Husband inside, lover outside,
> I can't manage them both.
> This world and that other,
> cannot manage them both.
> O Lord Chennamallikarjuna,
> I cannot hold in one hand
> both the round nut and the long bow.

(Ramanujan 1973)

~

> Why do I need this dummy
> of a dying world?
> Illusion's chamberpot,
> hasty passion's whorehouse,
> this crackpot
> and leaky basement?
> Finger may squeeze the fig to feel it,
> yet not choose to eat it.
> Take me, flaws and all,
> O Lord Chennamallikarjuna.

(Ibid.)

How, you may ask, did Mahadevi bear this contrary union?
Harihara, the author of *Mahadeviyakkagala Ragale*, tells us that it was
like a union experienced in a bad dream and Mahadevi's spirit looked
upon the body's torture as a *'sakshin'*, a passive witness. We understand

that she agreed to marry Kaushika solely to save her parents, but then surely she knew the consequences of her act? Going by her *vachanas*, however, it is of crucial importance to note here that Mahadevi did not convert this tension into a religious conflict between the spirit and flesh; rather, given her ineluctable circumstances, in all probability she took a practical view of things, lived the best way possible at Kaushika's palace, prayed and waited for a sign.

We do not know for how long Mahadevi lived with Kaushika. It appears Mahadevi did not have any children, and the marriage did not last long. And the break in her marriage came perhaps sooner than she had expected.

One day, a few *maheshwaras* arrived at the palace and sent word for her. It so happened that Mahadevi was resting at the time, so Kaushika, who had by then become quite irritated by the frequent visits of these devotees, shouted at the servant not to wake Mahadevi but to send the *sarana*s away. The clamour awakened Mahadevi and she went wild with anger at Kaushika for coming in the way of her meeting with the *maheshwara*s. The first condition she had laid upon him was thus broken, but upon his imploring, legend says she forgave him.

Another day, while Mahadevi was in Kaushika's chamber, her guru happened to come to the palace to see her. Kaushika wouldn't let her go, insisting that as his wife it was her duty to be entirely devoted to him, especially when she was in his chamber. She stood firm and demanded that he let her go and see her guru right away. In a fit of rage, Kaushika shouted at her: 'Leave this moment if you can't be my wife.' Thus the second condition was broken, but again Mahadevi forgave him.

Then one day, the third condition too was breached. When after her morning bath, Mahadevi sat in meditation, the sacred linga cupped in her raised left palm, Kaushika broke in on her sacred hour and tried to take her by force. Mahadevi's eyes flew open and her whole body burned in sudden rage. Pushing him away, she leapt to her feet with fire in her eyes. With one firm tug, Mahadevi loosened the sari at her waist and naked she stood, like a furious sun in a cloudless sky. 'This is what you want, what you lust for, this body, this bag of flesh and bones,' she cried. Kaushika lay sprawled on the floor. He had broken his promise, broken the last condition that had been laid upon him if he wanted her to live with him. He had in fact violated all three conditions of their marriage. He had agreed that if he were to break all three conditions, she could go free.

So now, with the bond between them broken, like a bird at last freed from her cage, Mahadevi turned and walked away and out of Kaushika's life, from her hitherto incarcerated existence as the queen in the palace, from her past that now seemed a heap of ash. She strode through and out of the corridors of the palace, hearing and not hearing the cries and pleas of her maids, past the guards who stood aghast, her breasts bouncing with pride, her eyes aglow with the new-found joy and freedom.

Like a snake that sheds off its old skin, Mahadevi shed her needless modesty and cumbersome sari. Like Shiva, his skin burning and shining like burnished gold, who walked naked through the pine forest looking for Sati, Mahadevi, giving a strange twist to the tale, sky-clad, walked past the civilized world, in search of Shiva, the Lord of the Peaks. Legend relates that her guru, parents and well-wishers, aghast at what she had done, tried to dissuade her from leaving Kaushika. Her parents begged her to put on some clothes and at least stay with them. But for Mahadevi all was over, there was no turning back.

> I am no helpless woman,
> I utter no futile threats,
> I cannot be daunted.
> I shall dare hunger and pain,
> I shall steal out of withered leaves,
> a wholesome meal,
> and on pointed sword,
> shall make my bed.
> I am ready to dare the worst,

to die this instant.

The readiness is all.

(His Holiness Mahatapsvi Shri Kumarswamiji 1992)

Mahadevi's Trial

Legend recounts that from Uduthadi (a small village in Shivmoga district) Mahadevi trekked nearly eight hundred kilometres to reach Kalyana (in Bidar district). Without the protection of clothing how did she endure heat and cold, quench her thirst and satisfy hunger, rest during the night? Did she move on the outskirts of towns and villages, avoiding contact with people, or did she bravely walk through towns and villages? The old texts do not talk about the likely hardships she must have endured, or the dangers she may have escaped. Some of her *vachana*s, however, give a broad hint of the hardships she endured; of her unwavering resolve not to succumb to pressure and adversity; and of the unflagging perseverance that led her to achieve her spiritual goal.

She went to Kalyana to meet with Basavanna, Allama Prabhu and other *sarana*s. But her ordeal did not end on reaching there. Kinnari Bommayya, a senior *sarana*, escorted her to the Anubhava Mantapa, the Hall of Experience, where the likes of Allama and Basavanna had already gathered and were waiting to see her. No sooner did she enter the hall than she was quizzed about her personal integrity and spiritual merit by none other than Allama Prabhu himself. A telling, compelling dialogue ensued between the two, forming, definitely, one of the most illuminating chapters in the annals of Indian spiritual narrative. Here is a brief account of that dialogue, adapted from the fifteenth century text *Sunya Sampadane*, and from a modern narrative, *In Search of Shiva* (Rao 2010).

At one end of the hall seated on a massive, magnificent throne, was a bearded figure in a long ochre robe. Flanking him, two on either side, sat four men, gazing at her. Mahadevi probably knew by then that the personage on the throne was none other than Allama

Prabhu. On his left, head adorned with a turban and face wreathed in a warm smile, sat Basavanna. The other *saranas* were the legendary Guru Siddarama and the young scholar Chenna Basava.

Allama knew about Mahadevi and her controversial background. The news of her arrival had reached Kalyana much before she appeared at the Anubhava Mantapa. Legends recount that Allama had to interrogate her not so much to clear his misgivings about her spiritual maturity, as to dispel the possible doubts of the *saranas*. Or, could it be that he himself was in doubt and so he had to interrogate Mahadevi?

Allama: 'What is all this fanfare about? Why have you come here instead of going to your husband's house?'

Mahadevi: '*Prabhu*, you ask a strange question. Still, if I have to answer it, I have come here as the daughter-in-law of this house.'

Allama: 'Daughter-in-law? But, tell me, who is this husband of yours?'

Mahadevi: 'Of what use have I of husbands who die and decay? Throw them into the kitchen fire. The One with no bond nor fear, no clan nor land, no birth nor death, no place nor form, my Lord Chennamallikarjuna, He is my husband.'

Allama: 'Ah, you speak well! The whole world can see that you are quite young, and beautiful, too. Umm, a mere little girl, and you speak of Chennamallikarjuna and Kadali in your *vachanas*! Tell me, what do you know of Kadali? What is your experience?'

Mahadevi: '*Prabhu*, are you really troubled by my young age and body? And don't you know what Kadali is? Kadali is this body, this mind and five senses. Kadali is this dense world and impenetrable forest. I have penetrated this forest and triumphed over this world, and in every pebble and every leaf I have seen the face of my Lord

Chennamallikarjuna. I am nothing but His now, lodged in His lotus heart.'

Allama: 'Do not think I'm impressed by your fine words. You still have not answered my question. The whole world knows that you were married to King Kaushika, that you betrayed his trust in you and ran away. You think our *saranas* here will be impressed by a woman like you?'

Mahadevi: 'I did not betray Kaushika. In fact, he betrayed my trust in him. He broke his promise. While I was into my prayers, breaking his word, he came in and pulled at my sari. And I walked out. We had agreed that if he were to break his word of honour I would go free. So I walked out free. This is my story and this is the truth.

'And, *Prabhu*, think of this, men and women blush when a cloth covering their shame comes loose. But when the entire world is the eye of the Lord, overlooking everything, what can you cover and conceal?

'*Prabhu*, there is nothing that I can call my own. Absolutely nothing, not even this body. Everything is His. And when everything is His, what is there to hide? When this body, cleansed of all impurities, has become one with the Lord, what does it matter how it looks?'

Allama: 'Clever, very clever. You say you are nothing and speak as if you have gone beyond the consciousness of your body. Why then have you covered yourself? If there is nothing to hide, why then do you hide your body behind those tresses of yours?'

Mahadevi: '*Prabhu*, I cover myself for the sake of the world, lest people see in my body what is not there. And it is to protect others and not myself, nor to hide anything. Does that trouble you, *Prabhu*? Are you still not satisfied with my answers?'

Allama: 'No, I'm not convinced. You speak as if you don't have
a body, as if you don't exist. It is like a dead body declaring itself
dead, like curdled milk claiming sweetness. Is that possible?'

Mahadevi: 'But *Prabhudeva*, when one wakes from a dream
in which one has died and talks about it, isn't it like a dead one
speaking of one's own death? When curdled milk is boiled, isn't
there sweetness in it? Should this matter be argued further, *Prabhu*?
But then I have nothing more to say.'

Allama: 'There are no more questions to be asked. You have solved
the unsolvable, answered the unanswerable. You may be young
by years, but in your maturity and vision, you are our elder sister,
our *akka*.'

'Akka, Akka, Akka Mahadevi...' Cries of joy burst forth in the
hall, like a sudden rain pattering down from the heavens. Since
then Mahadevi was referred to as Akka Mahadevi.

(Rao 2010)

Akka Mahadevi did not give much importance to tradition, rather
she moved and lived the way she did, in light of her own experiences.
After she left Kaushika, she went to Kalyana, curious to meet with
the likes of Basavanna and Allama Prabhu. However, it appears
that by the time Mahadevi reached Kalyana she was more or less
finished with her spiritual seeking, and it's quite possible that her
interactions with the likes of Allama Prabhu completed the process
of awakening in her. If she wanted she would have stayed back
among the kindred spirits in Kalyana, but she didn't. Instead, she left
for Srisailam, where she is believed to have attained union with her
Lord Chennamalikarjuna.

Today she may be seen as one of the great leaders of the Virashaiva/
Lingayat sect, though in actuality she was not. She did not have a guru

nor did she become one to others. She did not give importance to Virashaiva/Lingayat beliefs and rituals, and like Allama, she was no believer in *ashtavarna* (literally eight spiritual coverings: guru, linga, *jangama, padodaka, prasada, vibhuti, rudraksha* and mantra), nor a follower of the *shatsthala* doctrine. One may pick out *vachanas* to show that she did believe in the notions of *ashtavarna* and *shatsthala*, but there's a strong doubt if she was really the author of those *vachanas*. For all you know it could have been the work of overzealous scribes to fit her into the framework of Virashaivism.

Mahadevi just cut loose from these initiations and stages of *becoming* and came upon that which has no name and no form. Her bhakti was the path, her inner voice the guru, and she promptly moved from bhakti to *arivu*—awareness that all is one.

Srisailam

Srisailam is located in Nallamala hills in the Kurnool district of Andhra Pradesh. In the deep and mountainous part of the forest at Srisailam, in one of the caves there, Akka Mahadevi is supposed to have lived her last days, attained *aikya* and breathed her last. The cave was her home, her resting place, and for company she had the deep forest and hills and the Krishna River flowing by, away from the prying eyes and chattering tongues.

> Every tree,
> the all-giving tree.
> Every bush,
> the life-reviving herb.
> All the water,
> the elixir of life.
> Every beast,
> the golden deer.
> Every pebble I stumble on,
> the wishing crystal.

Thus, walking round
I happened on
Chennamallikarjuna's beloved hill.

(Sreekantaiya 1979)

Months after Akka Mahadevi settled down in the forest to an uninterrupted life of prayer and contemplation, her parents, legend says, came looking for her. Moved to tears by the hard ascetic life their young daughter was leading, they begged her to return home. The mother pleaded, 'At our age we'll at least have the satisfaction of having you in our presence. That is all that we ask of you. This forest is too dangerous for you to live by yourself.' But Mahadevi said she was safe and at peace with herself and at home in the company of her Lord, and bluntly told them to return home and never ever bother her again.

Soon after her parents departed, the lovesick Kaushika arrived and refused to leave without her. He came attired in the garb of a Shiva devotee, wearing an ochre robe and sacred beads, with ash smeared on his forehead and arms. 'See, I have fulfilled your condition, I'm a Shiva bhakta now,' he said and implored her to return with him to Uduthadi. Just as she had refused to return with her parents, she firmly refused him as well. Other ascetics who lived in Srisailam, who knew Akka was a spiritually advanced yogini, advised Kaushika to leave her alone and go back.

We do not know for how long Akka Mahadevi lived in that cave. But what we know is that it was here, in this dense forest of Srisailam, living in tune with the natural world, that Akka attained the state of tranquillity, or wholeness. Going by her later *vachanas*, probably heard and recorded by occasionally visiting *maheshwaras*, Akka, not surprisingly, ceased speaking of Chennamallikarjuna, of her agony of separation and yearning for union. Suddenly, the search, the struggle, the yearning were all over and done with, and then, as suddenly, her life story too ended. There is no evidence of the manner of her death. It remains a mystery.

Towards Anubhaava

Akka's journey started with *bhava*: the agony of separation, the search, and the eventual realization that the binary mind is indeed an impediment to gain entry into that space within the heart, where there is neither word nor thought, neither the transcendent nor non-transcendent, not even God. It was a journey from *bhava* to *anubhaava*—the unmediated experience or vision of the Absolute Infinite Principle. No doctrine, no stages or levels to reach and progress. All she knew was to go where her heart took her, and with single-minded burning devotion to her Lord, she moved swiftly, shedding the 'unessential' as she moved from Uduthadi to Kalyana to Srisailam. From bhakti or devotion, to *arivu* or awareness, to *bayalu* or emptiness; from what may be called *saguna* Brahman (with form and attributes or *gunas*), to *nirguna* Brahman (the formless, attributeless).

Bhava is joy, also pain. The play of emotions, even ideations, takes place on the ground of duality. Without duality there is no art, no music, no love, no samsara and no search or enquiry, either. The end of play is the cessation of duality, but the play doesn't end so easily. And we start enjoying the play and don't want it to end. Likewise, the play of bhakti, or the pursuit of knowledge, may become an end in itself, and we find pleasure in it. For some bhaktas, however, there comes a point during this journey when there is a sudden shift in consciousness that ends the pursuit, the pain-pleasure movement, and they find themselves in a state of being where there is no duality. See for instance, the following *vachanas*:

> The sun is the seed
> for the worldly mischief,
> the mind is the seed
> for the human mischief.
> My mind rested in You,
> O Lord Chennamallikarjuna,
> I have no desire, nor fear;

this worldly life is not for me.

(Author's translation)

~

Not seeing you,
in the hill, in the forest,
from tree to tree,
I roamed,
searching, crying: Lord, my Lord,
where is your kindness?
Give me a clue to your hiding place,
come, show me your face,
O Lord Chennamallikarjuna.

(Author's translation)

~

Husband inside, lover outside,
I cannot manage them both.
This world and that other,
I cannot manage them both.
O Lord Chennamallikarjuna,
I cannot hold in one hand
both the round nut and the long bow.

(Ramanujan 1973)

~

Till you know it is lust's body,
site of rage and ambush of greed,
house of passion, fence of pride
and mask of envy;
till you know and *lose* this knowing,
you've no way of knowing
our Lord Chennamallikarjuna.

(Ibid.)

~

When I didn't know myself,
where were you?

Like the colour in the gold
weren't you in me?
I saw in you,
O Lord Chennamallikarjuna,
the paradox of your being in me
without showing a limb.

(Ibid.)

The above five *vachanas*, chosen from among several expressing more or less the same *bhava*, are only indicative of the likely shift in her consciousness, from an acute sense of separation and love to the realization of the unreality of separation.

It's a path hard to cross, difficult to tread. She knew the mind was the seed for mischief, and it wouldn't go away so easily. However, the search was on, but she had no clue as to how the pain of separation could be ended. The conflict persisted, between this world (husband) and the other, the body-mind was torn between the two and she was overcome with disgust at herself. It was a moment of spiritual crisis and she could not resolve it, except pray: Take me, flaws and all, O Lord Chennamallikarjuna. The sheer helplessness and total yet humble submission seemed to open up a chink of light that enabled her to *see* that while she had been looking for the Lord outside, He actually was within her being, like the colour in gold. It's a paradox, because her very search was taking her away from the truth.

Now contrast the six *vachanas* quoted above, with the two *vachanas* quoted below. These two *vachanas* were probably composed or uttered while Akka was in Srisailam. They clearly indicate a possible transformation that dissolved the sense of separation, after which there was nothing more to achieve, or to know and experience, and no words to describe that state of being.

I am a *bhakte*,
but I cannot tell
there is a devotee and lord.

I do not know vows and rituals
or what even *anubhaava* means.
I am a *sarane*
but there's no surrender nor holding on to anything,
the thought *sarana-sati linga-pati* doesn't exist,
there is no separation,
all that exists is one.

(Author's translation)

~

I do not say it is the *linga*.
I do not say it is oneness with the *linga*.
I do not say it is union,
I do not say it is harmony.
I do not say it has occurred.
I do not say it has not occurred.
I do not say it is I.
I do not say it is You.
I do not say anything,
for there is nothing to say.

(Ibid.)

Bhakti or bhakti poetry, by its very nature, is intensely iconic and a powerful *bhava*, yet the impulse, the deep urge within it, is defiantly aniconic, often rising towards *anubhaava*, especially in the case of Akka Mahadevi.

All spiritual journeys start the same way, with *bhava* but end differently for different bhaktas. The journey starts with agony of separation and yearning for union, there is a goal to be achieved, the yonder shore of union or tranquillity. In other words, the seeker, Akka Mahadevi, moves and expresses herself within the structure, but somewhere along the way the 'structure' falls by the way side and the bhakta finds herself in a state of tranquillity. There is no goal, no yonder shore to reach, for you realize you are always already there!

Akka Mahadevi's *Vachanas*

My body is ready for you,
my mind is ready for you,
my life breaths are ready for you,
still you don't turn up.
Why, my lord,
are you annoyed with me?

~

I burned in fireless heat,
I suffered gash-less wounds,
I felt drained without pleasure,
in love with Chennamallikarjuna
I lived through lives yet to come.

~

Offering the limbs to the *linga*,
I became limbless!
Offering my self to *jnana*,
my mind dissolved.
Since my limbs and my mind were annihilated,
the body ceased to be,
we became the ideal couple,
and I reside in Him, my husband,
Lord Chennamallikarjuna.

~

Sagging breasts, untied hair,
sunken cheeks and withered arms,
brothers,
why do you leer at me?
I'm a woman who has lost
caste and pride,
is dead to the world
and become a devotee.
Fathers,

why do you stare at me?
I'm a woman who uniting with Chennamallikarjuna,
has lost status and pride.

~

The arrow of love when shot
should penetrate so deeply
that even the feathers do not show.
And when it hugs the body of the lord tightly
the bones must crunch and crumble,
weld to the divine until the very welding disappears.

~

Look,
the Vedas and *Shastras*,
Aagamas and Puranas,
are but grist and husk ground in the mill.
Why grind, why winnow?
If one can sever
the head of the mind,
that hops here and there,
then,
O lord Chennamallikarjuna,
there is nothing
but utter void.

~

If one could
draw the fangs of a snake,
and charm the snake to play,
it's great to have snakes.
If one could purify
the body's senses,
it's a blessing to have a body.

Lalleshwari

What the books taught me, I've practised.
What they didn't teach me, I've taught myself.
I've gone into the forest and wrestled with the lion.
I didn't get this far by teaching one thing and doing another.

(Hoskote 2013)

Among women saints, mystics and sages, along with Akka Mahadevi, and Anandamayi Ma in modern times, Lalleshwari stands out as a complete sage, who blazed a path all her own. She did not teach any particular creed or dogma or propound a philosophy, she lived in tune with the dictates of her heart and spoke straight from the depth of her being. In a sense, she was the Allama of Kashmir, direct, explosive, and illuminating. It is strange that so outstanding a personality as Lalleshwari, who was a household name in Kashmir until recent times, should be hardly known even in Kashmir today, let alone outside Kashmir, and that there should be very little literature available on her. Nonetheless, there's no doubt that she is one among the greats this country has produced and her words continue to speak to us and illumine the path to the fullness of life.

Lalleshwari (1320–92 CE), known as Lalla Arifa to Muslims and Lalla Yogishwari to Hindus, is generally and more popularly referred to as Lal Ded, which means 'Grandmother Lal', or, simply as Lalla. Legend recounts that she was born in Pandrethan, near Srinagar, in a Kashmiri Pandit family. She was a girl with a strong spiritual streak, but, as was the custom at the time, she was married off at the young age of twelve. It was not a happy marriage. It is said that Lalla's husband and mother-in-law took umbrage at her meditative absorptions and visits to shrines, treated her cruelly and often starved her. They had no clue about her spiritual maturity.

This puts us in mind of Anandamayi's troubles during the early period of her married life. Anandamayi, too, was married at the early age of thirteen. Even as a young girl she would often slip into a trance and this 'odd behaviour' created a huge problem in her married life. Later, Anandamayi, in a polite and gracious way, negotiated her problems and won the hearts of her husband and relatives and they turned into her admirers and disciples. Here the similarity between Lalleshwari and Anandamayi ends. Lalleshwari was not as lucky. We have no clue about the troubles and traumas she had to bear. At the age of twenty-four, however, she left the family, renounced all her ties with samsara and took to a life of *sannyasa*. She joined the ashram of Siddha Srikantha, a Shaivite guru, and sought spiritual guidance.

She probably stayed at the ashram for some years before she came into her own and turned into a wandering yogini. Indifferent, like Akka Mahadevi, to social strictures, it is said that she walked nude oblivious to the world, and was given to singing and dancing in a state of ecstasy. Her compositions (called *vakh*—corresponding to Vedic-Sanskritic '*vak*', 'speech', and to '*vachana*' of the twelfth century *saranas*, meaning 'what is said', an utterance), are marked by vehemence, fervour, even fury and apparent arrogance, which may remind us of Allama Prabhu's *vachanas*. Those of her *vakhs* that express the agony of separation, a feverish longing to unite with her lord and her eventual leap from *bhava* to *anubhaava*, run almost parallel to Akka Mahadevi's spiritual odyssey.

In one of her early *vakhs*, she describes her life as sailing on a boat through the murky waters of the sea of samsara, praying constantly to her lord to help her cross over to the shore. Her life, she laments, is like an unbaked earthen pot with water slowly seeping through it, threatening to fall to bits, but she will not give up until she is liberated from the agony of separation and reaches her real *home*.

That thou art my destiny.
Learning by rote, my tongue and palate dried,
I found not the right way,
to act and reach thee.

Telling the beads,
my thumb and finger,
wore out; and, my friend,
I couldn't get rid of
the duality of mind.

(Razdan 1998)

~

I, Lalla, searched and sought Him,
and even beyond my strength I strove.
Finding His doors bolted and barred
I longed to see;
firmly resolved, I stood just there
with tears and love,
fixing my gaze upon His door.

(koausa.org)

Before long we see her move beyond the state of feverish longing or the state of the pining bride, lamentation giving way to reflection and meditation on life and the mystery of truth. It is quite possible that at this stage of her life, she came upon 'life-altering' experiences, into glimpses of unitary consciousness or oneness.

Truly, the trials and tribulations of her married life, her daring spiritual journey and eventual attainment of wholeness make for a fascinating story. Ranjit Hoskote, in his erudite work (2013) on Lalleshwari, states that she lived through 'a time of seismic turbulence', through 'rapid sequences of political catastrophes'. So one may wonder how, in a time of political upheavals and patriarchal prejudices, Lalla moved around singing her profoundly moving yet provocative songs and dancing in ecstasy. Surely it was not so much an act of supreme will or courage as 'spiritual madness', or holy indifference.

They may abuse me or jeer at me,
they may say what pleases them,

they may with flowers worship me.
Let the world do what it wants,
I am indifferent to praise and blame.

(Ibid.)

And, like Allama, she did not mince words when she, to quote Ranjit
Hoskote (2013) again, took on 'arid scholarship, soulless ritualism,
fetishised austerity and animal sacrifice'; in short, the absurdity of
an elaborately constructed punditry and ritualism that served only
as an hopeless substitute for the real thing, and even destroyed the
possibility of coming upon *that* which cannot be manipulated and
programmed.

The idol is but stone,
the temple is but stone,
from top to bottom all is stone.
Whom will you worship, O foolish pandit,
let go and let *prana* and the mind unite.

(koausa.org)

~

Should you, in this body, seek
the Supreme Self that dwells within,
remove greed and illusion,
lo, a halo of glory will surround
this very body of yours.

(Ibid.)

Lalla was not a mere bhakti poet. Her *vakh*s were not just
outpourings of her devotion to God, or 'brimming over with devotional
expressions'; rather, there was bhakti as well as *jnana* and these two
streams merged perfectly in Lalla. Her penetrating insights illumined
the path of *adhyatma*, offering one a taste of that which cannot be
described.

In her philosophical *vakhs* she creatively deployed expressions from Sankhya philosophy, Shaiva Siddhanta, Tantra Yoga, the Mahayana philosophy of *sunyata* and Sufism to drive home the irrelevance of beliefs and rituals, tantras and mantras in the quest for mystic union. Even among the twelfth-century *vachanakaras* we have seen how some used concepts borrowed from Hindu tradition as well as Buddhist philosophy. Since these different schools of philosophy or thought formed the living background of many of these mystic-poets, they naturally picked these concepts to make sense of their transcendental experiences and in order to communicate.

To go behind these concepts in order to historicize the journey is quite unnecessary, for such exercises at times can only distract us from the core issue, which is to understand and appreciate the different spiritualities, the different paths that lead to the same goal, namely, attainment of a state of being where the division or separation has ended.

> Foulness from my mind was cleared
> as ashes from a mirror,
> then recognition of Him came to me
> unmistakable and clear.
> And when I saw Him from close,
> He was all and I was not.
>
> (Ibid.)

~

> Tantra dissolved and
> the mantra remained.
> The mantra disappeared,
> consciousness remained.
> Consciousness vanished,
> nothingness merged with
> nothingness of the Void.
>
> (Razdan)

~

Here there is neither word nor thought,
Transcendent nor non-Transcendent.
Vows of silence and mystic mudras
cannot gain you admittance here.
Even Shiva and Shakti remain not here.
What remains is the Truth,
to know and realize.
Here there is neither thou nor I,
nothing to contemplate,
not even God.

(Ibid.)

'Here there is neither transcendent nor non-transcendent ... neither
thou nor I, nothing to contemplate, not even God.' It's an explosive
discovery, or what may be simply called *seeing*, seeing through the
imprisoning structure of thought and transcending it. We seek, search
and tread a path, do sadhana and we realize we are going in circles and
that is a moment of 'crisis' that probably enables an Allama, an Akka,
a Lalla to give up, surrender. That's where it ends, both bhakti and
jnana marg, in absolute surrender. And you discover that *that* has been
always there. It's a magical moment which transforms the individual.

This terrific realization is not an object of knowledge, but a
tremendous awareness of one's own essential being where the
binaries and boundaries have dissolved, and that state of being cannot
be captured in words. Yet, *nirguna* poets such as Allama Prabhu,
Akka Mahadevi, Lalla and Kabir, give expression to what is actually
indescribable. It is a paradox, which when expressed poetically, turns
into a *rasa*. It is a moment of indefinable joy and wonder. Here are
three poems, the first from Lalla, followed by Akka Mahadevi and then
Allama Prabhu, expressing the sense of mystery and wonder.

Wrapped up in Yourself, You hid from me.
All day I looked for you

and when I found You hiding inside me,
I ran wild, playing now me, now You.

(Hoskote 2013)

~

When I didn't know myself,
where were you?
Like the colour in the gold,
weren't you in me?
I saw in you,
O Lord Chennamallikarjuna,
the paradox of your being in me,
without showing a limb.

(Ramanujan 1973)

~

In a blue sapphire,
I saw the three worlds hiding.
Yet, looking for your light,
I went hither and thither,
in and out, and it was like
a sudden dawn of
a million million suns,
a ganglion of lighting,
O Lord of the Caves.
But tell me,
if you are light, what am I?
O, there can be no metaphor.

(Author's translation)

The body is a liability, a weakness and an obstacle to be overcome
in the path of bhakti for many devotees such as, for instance,
Avvaiyar and Karaikalammaiyar, the saints and bhakti poets of sixth-
century Tamil Nadu. So Avvaiyar turns into an old woman and
Karaikalammaiyar into a *pey*, a ghoul, in order to pre-empt the lechery
of men and overcome the social conditioning that forced marriage

on women. For Akka Mahadevi the body was not a liability, or an impediment to bhakti, but the gender was, the social conditioning was, as it was to Avvaiyar and Karaikalammaiyar, but she would not seek an escape from it. Interestingly she compared the body to a snake. 'If one could draw the fangs of a snake, and charm the snake to play, it's great to have snakes' (Rao 2018). Similarly, 'if one could purify the body's senses', free it from destructive passions, 'it's a blessing to have a body' (Ibid.). And she walked naked in defiance of the societal norm and eventually moved beyond all binaries, including male-female, devotee-God.

For Lalla, too, the body was not a liability, not antithetical to spirituality or self-realization, it was not a prison of the mind or soul but the source and ground of intelligence and enlightenment. Expressing the idea differently, Ranjit Hoskote (2013) writes, 'Lalla treats the body as the site of all her experiments in self-refinement: she asserts the unity of the corporeal and the cosmic, as achieved through immersive meditation and the yogic cultivation of the breath.'

> I trapped my breath in the bellows of my throat:
> a lamp blazed up inside, showed me who I really was.
> I crossed the darkness holding fast to that lamp,
> scattering its light-seeds around me as I went.
>
> (Hoskote 2013)

~

> Should you, in this body, seek
> the Supreme Self that dwells within,
> remove greed and illusion,
> lo, a halo of glory will surround
> this very body of yours.
>
> (koausa.org)

~

My mind boomed with the sound of OM,
my body was a burning coal.
Six roads brought me to the seventh,
that's how Lalla reached the Field of Light.

(Hoskote 2013)

Towards the end of the fourteenth century, round about 1392 CE,
when she was in her seventies, Lalleshwari is said to have visited
Bijbehara town in Anantnag district in south Kashmir and breathed
her last there. Ranjit Hoskote (2013) writes, 'A total of 258 *vakhs*
attributed to Lalla have circulated widely and continuously in Kashmir
popular culture between the mid-fourteenth century and the present,
variously assuming the form of songs, proverbs and prayers.' Not all of
them were composed by Lalla, nevertheless they do reflect the essence
and spirit of Lalla. The *vakhs* were committed to writing about four
hundred years after Lalla's death. And the first English translation of
some of her *vakhs* came out in 1920.

A Selection of Lalla's *Vakhs*

My guru gave me but one *gurushabd*,
He told me to move within from without.
That hit the nail on my head;
I realized myself and shed the veil;
Self-realized, I began to dance in freedom.

~

Shiva is present everywhere.
Where lies the creek to distinguish
between a Hindu and a Mussalman?
Quick-witted if you are,
recognize yourself and realize God!

~

Thou are the sky, the earth and air,
Thou the day and night;
Thou art the grain, flowers and sandalwood,

Thee, the water, universe, all;
Then what remains to adorn Thee with
O Lord?

~

O, you dull pandit, you offer
a living ram that feeds on water,
natural grass, and crumbs,
to a lifeless stone.
It'll cover you in woollens,
shield you against cold.
Who advised you to sacrifice
a live-lamb as an offering
to a dead rock?

~

Learning by rote, my tongue and palate dried,
That thou art my destiny.
I found not the right way,
to act and reach thee.
Telling the beads,
my thumb and finger
wore out and yet, my friend,
I couldn't get rid of
the duality of mind.

∽

Anandamayi Ma

Nirmala, who came to be known as Anandamayi Ma, was the second
child of Brahmin parents and was born on 30 April 1896 in village
Kheora in erstwhile East Bengal, now a part of Bangladesh. Her parents
were devout Vaishnavas, worshippers of Vishnu. Her father Bipin

Bihari Bhattacharya, a traditionalist, was given to going on pilgrimages and chanting devotional hymns. Her mother Moksada Sundari, came from a family of pandits and was herself a poet, whose compositions of devotional songs were quite popular in the village.

The name Nirmala means immaculate beauty, which Anandamayi Ma embodied till her last days. Four brothers and two sisters were born after Nirmala, and the family lived in comparative poverty, dependent on an income from a minor landed property.

Nirmala was different from other girls, indifferent to happenings around her, yet always cheerful. It is said that when her mother fell seriously ill, she remained unaffected to the utter bewilderment of family members. She did hardly a year or two of schooling and didn't care to learn reading and writing. She had such a happy demeanour that she was called *Hasi Ma* mother of smiles, or *Khusir Ma*, happy mother. This cheerful temperament was her nature in all circumstances that later earned her the sobriquet Anandamayi Ma, Joy- or Bliss-permeated Mother.

Even as a girl Nirmala used to fall into a trance now and then, which was seen as 'absent-mindedness' by her parents and not as something 'abnormal' or 'supranormal', since otherwise she was extraordinarily obedient, cheerful and lovable, and performed household chores without complaint. Perhaps because she was the eldest child (her older sibling having died in infancy), she was burdened with more work than the other girls. In the later years, when she was no more required to do household work, she would cheerfully recall the days when she worked hard and practically took care of the family.

In 1909, at the age of thirteen, she was married to Raman Mohan Chakravarti, who was older to her by several years. He worked as a clerk in the police department in Atpara, East Bengal. Five years later in 1914, when she turned seventeen, she joined her husband in Astagrama, also in East Bengal, where he had found a new job with the Land Settlement Department. She called him Bholanath and the name stuck.

Bholanath had no idea that Nirmala often slipped into a trance. He had taken her to be a typical illiterate village girl, a little moody and melancholic, but given to hard physical work. Almost all biographical works report that the marriage was never physically consummated. Every time Bholanath approached her she would fall into a trance or deathlike state. It is quite possible that when this happened repeatedly Bholanath could have been both alarmed and alerted to the fact that his good-looking, cheerful, seventeen-year-old wife was no ordinary woman. To all appearances she was otherwise a most obedient wife, who scrubbed and cleaned the house, washed his clothes and cooked his meals with an endearing smile on her face. But when it came to sex she simply swooned and was not there for him.

Psychiatrists would say that Nirmala was probably a frigid woman and so fell into a trance-like state as a strategy to circumvent sex. Such an interpretation prevents exploring other possible reasons. Psychology and medical science may offer very significant and useful insights into the nature and functioning of the body-mind, but there's a lot more that these disciplines are yet to come to terms with and begin to understand.

Stepping off the frameworks of these disciplines, we need to consider other, alternative understandings of body-mind nature. For instance, in the light of Kundalini Yoga, we may understand that it's quite possible that with the rising of Kundalini energy or opening up of the chakras, or energy centres within the body, the sexual urge gets sublimated. In other words, the sexual glands undergo change which enables sexual transcendence. Such an individual is freed from the grip of sexual desire. This could be one way, perhaps the right way, to understand the 'asexual' behaviour of Akka Mahadevi, Anandamayi and Ramana Maharshi, among others. Surely such a thing must have happened to many more mystics and sages to whom sexuality was never an issue to be either fulfilled or overcome. Not because sex is anti-God or anti-spiritual but simply because sex as an urge or desire did not exist for these individuals.

Celibacy is based on the assumption that sex is an obstacle on the path of spirituality and that practising celibacy helps sublimate sexuality and attain higher states of consciousness. This belief and practice is built in emulation of the 'asexual' behaviour of sages. But such practices cannot lead to sexual transcendence, unless physical and physiological changes occur that make sex an impossibility, because there is no formation of desire.

Even as a girl Nirmala would have sensed the physiological changes taking place in her and that her body was being transformed into a field of energy. It is of importance to note here that it was not her 'will' or sadhana that brought this on, rather the mind was simply not involved at all in this transformative process. This could be the reason why Anandamayi always referred to herself as 'this body'. The body that had become a receptacle of divine energy and the seat of great intelligence.

Conditioned as they were by the Brahminical tradition, which expected women to be subservient to men and family in the name of *stridharma* or wifely duties, members of her family were unable to see and appreciate Anandamayi for what she was. If, on the one hand, the tradition denied women the right to asceticism, on the other, it glorified and worshipped woman as a self-sacrificing mother, chaste wife and obedient daughter. And by virtue of their selfless love and service and devotion to husband and family, tradition maintained that women would automatically attain liberation.

During the Bhakti Movement that spread and extended over several centuries (seventh to fifteenth century CE), women had a significant and radical presence that challenged the Brahminical tradition and the social order. Women saints, in particular, inverted and subverted the traditional ideals to rewrite spiritual history, wherein women claimed equal space and status with men. Not only were the classical ideals embodied in the Sitas and Savitris of Hindu theology negated, even sexual bifurcation was rejected and transcended, thus opening a new and different track for women for being and doing things in the world. Akka Mahadevi walked out of marriage and walked naked in defiance of the social norm and religious tradition. Mira Bai, like Gauri and Kururamma but in a different time and place, refused to acknowledge widowhood and refused to commit sati.

Several centuries down the line and despite a heritage of rebellion of women against patriarchal values, and living at a time when equality and autonomy of women were beginning to be seen as the mark of a mature culture and civilization, Nirmala had to face severe criticism and opposition from orthodox people and relatives. However, living in the traditional milieu of Bengal, where a wife was expected to be submissive to her husband, the gracious way in which she negotiated these problems makes for an extraordinary story which is all her own. She was obedient, yet not submissive. She went with her husband to different places whenever he changed jobs, cooked for him and cheerfully did the household work, but refused to sleep with him.

Bholanath's friends and relatives sensed that he was not a happy man and that he didn't have a 'normal' family life. They urged him to seek separation from Nirmala and find a suitable wife. To his credit, Bholanath never thought of breaking up the marriage, although he was a traditional creature and was given to wild tempers. Perhaps, deep in his heart he knew that Nirmala was not faking the trance, that she was not an ordinary woman and there was something deeply spiritual about her, which he was not yet able to grasp.

However, as more and more people came to know about her exalted spiritual state, they started to come for her darshan. Bholanath let her meet them without the purdah or veil, which women generally wore in traditional families, especially when men were around. And it's interesting to note here that more than women, men were drawn to her glowing presence. They prostrated in front of her and addressed her as 'Ma', as 'Goddess Durga'. And she was invited to grace public pujas and kirtans, where people now directly witnessed her going into a trance and felt a 'divine' presence. At times she would spontaneously start chanting Sanskrit mantras, which impressed the 'educated' class, too. And just as her popularity as 'Divine Mother' grew, 'orthodox' forces stepped in, calling her 'divine possessions' the work of evil spirits.

One of the reasons for such a suspicion could be that while she was in the state of trance, Nirmala's body would sometimes contort and take on different shapes. At the time Bholanath did not know that her body on its own was assuming difficult, at times seemingly impossible yogic positions, complex tantric hand positions and mudras, gestures. And he was persuaded to believe she might be possessed by evil spirits and so he called an exorcist to cure his wife.

The story goes that an *ojha*, exorcist, upon touching her, was seized with a pain and, realizing Nirmala was no ordinary woman, prostrated in front of her and sought her forgiveness. But Nirmala's troubles didn't end there. A distinguished physician was brought in to examine her. After studying her behaviour and examining her, the doctor is believed to have assured Bholanath and his relatives that Nirmala did not suffer from any mental illness—rather her 'eccentric' behaviour was a sign of 'God intoxication' (Lipski 2000).

The situation began to change drastically when Bholanath took up a new job in 1924, as manager of an estate, the Shah-bagh Gardens of the Nawab in Dacca. Nirmala continued to perform household tasks, though she was found in a withdrawn state of ecstasy much of the time. More and more people from all walks of life were now drawn to her 'divine' presence. Prominent government officials, medical doctors, Sanskrit scholars, professors from universities, writers and serious spiritual seekers as well as gurus came to sit at the feet of what they considered to be a new avatar of Divinity. Here is a report by Dr Nalini Kanta Brahma, which sums up the prevalent atmosphere and feeling at the time.

It was a cold evening in December 1924, when we had *darshan* of the Mother. She was sitting alone deeply absorbed in meditation. After about half an hour, suddenly the veil loosened itself and Mother's face became visible in all its brilliance and lustre. Hymns containing many seed mantras began to be recited by her. The stillness of the

night, the loneliness of the Gardens and the sublimity and serenity
of the atmosphere in the Mother's room—all combined to produce
a sense of holiness; an incredible elevation of the spirit, a silence
and a depth not previously experienced. (Ibid.)

Whilst living in the house in Shah-bagh Gardens, Nirmala, now
in her late twenties, was addressed as Anandamayi Ma or Blissful
Mother. She frequently fell into a trance, rather, samadhi, and this
happened even during darshan and kirtans. We may recall here the
story of Raman Maharshi. After his 'near-death' experience at the age
of seventeen, Ramana went to Arunachalam. There, in the Patala-
lingam vault of Arunachaleshwara temple, for about six weeks, he
went into such deep samadhi that he was unaware of the bites of
vermin and pests. He had to be carried out and forcibly fed. From then
on he stayed in different spots on Arunachala Hill, often absorbed in
samadhi. In 1921, he came down and settled at the foot of the hill—
where the present ashram is situated today—to live and teach.

What is samadhi? We could understand this state of being in three
ways.

One, in samadhi the individual is cut off from the surrounding
reality, the mind goes completely silent and there is bliss or pure
awareness, without the touch of thought.

Two, in samadhi the interference of the mind is completely
obliterated, the body takes over and transforms itself. The energy
centres within the body open up and transform the body-mind. It is
not the result of sadhana or will power, but something that occurs
spontaneously.

Three, it is the body's way of renewing itself. During this time the
stream of thought is cut, the person passes out and the body goes
through 'death'. It is not an experience but a physiological process of
a total renewal of the senses, glands and nervous system, after which
the body starts functioning at the peak of its sensitivity.

Hindu enlightenment tradition speaks about two kinds of samadhi:
Savikalpa samadhi, where the mind is completely absent and there is

only a bright Pure Awareness. And *Nirvikalpa* samadhi, where even the awareness is absent and that state is something that cannot be described, although sages have called it variously as *turiya* or *turiya avastha*, the fourth state, the substratum of the other three states (the state of waking consciousness, the state of dreaming and the dreamless sleep), which is 'unseen and ineffable, ungraspable'.

Like Sri Ramana, Anandamayi had no guru, no formal religious education, had not studied the scriptures, nor had any training in spiritual sadhana. Grace descended upon her, not from some benevolent God or an external agency, but from what may be called the spontaneous opening up of the inner nature or immanent potential, which transformed her.

In point of fact, years later, Anandamayi did speak about these physical changes, or what is generally referred to as the rising of the Kundalini energy in her body and the eventual transformations. Bhaiji, one of her close associates and biographer, in his *Mother as Revealed to Me*, writes about how she surprised him talking about the exact locations of the chakras, energy centres, and described in vivid terms their specific roles in bringing about the transformation. She even drew pictures of these chakras on the floor. And she said that while she sat down in a yogic posture, she could observe some lotus-like vital centres from the highest centre in the brain right down along the spinal cord to its lowest end. Further, she could clearly see from the lowest tip of the spinal cord upwards there lay many finer and finer centres, of which only the six chief ones she had drawn on the floor. In her words:

It is through these vital areas of interlacing nerves function the inherited impulses, acquired dispositions, emotions, various urges, thought-cycles, and notions of life and death, etc. Stream of life and of vital fluid course swiftly or slowly through those channels and guide the life-processes and thought-currents of man—

Just as you find that springs of water lying at the bottom of a well keep up a constant supply, so at the lowest end of the spinal

cord (*muladhara*) lies asleep the fountain of the giant vital forces.
(Dasgupta 2004)

Describing and explaining thus, Anandamayi goes on to explicate
how, when the energies start flowing upwards the primal urges and
samskaras, mental dispositions, fade away, attachments dissolve, and
when the energy reaches beyond the highest vital centre which is
situated between the eyebrows (*dvidalachakra*) the individual mental
powers merge in the supra-mental, the ego dissolves in *mahabhava*
(ecstasy) and then the individual goes into samadhi, a state of perpetual
bliss. Further, and most tellingly, she says:

As the various vital centres begin to open up, different sounds are
perceived inwardly and the individual comes to feel the sounds of
conches, bells, flutes, etc., all merging in the cosmic rhythm of one
great voice of infinite silence. At that stage, no thought or object
of the outside world can distract your attention. And then your
being gets dissolved in the bottomless depth of that blissful music
that pervades the whole universe and there is eternal peace. (Ibid.)

And then Anandamayi adds that when the question 'What are
these?' flashed across her mind at some point during this process, 'the
reply came from within and the inner structure of all those chakras
or plexuses became distinctly visible like the pictures you have put
before me.'

This brings to mind what U.G. Krishnamurti has said about
these chakras or energy centres. It is amazing to note here that like
Anandamayi, even U.G. could see vividly, with his naked eye, as it
were, these chakras or plexuses, which he called, in biological terms,
the endocrine glands. In light of what he has said, it appears that once
these energy centres open up the body takes over, in the sense the
human instinct revived and rejuvenated by the chakras, or the energy
centres, that take over. Chakras or ductless glands, such as the thymus,
the pituitary, the pineal glands, are the 'locked up' energy centres in

the body. Once the intrusion of the self has ended, the 'triggering device within the body' releases this locked-up energy, which in turn transforms the body.

In other words, once the parallel movement of thought, which is the self, comes to an end, the unitary movement of life begins to express itself. In this state there is no conflict, no fear, no death, because the dualistic mode of thinking and being has come to an end. In such a state, the dictatorship of the mind is finished, because it has realized, as it were, that it cannot solve the problems it has itself created. This is self-realization, enlightenment—where the unnatural movement of the self ends, and the natural movement of life begins to express itself.

The life of such an enlightened person is directed not by the divisive or binary mind but by something else. U.G. Krishnamurti said that it is the pineal gland, the *ajna chakra*, also called the 'third eye', that takes over once the interference of thought is gone. It is this pineal gland, situated over the forehead and between the eyebrows, which becomes active in the natural state. It is this gland, not thought, that controls all the functions that the body performs. That's why, he said, it is called the *ajna* (command) *chakra*.

Anandamayi simply called it *kheyala*, a sudden thought-feeling or an urge, or what may be called 'inner voice' that inspired and prompted her to act in a certain way, and she would brook no opposition to her *kheyala*. The Bengali word '*kheyala*' added poetry and drama to her life and offered an apparent 'reason' for her actions. *Kheyala* nudged Anandamayi Ma to travel and visit religious centres and meet with people who were interested in speaking to her. More and more people now flocked around her, seeking her blessings, soaking in her blissful presence. In 1928, an ashram was built at Siddhesvari in Dacca, the first of a network of ashrams that were going to be established all over northern India to carry forward her message. She offered no teaching as such, but through telling stories with spiritual messages, through kirtans, and her cheerful, smiling presence, she taught what had to be taught. Her joyful smiles and her body radiating an uncommon glow touched the hundreds and thousands of people who sought her darshan.

Bholanath, who in many ways characterized the 'patriarchal' prejudice and opposition to Anandamayi Ma going into samadhi and her *kheyala*, was eventually swept up by the 'blissful' waves that rose around Anandamayi Ma. In 1922, she 'initiated' him and the husband turned into a disciple. During darshans and kirtans, he would stand among other devotees, his palms folded in reverence. It's an amazing story, which, yet again, speaks volumes about the charming yet compassionate way Anandamayi negotiated the obstacles on her path.

Sometime after his death, when a devotee asked Ma about Bholanath and if she did not love him a little more than others, she emphatically replied that it was incorrect to think so. She said:

> All of you know that Bholanath was prone to fits of great anger. It is said that even *rishis* were subject to the emotion of anger. Not that I am saying that Bholanath was a *rishi*. If I did, people would think I was praising my husband. But you have all seen yourselves that he led an extraordinary life of self-denial and rigorous asceticism. (Lipski 2000)

Although Anandamayi Ma never offered a teaching as such, her whole life, which was an embodiment of joy and compassion, was a message in itself. Her informal talks and conversations in Bengali with people were recorded by her devotees, some of which were later translated into English and other languages. She did not advocate any specific method or sadhana, did not encourage renunciation when people sought her advice. She responded to people spontaneously and answered their queries with compassion. Importantly, she advocated spiritual equality for women and encouraged women to wear the sacred thread, a practice performed only by men for centuries. And it is not surprising to note here that spiritual seekers and masters from Shaivite, Tantric, Vaishnav sects, and even people from Islamic, Christian, Zoroastrian and Buddhist faiths, found in their interactions with her that her 'teaching' or message in fact highlighted the essential philosophy of their own religion or faith.

Paramahamsa Yogananda was one of the famous gurus who met her at the time. In his celebrated work *Autobiography of a Yogi*, he wrote about his meeting with Anandamayi Ma and how truly she was a 'Joy-Permeated Mother'. Talking about herself, she said to him:

Father, there is little to tell. My consciousness has never associated itself with this temporary body. Before I came on this earth, Father, I was the same. As a little girl, I was the same. I grew into womanhood, but still I was the same. When the family in which I had been born made arrangements to have this body married, I was the same... And, Father, in front of you now, I am the same. Ever afterward, though the dance of creation change around me in the hall of eternity, I shall be the same. (Yogananda 1946)

Anandamayi Ma died on 27 August 1982 in Dehradun. She was eighty-six years old at the time.

Selected Sayings

As you love your own body, so regard everyone as equal to your own body. When the Supreme Experience supervenes, everyone's service is revealed as one's own service. Call it a bird, an insect, an animal or a man, call it by any name you please, one serves one's own Self in every one of them.

~

With earnestness, love and goodwill carry out life's everyday duties and try to elevate yourself step by step. In all human activities let there be a live contact with the Divine and you will not have to leave off anything. Your work will then be done well and you will be on the right track to find the Master.

~

Whatever work you have to do, do it with a singleness of purpose, with all the simplicity, contentment and joy you are capable of.

Thus only will you be able to reap the best fruit of work. In fullness
of time, the dry leaves of life will naturally drop off and new ones
shoot forth.

~

The lute of man's short life is strung with so many strings; they
have to be cut asunder. There is no real substance to these many
strings. It is futile to let one's thoughts be occupied with the ties by
which one is bound. Why behave like a fool and return again and
again to this world of illusion?

~

Man appears to be the embodiment of want. Want is what he
thinks about and want indeed is what he obtains. Contemplate your
true being—or else there will be want, wrong action, helplessness,
distress and death.

~

Why speak of Self-realization in the future? It *is* here and now—
only the veil that hides it has to be destroyed. That which in any
case is doomed to destruction is to be destroyed. When the veil falls
to pieces *That* which eternally *Is* shines forth—*One*, Self-luminous.

The Mother

There was something exceptional about Blanche Rachel Mirra Alfassa.
She was an accomplished painter, talented musician and writer, with
a strong spiritual streak that eventually set her up on a long spiritual
journey which ended in 1914 at the age of thirty-six following her
meeting with Aurobindo. On meeting Aurobindo at Pondicherry
(now Puducherry), she at once recognized him as the master who had
appeared in her dreams over the years and had inwardly been guiding
her spiritual development.

Mirra Alfassa was born on 21 February 1878 in Paris to a Turkish Jew father, Moïse Maurice Alfassa, and an Egyptian Jewish mother, Mathilde Ismalun. A year before Mirra was born, their marriage fell apart and Mirra grew up with her grandmother Mira Ismalun. She was a voracious reader and it is said that by the age of fourteen she had read most of the books in her father's library.

She studied art and soon became an accomplished painter. In 1897, she married Henri Morisset, also an artist. Even as a girl, Mirra recalled later, she had various 'occult' experiences when she knew nothing of the subject or its significance. She kept these to herself. She was not a particularly religious person and had doubts about the existence of God and other religious matters, and yet she continued to have these experiences which seemed to come over her spontaneously.

It was only in her late twenties that she developed an urge to know about such 'mystical' happenings and read Swami Vivekananda's *Raja Yoga* and the Bhagavad Gita in French. During this time, she also came in touch with the Cosmic Movement, a group led by Max Theon. She separated from Henri in 1908, and her involvement with the group eventually led her to meet with Buddhists and other spiritually oriented people.

In 1911, she married again, one Paul Richard, a member of a circle of friends interested in philosophy and spirituality. In 1914, along with Richard, she travelled to India and visited Pondicherry, then a French colony. The husband and wife met Sri Aurobindo who had by then settled in Pondicherry. At their very first meeting, Mirra realized that the dark figure of a man who had appeared in her dreams was none other than Sri Aurobindo and her life changed that day.

It was about the time World War I broke out, and Richard and Mirra had to leave for Paris. The couple also lived for some years in Japan and in 1920, Mirra finally returned to Pondicherry, never to leave India again. She moved into the guest house at Rue Francois Martin, to live near Aurobindo. Richard returned to France and after divorcing Mirra, he remarried.

Initially Mirra encountered a general feeling of resistance from the other inmates of Aurobindo house. She was seen as an outsider. But once Aurobindo, who considered her to be of equal yogic stature, called her 'the Mother', the resistance melted away and the inmates looked upon her as a gifted yogini. It was at this time the foundation of the ashram was laid.

At first, both Sri Aurobindo and the Mother were not sure if they should call their place an 'ashram'. The term 'ashram' was traditionally associated with renunciation and asceticism, while what they had in mind was a space within society, a kind of spiritual laboratory, where fullness and prosperity, equality of the sexes and a life-affirming attitude were to be cultivated; where, more importantly, 'the new integral, divine life was to be tried on a much larger scale than had ever been attempted before.' However, eventually, Sri Aurobindo accepted the term, since it connected with spirituality and God-realization, though the model here was going to be different.

In 1926, when Aurobindo withdrew from all activities to concentrate on his Integral Yoga, Mirra, who was now called the Mother, took charge of running the ashram and offering guidance to the *sadhaks*. Under her guidance, which extended over nearly fifty years, the ashram grew into a large, many-faceted community. The Mother also founded the Sri Aurobindo International Centre of Education in 1951 and the international township Auroville in 1968. It was the Mother's dream that:

There should be somewhere on earth a place where no nation could claim as its own ... a place of peace, concord and harmony ...
In this ideal place money would no longer be the sovereign lord; individual worth would have a far greater importance than that of material wealth and social standing.

(Alfassa 1978)

Five years before her death, on 28 February 1968, representatives of 124 nations, including twenty-three Indian states, brought with them some soil from their homeland, to be mixed in a white marble-clad, lotus-shaped urn, now sited at the focal point of the amphitheatre which is close to Matrimandir. There were about five thousand people on that day. Although originally intended to house 50,000, the actual population in Auroville today is about two thousand people from 44 nationalities, 836 of whom are supposed to be of Indian origin.

Salvation is Physical

After Sri Aurobindo's passing away in 1950, till her death on 17 November 1973, the Mother carried on the work she had started along with him, with unexpected but revealing discoveries. The reports of her experiences and the tremendous physical changes she underwent offer an account of the biological foundation of enlightenment.

Mother's Agenda (1979) is a massive thirteen-volume, 6,000-page journal of the Mother's spiritual and physical experiences, recorded by Satprem from 1962 until her passing in 1973. From 1957 until 1962, the Mother met Satprem twice a week, and from March 1962 onwards, when she permanently retired to her room, the interviews were conducted at her office by Satprem. In these pages the Mother describes in detail the changes, in particular, the physical changes she underwent, or what she called 'cellular changes' from 1962 onwards until her death. *The Mind of the Cells* (1982) by Satprem is a distilled but a more cohesive account of these very same changes.

In 1962, after what seemed like a brief illness, she began to sense signs of her body undergoing biological mutation: 'a sort of decentralization…as if the cells were being scattered by a centrifugal force.' She would feel terribly weak at times, yet, something, untouched, was fully conscious of what was happening, 'witnessing everything … like matter looking at itself in a whole new way' (Ibid.).

Taste, smell, vision, touch, sound—the sensory perceptions began to undergo a complete change. Now and then she experienced bursts of energy that caused pain. At times she would feel that she was dying, that she was going to explode. The sensation was not what religious people assumed to be joy or bliss, she asserted, but a sense of alarm, fear, anxiety, pain. She said, 'it's really and truly terrifying … it's truly a journey into nothing … You are blindfolded, you know nothing' (Ibid.).

It was the body that was involved in the process, not the mind. There was a struggle within the cells between the old habits and something new that was trying to emerge. In other words, it was the struggle of the body to cleanse itself of the *habit* developed over thousands of years of 'separate existence on account of ego'. Now it had to learn to continue without the ego, 'according to another, unknown law, a law still incomprehensible for the body. It is not a will, it's … a way of being …' and she felt that the body was everywhere. 'I am talking here about the cells of the body, but the same applies to external events, even world events. It's even remarkable in the case of earth quakes, volcanic eruptions, etc., it would seem that the entire earth is like the body'(Ibid.).

Everything is interconnected. The sense of separation is complete falsehood. The mind divides everything up. But here, in the body, the Mother asserted, everything is one:

> The speck of dust you wipe off the table or ecstatic contemplation, it's all the same … It's not a product of thought or imagination … Dreaming, meditating, soaring into higher consciousness is all very well, but that seems so poor in comparison, so poor, so limited. … In the mental world, you think before doing the thing; here it's not that way. … No more memory, no more habits … it's all spontaneous … it comes, it comes in facts, in actions, in movements. (Ibid.)

'Salvation is physical,' the Mother declared. The 'I' or the individual had no role to play in this process. It was the body with its innate intelligence *taking over and doing what had to be done*. She wondered why the spiritual teachers of the past sought liberation by abandoning their body, and why they had to talk of nirvana as something outside the body? 'The body is a very, very simple thing,' said the Mother. 'It does not need to "seek" anything. Why did men never know of this from the start? Why did they go after all sorts of things—religions, gods, and all those ... sorts of things?'(Ibid.)

'The physical is capable of receiving the Superior Light, the Truth, the true consciousness and to manifest it,' asserted the Mother. But it is not easy, she warned, 'it requires endurance and will come when it will be totally natural. The door has just—just been opened—that's all; now we must go ahead' (Ibid.; also see Joshi 1996).

On 17 November 1973, at the age of ninety-five, the Mother died, leaving behind an inspirational and challenging legacy. With the passing away of Aurobindo, the unfulfilled task of bringing about the supra-mental manifestation had been passed on to the Mother. When the Mother underwent the physical changes, it was felt that she would be the first of a new type of human individual, the new species, incarnating the Supra-mental Truth Consciousness that Sri Aurobindo had allegedly discovered.

Perhaps the Mother did not live long enough to forge ahead on the path she had discovered, and for these cellular changes to come to full fruition. How that would have spanned out could only be a matter of speculation today. However, in modern times, along with Pandit Gopi Krishna and U.G. Krishnamurti, the Mother was one of the first people to have discovered and articulated in a plain and definitive language the biological foundation of nirvana.

Words of the Mother

Do not take my words for a teaching. Always they are a force in action, uttered with a definite purpose, and they lose their true purpose when separated from that purpose.

~

What you must know is exactly the thing you want to do in life. The time needed to learn it does not matter at all. For those who wish to live according to Truth, there is always something to learn and some progress to make.

~

The true aim of life is to find the Divine's Presence deep inside oneself and to surrender to It so that It takes the lead of the life, all the feelings and all the actions of the body. This gives a true and luminous aim to existence.

~

Never forget that you are not alone. The Divine is with you helping and guiding you. He is the companion who never fails, the friend whose love comforts and strengthens. Have faith and He will do everything for you.

~

Our human consciousness has windows that open on the Infinite but generally men keep these windows carefully shut. They have to be opened wide and allow the Infinite freely to enter into us and transform us.

~

The one you love must have the right of freedom in her feelings and if you want the truth you must understand this right and accept it. Otherwise there will be no end to your miseries. This is an occasion to surmount your egoism and to open to the true life. If you decide to make this effort my help will be with you.

~

You should not confuse a calm mind with a silent mind. You can calm your mind and stop its ordinary activity, but it may still be open to ideas coming from outside and that too disturbs the calm. And for the mind to be completely silent, you must not only stop its own activity but shut out all that comes from other minds.

Eight

Modern Sages

Sri Ramakrishna Paramahamsa

Sri Ramakrishna Paramahamsa was one of the most remarkable and lively of the modern sages. Looking at his life from the outside, and if one has little understanding of spirituality, Sri Ramakrishna might appear as one who was mostly 'mad' but with a strong spiritual streak in him. Indeed he was *spiritually mad*, a saint, who embodied a bewildering range of pietism. He was, in another sense, all the four acharyas, Shankaracharya, Ramanujacharya, Madhvacharya and Nimbarkacharya, rolled into one! The teachings of Advaita, Dvaita, Vishishtadvaita and Dvaitadvaita permeated and found vibrant expression in the unrelenting play of the fifty years of his existence in Calcutta (now Kolkata). It's an incredible story.

Ramakrishna, named Gadadhar after Lord Vishnu, was born to Kshudiram Chattopadhyay and Chandramani Devi on 17 February 1836, in the village of Kamarpukur in the Hoogli district of

West Bengal. The fourth among five children, he attended a village school for about twelve years and then, losing interest, dropped out.

Even as a boy he was of a spiritual bent of mind and given to falling into trances. Years later, Ramakrishna himself recalled the first mystical experience he had at the young age of six. Once, while walking along the paddy fields, he saw a flock of white cranes flying against a backdrop of dark clouds. He became so absorbed by the sight that he was thrown into a state of indescribable joy and then lost consciousness.

The village of Kamarpukur was a transit point for monks and pilgrims to rest en route to the holy place, Puri. Ramakrishna would go and meet these holy men and it is from them he is believed to have picked up his knowledge of the Puranas, the epics and stories of saints and sages. He was hardly seven when his father died. The responsibility of the family fell on the shoulders of his eldest brother, Ramkumar. Ramakrishna, it is said, was drawn closer to his mother and assisted her in household activities.

He had a phenomenal memory and would regale his friends with the stories he heard from itinerant monks, and the religious plays he had watched. In fact, he took great interest in religious/mythical plays and even joined an amateur drama company. Once, it is said, he was persuaded to play the role of Shiva. Ash smeared all over his body, he went on stage only to fall into a trance. It is interesting to note here that he loved enacting female roles, and that women in particular grew very fond of him.

He was restless, buoyant, talented, mischievous, forthright and gifted with extraordinary intelligence. And, of course, he could go into a meditative state and enter a state of trance effortlessly. This phenomenon, rather the physical process of going into trance, more exactly samadhi, became a frequent occurrence from the age of eleven and continued until his last days. You will recall here that even Anandamayi Ma, as a young girl, used to go into samadhi and continued to do so almost until the end of her life. Parents, siblings, other family members and later even her husband thought she was mentally ill, or subject to possession by spirits, and only later began to accept that it was a case of 'God-intoxication'.

More or less the same thing happened in Ramakrishna's case too. People thought he was epileptic, mentally imbalanced, even mad. His behaviour used to be so out of the ordinary that even young Narendra (the famous Swami Vivekananda of later years) thought, during the first couple of meetings, that Ramakrishna could be a little insane.

The eldest brother, Ramkumar, had moved to Calcutta after his wife's untimely death, and started a Sanskrit school there, while also working as a family priest. Back home, the burden of the family now fell on the second son, Rameshwar. In 1952, when Ramkumar complained that he could not manage priestly work along with teaching in school, Ramakrishna, now seventeen, agreed to assist his brother in priestly duties. Within three years, Ramkumar also became the priest of Dakshineswar Kali Temple, which, incidentally, had been built by Rani Rasmani, a Shudra by caste. Ramakrishna, along with his nephew Hriday who was to become his close companion and attendant for the next twenty-five years, moved in as Ramkumar's assistant.

A year into this work Ramkumar died and Ramakrishna was asked to take over as the temple priest. At first, Ramakrishna did not agree. Living in the garden of the temple premises he had taken to meditation during his spare time. Temple services would be a heavy responsibility, especially taking charge of the valuable ornaments of the goddess, and he was afraid it would all come in the way of his sadhana. But when Hriday agreed to assist him, he agreed and his life changed forever.

His time was now divided between his duties as the priest and in pursuit of his sadhana. To him now, the statue of Kali was not just a figure in stone but his virtual mother, the mother of the universe. And while worshipping the goddess he often went into samadhi. However, during his free time in the afternoon, and especially at night, he continued his sadhana under a large Amalaka tree inside a nearby jungle referred to as Panchavati. It was low, uneven land, dense with tall trees and thick shrubs. He would sit naked under the tree, lost in meditation for hours. Realization of God, coming face-to-face with the Divine Mother, became his only passion and purpose of existence.

One day, unable to bear the agony of separation from the Divine Mother, he decided to end his life. In his words:

> I felt as if my heart were squeezed like a wet towel. I could not bear the separation any longer. Suddenly my eyes fell on the sword that was kept in the temple. Determined to put an end to my life, I jumped up like a madman and seized it, when suddenly the blessed Mother revealed Herself to me, and I fell unconscious on the floor. What happened after that, I do not know, but within me there was a steady flow of undiluted bliss, altogether new, and I felt the presence of the Divine Mother. (Nikhilananda [Transl.] 2002)

A few days later, he experienced the following: 'The building with its different parts, the temple, and all vanished from my sight, leaving no trace whatsoever, and in their place was a limitless, infinite, effulgent ocean of consciousness. ... I was panting for breath. I was caught in the billows and fell down senseless'(Ibid.).

It was only the beginning of a series of such experiences that he would undergo over the next few years. Like a child he constantly yearned for the vision of the Divine Mother. Like one gone mad he would sing, shout, joke, laugh, weep and even dance, holding the image of the Mother in hand. Sometimes he would approach the idol with a morsel of food in hand and insist that the Divine Mother eat. Or, he would deck himself with flowers meant for the goddess and eat the food offering and then lie down in Her bedstead. It all seemed a sacrilege to many and soon rumours spread that Ramakrishna had become unstable as a result of his spiritual practices at Dakshineswar. It was what they later reckoned as *prema*-bhakti: 'the state of being blasted by an excess of Light'.

In the years to follow he was to go through other forms of bhakti, such as *shanta* (serenity, calm), *sakhya* (friendship), *dasya* (the relation of servant to master), and *vatsalya* (fondness, affection, or the love a mother feels for a child)—all of which came in such a natural way that Ramakrishna himself was scarcely conscious of it. During one such phase, behaving like the monkey god Hanuman, he lived on fruits, and passed most of his time sitting naked on trees, calling out 'Raghuvir, Raghuvir'. During this phase he had a vision of Sita and felt her merge into his body.

The temple authorities were not without misgivings about his strange behaviour and arranged for his treatment by an expert physician. It did not help, rather his behaviour only grew deeper and more intense. He had stepped into his twenties then, and for the next three years he went through what later came to be identified as different phases of bhakti-*bhava*, like an artist playing out different avatars on stage.

When the news reached his home in Kamarpukur, mother Chandra Devi and elder brother Rameshwar were naturally worried and decided to get Ramakrishna married. They believed that marriage would be a good steadying influence, force him to take up responsibilities, and keep his attention on family affairs rather than on chasing spiritual experiences. He was duly called home, and treated with medicines given by vaidyas (doctors practising Indian systems of medicine). Thereafter, occult cures were tried, exorcists consulted and religious rites performed, hoping to bring him back to a 'normal' state. But Ramakrishna's feverish zeal for God only grew in leaps and bounds. Nevertheless, he didn't want to cross his mother and agreed to marry.

And so, at twenty-three Ramakrishna was married to a five-year-old bride, Saradamani, later to be known as Sarada Devi, the Holy Mother. After the marriage, for the next thirteen years or so Saradamani stayed at her father's place—for short periods at Kamarpukur, too—and joined Ramakrishna in Dakshineswar at the age of eighteen. But the marriage was never consummated since Ramakrishna, who was in his mid-thirties at the time, had already embraced the monastic life of a sannyasi. We do not know how Saradamani viewed her marital status, but what we know is that by then she knew that her husband had turned deeply spiritual.

It is said that Saradamani became Ramakrishna's devoted follower and his first disciple and he in turn regarded her as the Divine Mother in person and addressed her as Sree Maa (Holy Mother). And when, as a priest, Ramakrishna performed the ritual ceremony, the *Shodashi Puja*, Sarada Devi was made to sit in the seat of goddess Kali, and worshipped as the Divine Mother. Sarada Devi outlived Ramakrishna by thirty-four years and played an important role during the early phase of Ramakrishna Mission.

It was during this period—in his late thirties—that Ramakrishna went through rigorous sadhana in Vaishnava bhakti, tantra and Vedanta. In a sense, it was all like a play to Ramakrishna and he was keen to explore all the well-known modes of spiritual practices and experience the Divinity in all its forms and manifestations. For a period of time he even turned into a Muslim devotee. He lived outside the temple complex, dressed like an Arab Muslim, chanted the name of Allah, recited the namaz five times daily and immersed himself in Islamic practices. Three days into this sadhana, he had a vision of a 'radiant personage with grave countenance and white beard resembling the Prophet and merging with his body' (Nikhilananda 2002).

Soon after this he took to Christianity like a zealot. And he is believed to have had a vision of the Madonna and Child, and then of Jesus Christ, who, too, is supposed to have merged with his body.

When Sri Ramakrishna said that all spiritual paths ultimately lead to the same goal, namely, the experience of Godhood, he was speaking from experience and not verbalizing mere philosophy, since he himself had gone through all the different varieties of religious practices and experiences. That way, he was a spiritual empiricist of sorts, who wanted to test, verify and himself live through the truths of different spiritual disciplines and experiences. No wonder, therefore, that he was seen on the one hand as an authority and sagacious guide in spiritual matters, and, on the other, as an embodiment of different spiritualities, rather an embodiment of the deeper and profound unity of the different paths to God-realization.

To him the dual and non-dual were not contradictory but complementary to each other; form and formlessness were but attributes of God. For Ramakrishna, the great debate among the different schools of Vedanta merged in *bhava-rasa* (*bhava*, feelings or emotions; *rasa*, the aesthetic flavour that results from the emotions; in short, *rasa* is the state of mind produced by different *bhava*s or emotions). The following three episodes from his life should explain how he resolved the great spiritual conundrum and came into his own.

In 1864, Ramakrishna practised both *vatsalya* and *madhura bhava* (the attitude of Radha and the *gopika*s towards Krishna), as per Vaishnava faith. During this period, he worshipped the image of Ram Lalla (Rama as a child) in the attitude of a mother and felt the presence of child Rama as a living God. Later, in the practice of *madhura bhava*, he often fell into samadhi. During this period, he dressed himself in women's attire and regarded himself as one of the *gopika*s of Vrindavan in love with Krishna. It is said, towards the end of this sadhana, Ramakrishna believed to have attained *savikalpa* samadhi—vision and union with Krishna.

The second episode occurred shortly after his experience of *vatsalya* and *madhura bhava* when, under the guidance of Bhairavi Brahmani, Ramakrishna set himself to learn all about tantra. She put him through all the exercises mentioned in tantra books. It generally took years and even decades for *sadhakas* to experience higher states of consciousness, but Ramakrishna went through several mystical states in quick succession in an incredibly short period of time and then all of that culminated in the rise of the Kundalini Shakti. Speaking about that phase to his close associates, he described that it was something like a tingling sensation that rose from the feet to the head. So long as it did not reach the brain he remained conscious, but the moment it did so, he was dead to the outside world. Even the functions of the eye and ears, he explained, came to a stop, and speech was completely out of the question. In his words:

Who should speak? The very distinction between 'I' and 'thou' vanishes. Sometimes I think I shall tell you everything about what I see and feel when that mysterious power rises up through the spinal column. When it come up to the heart and the throat it is possible to speak, which I do. But the moment it has gone above the throat, somebody stops my mouth, as it were, and I am adrift ... Well, I sincerely wish to tell you everything, Mother won't let me do so. She gagged me! (Ibid.)

The third episode took place two years later in 1866, when Ramakrishna was initiated into Advaita Vedanta by Totapuri, an itinerant monk and Naga sannyasi well-versed in the non-dual philosophy. By Ramakrishna's own report, Totapuri first guided him through the rites of *sannyasa* (renunciation of all ties to the world) and then taught him about Advaita Vedanta. Totapuri did not approve of image or idol worship. Brahman is formless, he insisted and that bhakti *bhava* was an aspect of maya and Ramakrishna should get out of it. And he instructed him to chant and contemplate on the following *mahavakyas*:

Brahman alone is real, and the world is illusory.
I have no separate existence
I am that Brahman alone.

Chanting and meditating on these, Ramakrishna reportedly experienced *nirvikalpa* samadhi. It is said that *savikalpa* samadhi is a state of being where thought or bhava is not entirely absent, rather, the self is present and you rest, as it were, soaked in a single thought or *bhava*. In *nirvikalpa* samadhi, let alone thought or *bhava*, even awareness is absent; name and form, which constitute the world, are dissolved. It is a state where there is no trace of the self, nothing exists—no multiplicity and no oneness either. *Nirvikalpa* samadhi is considered to be the highest state of spiritual realization.

> The naked one taught Advaita Vedanta and asked me to concentrate on Atman. Despite all attempts I could not cross the realm of name and form. Every time I tried to concentrate my mind upon the Advaita teachings, the Mother's form stood in my way ... Then, with a stern determination I used my discrimination as a sword and with it severed it in two. There remained no more obstruction to my mind, which at once soared beyond the relative plane, and I lost myself in samadhi. (Nikhilananda [Transl.] 2002)

Three days passed and still Ramakrishna remained immersed in *nirvikalpa* samadhi. Totapuri could not believe what he was witnessing—that Ramakrishna could attain in the course of a single day a state which had taken him forty years of strenuous sadhana to achieve. Ramakrishna remained on and off in the state of *nirvikalpa* samadhi for six months, and then as his fate would have it, the Divine Mother commanded him to 'remain on the threshold of relative consciousness for the sake of humanity'.

As his name spread, people came to know that a Paramahamsa—a great swan, the best among all categories of sannyasis, but generally seen as a realized soul who behaved like a child—lived in a garden house at the Kali temple in Dakshineswar. An ever-shifting crowd from all classes and castes started visiting Ramakrishna. Even prominent cultural leaders and scholars, intellectuals and writers such as Michael Madhusudan Dutt, Bankim Chandra Chatterjee, Keshab Chandra Sen and members of the Brahmo Samaj, Girish Chandra Ghosh and many such noted people visited Ramakrishna. And in between came spiritual seekers and sceptics, among them Narendra, Rakhal, Yogin, Baburam, Niranjan, Tarak and Kali, to name a few, who were to be transformed by the magical touch of Ramakrishna and then go on to become torchbearers of Ramakrishna Mission.

Ramakrishna's method of teaching was simple, straightforward and informal. He used rustic Bengali, reminisced a lot about his spiritual journey and experiences, narrated tales, cracked jokes, broke into songs and even used 'abusive' words (which were later cleaned up in English translations), to drive home a point. He raised critical questions and answered them himself, explained problematic Vedantic concepts or some knotty philosophical issue by drawing examples and illustrations from everyday life as well as from spiritual texts.

To Ramakrishna it did not matter if a seeker approached God as the formless Absolute Infinite Principle, or sought Truth in different forms through bhakti; rather, what mattered was a single-minded devotion to the ideal. If one was really serious, he would declare, one would surely find God. Once, a seeker approached Sri Ramakrishna and said that he had been yearning to see God for years. Sri Ramakrishna is believed to have led the man to a nearby river and held his head under water. A minute later he released the man from water and asked, 'What were you feeling?'

The man cried, 'What could I feel or think in such a terrible situation? I was gasping for breath.'

Then Sri Ramakrishna said, 'If and when you yearn for God the way you gasped for a breath of air, you'll see God.'

Towards the end of his life, Ramakrishna seemed to be in a hurry to complete his mission in life. He was clairvoyant and more, and he could tell the disposition of a person by merely gazing at the body. The day Narendra appeared on the scene—he, who would become Swami Vivekananda and storm the world with his blazing message of spiritual growth and liberation—Ramakrishna cried out, 'Ah, you came so late! How could you be so unkind as to keep me waiting so long? Oh, I am panting to unburden my mind to one who can appreciate my innermost experiences' (Chetanananda 1999).

And he did unburden, pour out all his knowledge and power to Narendra. Though at first sceptical (Narendra thought that Ramakrishna might be a little barmy, but certainly eccentric), he eventually saw the light and accepted Ramakrishna as an avatar. More than the words it was the magical touch of Ramakrishna that quickened the change in Narendra and enabled him to come into his own.

Sages such as Sri Ramakrishna and Sri Ramana were receptacles of great spiritual energy that could lighten the burden, change, give a glimpse of the oneness of reality and energize people to surge forward on the path of self-realization. Here is a report from Vivekananda:

> Muttering something to himself, with his eyes fixed on me, slowly he drew near me and in the twinkling of an eye he placed his right foot on my body. The touch at once gave rise to a novel experience within me. With my eyes open I saw that the walls, and everything in the room, whirled rapidly and vanished into nought, and the whole universe together with my individuality was about to merge in an all-encompassing mysterious void! I was terribly frightened and thought that I was facing death ... (Chetanananda 1999)

This was a 'near-death' experience that opened up Narendra to higher spiritual experiences, to possible activation of the Kundalini power in him, which would transform him completely. Preparedness is all that is required to receive such blessings. When one is vulnerable, empty and open, then the grace descends on you. Ramakrishna touched many, transformed a few; Narendra, in particular, was perhaps most ready and it happened to him like magic. No wonder then that Ramakrishna should choose Narendra to be the lead torchbearer of the message, not Ramakrishna's message, but the universal message that it is possible to end conflict and suffering and come upon the unitary experience.

On completion of his forty-ninth year, Ramakrishna fell seriously ill. In the beginning doctors thought that he suffered from clergyman's throat caused by bad weather and his constant talking, singing and frequent recurrence of 'bhava-samadhi'. But on detailed examination he was found to have throat cancer. Dr Mahendra Lal Sarkar, an allopath, was entrusted the treatment of Ramakrishna. Medication and 'proper' diet were prescribed, and the master was told to give rest to his vocal organs. None of which Sri Ramakrishna could or did follow consistently.

When the discomfort and pain became acute, a further diagnosis revealed that the cancer had turned worse. All sorts of medications, including homoeopathy, were tried. But Sri Ramakrishna being what he was he could never give rest to his vocal chords. And the recurrences of his samadhi seemed to only aggravate the disease. It was as if the rush of energy only added to the life and fast multiplication of cancer cells, instead of destroying them. The manner in which twelve young disciples close to Sri Ramakrishna, including Narendra, took care of him in his last days, makes for a moving story.

Ramakrishna was not a rich people's guru. The only money he came by was a paltry sum he drew as a 'retired' priest at the Dakshineswar temple. Every time Ramakrishna and his disciples moved to a new place, in order to pay the rent and meet other household expenses, the disciples had to raise funds, sometimes pledging their belongings. But why should their master suffer from such a deadly ailment? Couldn't the power of Mother Durga cure him? Couldn't he cure himself with his spiritual powers which could send people into trance in no time? Or, was it all a play, a Divine lila?

One group of close disciples felt it was all the master's play to test the devotion of the disciples, to strengthen their character and lead them on to the path of renunciation. The other group thought it was all the doings of the Divine Mother, the purpose of which the master himself could not fathom. The third group, led by Narendra, took a rational view of the whole matter and reasoned that Sri Ramakrishna's physical form, like all other forms of life, like all other human bodies, was naturally subject to the laws of nature. It would be futile to ascribe esoteric meanings or mystical reasons to his illness.

Despite these differences of opinion the disciples did believe that the master had probably taken the 'sins' or disease of some devotee upon himself, or that the 'impure' bodies of people who came and touched him had affected him adversely. This belief was partly strengthened by Ramakrishna himself, who had once chided Mother Durga thus: 'Why dost Thou bring here these worthless people who are like milk adulterated with five times its quantity of water? My eyes are almost gone by blowing into the fire to dry up the water, and my health is shattered' (Nikhilananda 2008).

For some time, the disciples tried in vain to prevent strangers from touching the master's feet. But the master himself was not cooperative. He talked and talked, even when he was in pain. He did not stop giving spiritual instructions, he even sang and danced with the disciples, and almost every day, as a rule, fell into samadhi. When the disciples pleaded, 'You must cure yourself, for our sake at least,' he replied, 'Do you think that I have been undergoing this suffering voluntarily? I do wish to recover. But how is that possible? It all depends upon Her will.'

'Your will is at one with Hers!'

'It won't do any good. How can I ask Her for anything when my *will* is entirely merged in Hers?'

The flow of old associates, devotees and admirers only increased tenfold. He did not stop speaking. The recurrence of his samadhi and mystical visions amazed and humbled the disciples. He was once heard saying to himself: 'Had this body been allowed to last longer, many more people would have been spiritually awakened.' Then after a pause: 'But Mother has ordained otherwise. Lest people should take advantage of my simplicity and illiteracy, and prevail upon me to bestow the rare gifts of spirituality. She will take me away. And this is an age when devotional exercises are at a sad discount' (Ibid.).

As days passed into weeks and weeks into months, his body shrank, the pain grew acute, and internal bleeding aggravated the condition. But he refused to be bedridden, for he knew his days were numbered and he had one last task to perform. He presented saffron robes to the

inner circle of disciples, who were eager and ready, and initiated them
into *sannyasa* with mantra *diksha* (bestowing upon them a mantra
each). One day he made Narendra sit in front of him, and gazing at
him Ramakrishna fell into samadhi. Narendra, who later became
Vivekananda, reported that he 'felt a subtle force like electric current
penetrate his body', and lost consciousness. When he came back to
normal state, he saw the master in tears (Chetanananda 1999).

'Today I have given you my all and have become a fakir!' whispered
the master. 'Through this power you will do immense good to the
world, and then only shall you go back' (Ibid.).

In the early hours of Monday, 16 August 1886, Sri Ramakrishna fell
unconscious and his body turned stiff. The stiffness was something
unusual and some of the disciples thought that the master had
only entered into a state of deep samadhi. They massaged his back
and limbs, hoping against hope the master would return to normal
consciousness. Hours later, Dr Mahendra Lal Sarkar, who had attended
to the master before and had now become his great admirer, declared
Sri Ramakrishna Paramahamsa dead.

The Teaching

> I have practised all religions—Hinduism, Islam, Christianity—and
> I have also followed the paths of the different Hindu sects. I have
> found that it is the same God toward whom all are directing their
> steps, though along different paths. You must try all beliefs and
> traverse all the different ways once. Wherever I look, I see men
> quarrelling in the name of religion—Hindus, Mohammedans,
> Brahmos, Vaishnavas, and the rest. But they never reflect that He
> who is called Krishna is also called Siva, and bears the name of the
> Primal Energy, Jesus, and Allah as well—the same Rama with a
> thousand names.
>
> ~
>
> It has been revealed to me that there exists an Ocean of
> Consciousness without limit. From It come all things of the

relative plane, and in It they merge again. These waves arising from the Great Ocean merge again in the Great Ocean. I have clearly perceived all these things.

When I think of the Supreme Being as inactive—neither creating nor preserving nor destroying—I call Him Brahman or *Purusha*, the Impersonal God. When I think of Him as active—creating, preserving and destroying—I call Him *Sakti* or *Maya* or *Prakriti*, the Personal God. But the distinction between them does not mean a difference. The Personal and Impersonal are the same thing, like milk and its whiteness, the diamond and its lustre, the snake and its wriggling motion. It is impossible to conceive of the one without the other. The Divine Mother and Brahman are one.

~

Truth is one; only It is called by different names. All people are seeking the same Truth; the variance is due to climate, temperament, and name. A lake has many ghats. From one ghat the Hindus take water in jars and call it '*jal*'. From another ghat the Mussalmāns take water in leather bags and call it '*pāni*'. From a third, the Christians take the same thing and call it 'water'. Suppose someone says that the thing is not '*jal*' but '*pāni*', or that it is not '*pāni*' but 'water', or that it is not 'water' but '*jal*', it would indeed be ridiculous. But this very thing is at the root of the friction among sects, their misunderstandings and quarrels. This is why people injure and kill one another, and shed blood, in the name of religion. But this is not good. Everyone is going toward God. They will all realize Him if they have sincerity and longing of heart.

~

God is directly perceived by the mind, but not by this ordinary mind. It is the pure mind that perceives God, and at that time this ordinary mind does not function. A mind that has the slightest trace of attachment to the world cannot be called pure. When all the impurities of the mind are removed, you may call that mind Pure Mind or Pure Ātman.

Aphorisms

I am everybody's disciple. All are the children of God. All are His servants.

~

The devotee of God wants to eat sugar, and not become sugar.

~

One cannot think of the Absolute without the Relative, or of the Relative without the Absolute.

~

Brahman and Śakti are identical. If you accept the one, you must accept the other.

~

As a piece of rope, when burnt, retains its form, but cannot serve to bind, so is the ego which is burnt by the fire of supreme Knowledge.

~

As a boy holding to a post or a pillar whirls about it with headlong speed without any fear or falling, so perform your worldly duties, fixing your hold firmly upon God, and you will be free from danger.

~

The more you dwell on worldly things, the greater will be your attachment. Smear your finger with oil if you want to open the jackfruit, or the milky exudation will stick to them. Devotion to God is like this oil.

~

So long as the bee does not sit on the flower, it buzzes. When it has begun to sip the honey, it is quiet. Sometimes, however, after drinking its fill, it hums out of sheer joy.

~

When a pitcher is dipped into a pond, it makes a gargling noise. When full, it makes no more sound. But [if] the water is poured into another pitcher, again there is sound.

~

Sri Aurobindo

Aurobindo was a great experimenter in spirituality, a spiritual scientist and a spiritual empiricist who, for twenty-three years or more, experimented, tested and probed into the depths of his own body-mind, exploring 'planes of consciousness', to bring home what he called the Supra-mental Being. Almost in the style of Marx, Aurobindo too could well have said: The world over saints, mystics and poets have hitherto only talked about their ineffable experiences, their god-experiences and beyond, but it is now time to surge ahead and transform the very human creature into a Supra-mental Being and thus create a new world!

In his scheme of things, Indian spiritualities were all great spiritual adventures in consciousness but they could not bring about a 'terrestrial realization' or evolution on earth. In other words, blessed and strengthened by the spiritual development achieved so far, we must now prepare ourselves for the next evolutionary stage and move beyond the religion-centred transformation of the individual to the spirituality-centred transformation of humanity, where nothing is excluded, all is heightened and widened.

Aurobindo Ghose was born in Calcutta, to Krishna Dhun Ghose and Swarnalata Devi, on 15 August 1872. Krishna Dhun Ghose was then an assistant surgeon in Rangpur in Bengal and an avowed anglophile. Aurobindo had two older siblings, Benoybhusan and Manmohan, a younger sister, Sarojini, and a younger brother, Barindrakumar. Krishna Dhun Ghose wanted his sons to enter the Indian Civil Service (ICS) and join the British Government. But only Aurobindo came close to fulfilling his father's aspirations. He studied at King's College, Cambridge, where he excelled in the classics, literature and history, and topped in Greek and Latin. He passed the ICS written examination although his heart was not in it. And he went purposefully late to the horse-riding practical examination to get himself disqualified for the service.

Instead, Aurobindo joined the Baroda State Service in 1893 and, after working in various departments, took to teaching and eventually became the vice principal of the Baroda College. During this period, he started taking an active interest in the politics of India's independence struggle against British rule, but worked behind the scenes as his position in the college barred him from overt political activity. He linked up with radical political activists and helped to organize resistance groups in Bengal.

In 1901, aged twenty-eight, he married Mrinalini, the fourteen-year-old daughter of Bhupal Chandra Bose, a senior official in government service. It was not a happy marriage. Separated from her husband for years, Mrinalini suffered loneliness and depression. She died of influenza in December 1918, a few days after she was told to join her husband.

Between 1906 and 1908, Aurobindo played an active role in the freedom struggle. He met Congress leaders such as Bal Gangadhar Tilak, sided with extremists, gave speeches and wrote articles in support of the struggle. In 1908, he was arrested on charges of plotting and overseeing a bomb attack on a sitting judge. He was imprisoned in solitary confinement in Alipore Jail. The Alipore Bomb Case trial went on for a year, but eventually he was acquitted on 6 May 1909.

Two significant events stand out during this period. The first occurred just before his arrest when he met Vishnu Bhasker Lele, a yogi. This meeting seems to have had a great impact on him. The second, the mystical experiences that Aurobindo underwent during his incarceration in Alipore Jail, which changed the course of his life forever— he was 'visited' by Swami Vivekanand, who had passed away seven years earlier. In Aurobindo's words,

It is a fact that I was hearing constantly the voice of Vivekananda speaking to me for a fortnight in the jail in my solitary meditation and felt his presence.' Soon after this, he had his first transcendental

experiences. In his words again, 'I looked at the jail that secluded
me from men and it was no longer by its high walls that I was
imprisoned; no, it was Vasudeva who surrounded me' (Paranjape
1999).

Shortly after his release from Alipore Jail, he withdrew from the
political field and turned his full attention to yoga. Two years later, he
went into hiding and then reached Pondicherry, where he made his
spiritual home. Until his death in 1950, he pursued his Integral Yoga
with startling discoveries, and, in the words of Makarand Paranjape,
'fathering one of the great spiritual movements of modern India'.
However, it must be noted here that Mirra Alfassa, called 'The Mother'
and considered to be of equal yogic stature by Aurobindo, was an
integral part of this great spiritual movement. It was she who, after
Aurobindo's passing away, carried forward his work on Integral Yoga
and fostered the movement to what it is today.

We do not know how much of Nietzsche's criticism of religious
thinking and his idea of Superman were influenced by his reading
of the Upanishads and Buddhism. Similarly it is difficult to say if
Aurobindo borrowed the notion of Superman from Nietzsche.
However, Aurobindo acknowledged the fact that it was Nietzsche
who first talked about Superman, though the idea was extremely
problematic.

Aurobindo was quite unique and innovative in his ideas and in
the way he challenged some of the central notions of both Western
and Indian philosophy. For instance, he declared that nirvana was not
the end of the spiritual journey, but only a new beginning. He found
the traditional notion of moksha problematic and interpreted it as
a forward movement towards supra-mental manifestation. There is
no such thing as maya, he asserted, nothing unreal or false, but only
imperfect and incomplete (perception/realization of) realities. So,

what one needed was a 'constant heightening and widening' of one's understanding of life and truth.

His Integral Yoga was geared towards this 'constant heightening and widening' of our understanding of life and truth, which would eventually, he believed, result in the manifestation of the Supramental Being on earth. 'It is clear,' he wrote, 'that Mind has not been able to change human nature radically. You can go on changing human institutions infinitely and yet the imperfection will break through all your institutions ... It must be another power that can not only resist but overcome that downward pull' (Sri Aurobindo 1971a).

So he argued that we should go beyond Mind, beyond even Overmind which can at best create mystics and sages, great scientists and leaders. There is certainly more to nature's design, to this cosmic play:

The animal is a living laboratory in which Nature has, it is said, worked out man. Man himself may well be a thinking and living laboratory in whom and with whose conscious cooperation she wills to work out the superman, the god. Or shall we not say, rather, to manifest God? (Sri Aurobindo 1971b)

He had no doubt that nature was pushing humankind towards a grand terrestrial realization and fulfilment, towards the creation of new species on earth. It would not be an aristocracy of Mind, nor Overmind, but Supermind. The new man would not be a Nietzschean Superman or Zarathustra, but God! And this God, rather Aurobindo's Superman, would usher in not a better world, but a New World!

Aurobindo, while operating within these enlightenment traditions, strove to go beyond it by giving it what may be called a political twist. It was not enough for individuals to cut themselves off from the bonds of sorrow and become perfect, but they needed to work for the total transformation of humanity. This was a bodhisattvic ideal to which he added the idea of evolution to mean that the state of a mystic, even a sage, is only a transitory phase—though much evolved—and one should move beyond even the state of a sage to bring home the Supra-mental Being, who will be God, the end product or fulfilment of evolution on earth.

In mid-1940 Aurobindo was found to be suffering from prostatitis. It was at a preliminary stage and it is believed that Aurobindo cured himself. But after a few years it reappeared and he developed other complications, his condition becoming quite critical. 'Why don't you use your force and cure yourself, master?' asked one of his close disciples. He replied, 'Can't explain, you won't understand. (Purani 1987).

On 5 December 1950, frail of body, Aurobindo died of uraemia and kidney infection. He was seventy-eight years old. It is said that many of his disciples witnessed Aurobindo's body glowing with light and expected him to come back to life. They hoped that there would be a 'resurrection' and Aurobindo would go on to live in his supra-mental body. But that was not to be. The light faded on the fifth day, and on the evening of 9 December 1950, Aurobindo's body was laid in a vault under the copper-pod tree which is where the samadhi stands today.

The Teaching

> The spiritual life (*adhyatma-jivana*), the religious life (dharma-*jivana*) and the ordinary human life of which morality is a part are three quite different things and one must know which one desires and not confuse the three together.
>
> The ordinary life is that of the average human consciousness separated from its own true self and from the Divine and led by the common habits of the mind, life and body which are the laws of the Ignorance.

The religious life is a movement of the same ignorant human consciousness, turning or trying to turn away from the earth towards the Divine, but as yet without knowledge and led by the dogmatic tenets and rules of some sect or creed which claims to have found the way out of the bonds of the earth-consciousness into some beatific Beyond. The religious life may be the first approach to the spiritual, but very often it is only a turning about in a round of rites, ceremonies and practices or set ideas and forms without any issue.

~

The spiritual life, on the contrary, proceeds directly by a change of consciousness, a change from the ordinary consciousness, ignorant and separated from its true self and from God, to a greater consciousness in which one finds one's true being and comes first into direct and living contact and then into union with the Divine. For the spiritual seeker this change of consciousness is the one thing he seeks and nothing else matters.

~

The Unknown is not the Unknowable; it need not remain the unknown for us, unless we choose ignorance or persist in our first limitations. For to all things that are not unknowable, all things in the universe, there correspond in that universe faculties which can take cognisance of them, and in man, the microcosm, these faculties are always existent and at a certain stage capable of development. We may choose not to develop them; where they are partially developed, we may discourage and impose on them a kind of atrophy. But, fundamentally all possible knowledge is knowledge within the power of humanity. And since in man there is the inalienable impulse of Nature towards self-realization, no struggle of the intellect to limit the action of our capacities within a determined area can for ever prevail.

~

Your practice of psycho-analysis was a mistake. It has, for the time at least, made the work of purification more complicated, not easier. The psycho-analysis of Freud is the last thing that one should associate with yoga. It takes up a certain part, the darkest, the most perilous, the unhealthiest part of the nature, the lower vital subconscious layer, isolates some of its most morbid phenomena and attributes to it and them an action out of all proportion to its true role in the nature. Modern psychology is an infant science, at once rash, fumbling and crude. As in all infant sciences, the universal habit of the human mind—to take a partial or local truth, generalize it unduly and try to explain a whole field of Nature in its narrow terms—runs riot here. Moreover, the exaggeration of the importance of suppressed sexual complexes is a dangerous falsehood and it can have a nasty influence and tend to make the mind and vital more and not less fundamentally impure than before.

Aphorisms

The first principle of true teaching is that nothing can be taught.

~

True knowledge is not attained by thinking. It is what you are; it is what you become.

~

When mind is still, then truth gets her chance to be heard in the purity of the silence.

~

What the soul sees and has experienced, that it knows; the rest is appearance, prejudice and opinion.

~

By your stumbling, the world is perfected.

~

Life is life—whether in a cat, or dog or man. There is no difference there between a cat or a man. The idea of difference is a human conception for man's own advantage.

~

The existence of poverty is the proof of an unjust and ill-organised society, and our public charities are but the first tawdry awakening in the conscience of a robber.

~

The anarchic is the true divine state of man in the end as in the beginning; but in between it would lead us straight to the devil and his kingdom.

~

The whole world yearns after freedom, yet each creature is in love with his chains; this is the first paradox and inextricable knot of our nature.

~

In order to see, you have to stop being in the middle of the picture.

~

Ramana Maharshi

Once, a devotee asked Ramana: 'The Upanishads say that he alone knows the Atman whom the Atman chooses. Why should the Atman choose at all? If it chooses, why some particular person?' And he quoted the following lines from the *Katha Upanishad*:

This Atman is not attained by instruction
or by intelligence or by learning.
By him whom *it* chooses is the Atman attained.
To him the Atman reveals his true being.

Ramana said: 'When the sun rises some buds blossom, not all. Do you blame the sun for that? Nor can the bud blossom of itself; it requires the sunlight to enable it to do so' (Godman 1999).

Ramana was that bud that blossomed in the light. It was natural, yet a miracle. In the story of Ramana we don't get to hear of any astrological prediction of his future greatness, or about some mysterious guru telling the parents of their son's future eminence in the spiritual world. Generally, in the lives of many sages we discern phases of disillusionment, quest, sadhana, and 'near-death experience' that eventually lead them up to the state of nirvana or moksha, but in the case of Ramana there was no search, absolutely no sadhana, no phases. He didn't knock on the door, yet the door opened by itself and he walked through it. 'Grace' descended upon him unasked and his life was transformed.

Born to Alagamma and Sundaram Iyer on 30 December 1879 in a village in present-day Tamil Nadu, Ramana was actually named Venkataraman Iyer. He grew up as a normal child. His early schooling took place in his native place and then at Dindigul. However, after the sudden death of his father in 1892, Venkataraman and his older brother were taken by their uncle Subba Iyer to his home in Madurai, where Venkataraman joined the American Mission High School. He did not take his studies seriously, and there was little to show that he was spiritually inclined, either. He had, though we cannot be too sure, probably read *Periapuranam* (a hagiography on the lives of the Nayanars, the sixty-three saint-poet devotees of Shiva said to have lived between the sixth and eighth centuries CE). However, on 17 July 1896 Venkataraman underwent a near-death experience and his life changed forever.

He was about seventeen years old when it happened. He was sitting in a room on the first floor of his uncle's house. All of a sudden he was seized by a terrible fear of death. He knew he was going to die, yet, strangely, he did not panic, did not call for help. The shock of death turned his mind inwards and he thought to himself: 'Now death has come; what does it mean? What is it that is dying? This body dies.' And just like that, he stretched his limbs out on the floor, held his breath, kept his lips tightly closed, and said to himself:

'Well, this body is dead. It will be carried to the burning ground and there reduced to ashes. But with the death of the body, am I dead? Is the body I? It is silent and inert, but I feel the full force of my personality ... and even the voice of I within me, apart from it.'

All these flashed through me vividly as living truths which I perceived *directly* ... all the conscious activity connected with the body was centred on that I. Then the 'I' or Self focused attention on itself by a powerful fascination. Fear of death vanished once and for all. (Osborne 2010) (Italics mine.)

After this 'life-altering' experience, he lost interest in school, studies, friends and relations and fell increasingly into fits of self-absorption. He turned meek and humble in his dealings with people and started visiting temples. Years later, recalling the phase, Ramana said that at the time he would go almost every evening to the nearby Shiva temple. He would go alone and stand before Shiva or Meenakshi or Nataraja or the sixty-three Nayanar saints for long periods and feel 'waves of emotion' overcoming him. Sometimes he would pray to Shiva for his blessings, but mostly just stand there in silence and let tears flow down his face. At the time, he had no scriptural knowledge, he 'knew nothing of bondage or freedom'.

He was in class six then. One day at home, his brother saw him put the books away, close his eyes and start meditating. The brother scolded him for behaving like a yogi. The word 'yogi', Ramana recalled later, gave him the idea and he decided then and there to leave home and go to Arunachalam.

The next day, he left home in the morning and reached the railway station just in time to board a train to Tindivanam, thinking it was the town nearest to Tiruvannamalai. Discovering Tindivanam was not anywhere close to Tiruvannamalai, he detrained at Villupuram, then changing two trains, and two days later, reached Tiruvannamalai

early in the morning. From there he went straight to the temple of
Sri Arunachaleshwara, a massive temple dedicated to Lord Shiva
built in the thirteenth century by the Cholas and the Pandiyans of
Tamil Nadu. There, joining his palms, he stood before his 'Father', the
Arunachaleshwara, tears running down his cheeks, and he knew there
was no going back, he had come *home*.

Possessed by a spirit, as it were, he came out of the temple and had
his head shaven, threw away the sacred thread and clothes, and tore a
strip off his dhoti to serve as his *kaupina*, loincloth. Absorbed in the
Self, he stayed in the thousand-pillared hall of the temple for a few
weeks before he took shelter in a vault known as Patala Lingam.

The 'near-death' experience had set him up on this journey to
Arunachalam where he was to undergo a series of 'death' experiences
to come into *sahaja sthithi* or the state of a *jivanmukta*. The first one
occurred six weeks after he reached Arunachalam, in Patala Lingam
where he spent days absorbed in such deep samadhi that he was
unaware of the bites of vermin and pests. He had to be carried out and
forcibly fed. In 1899, he went up Arunachala Hill, which is close to the
temple, and took residence in Virupaksha Cave, where he stayed for
about seventeen years.

Gradually, as the days passed he returned to outward normality
and spoke a few words with Palaniswami, who was now dedicated
to taking care of the young 'Brahmin swami'. During this period
Ramana was exposed to a few spiritual texts, such as *Yoga Vasishta*,
Vedanta Chudamani and so on. He learnt Malayalam from Palaniswami,
Telugu from Gambhiram Seshayya and Sanskrit from Kavyakanath
Ganapati Sastry, all of whom visited him often. Incidentally, it was
Kavyakanath Ganapati Sastry who renamed the young swami:
Bhagavan Ramana Maharshi.

In 1912, when he was thirty-two, the second 'death' experience
took place on Arunachala Hill. In Ramana Maharshi's own words:

The landscape in front of me disappeared as a bright white
curtain was drawn across my vision and shut it out ... my

circulation and breathing stopped. The skin turned a livid blue. It got darker and darker. ... This state continued for some ten or fifteen minutes. Then a shock passed suddenly through the body and circulation revived with enormous force, and breathing also, and the body perspired from every pore. The colour of life reappeared on the skin. I then opened my eyes and got up and said, 'Let's go.' We reached Virupaksha Cave without further trouble. (Ibid.)

Then he had yet another 'death' experience during his stay in Skandasramam Cave (1916–22). During these 'death' experiences, otherwise called samadhi, the stream of thought is cut, the person passes out and the body goes through a sort of clinical death. As we have already said earlier, it is the body's way of renewing itself. By 1922, however, Ramana Maharshi was finished with all experiences. Whatever had to be done had been done. And he came down and settled at the foot of the hill—where the present ashram is situated today—to live and teach.

It is of interest to note here that at first Ramana Maharshi could not figure out the state of being he had come into. He had absolutely no knowledge of the scriptures, especially the Upanishads. At sixteen he had probably read a little of *Periapuranam* and the Bible, and bits of *Thevaram*, but knew nothing of the central concepts of Hinduism, such as Brahman, *Sat-Chit-Ananda*, samadhi, *sahaja* samadhi or *sahaja sthiti* and so on. It was only after interacting with Sanskrit pandits and after reading *Ribhu Gita* and other Hindu texts that he began to 'feel' that some of these texts were actually naming and describing the state of being he had come into. Thereafter, Ramana started to use the classical Hindu terms to describe his state of being and discuss spiritual matters.

In the Ramana Ashram, adjacent to the great samadhi hall, is an old well and by its side the nearly hundred-year-old rectangular room called the Hall, where Ramana gave audience. It was here that famous personalities like Paul Brunton, Paramahansa Yogananda, Somerset Maugham, Arthur Osborne and the incomparable U.G. Krishnamurti met Ramana. It was here that Ramana talked to people and drew people from all over the world, and it was within the precincts of this ashram that he lived, taught and breathed his last.

In 1902, when Ramana Maharshi was staying in Virupaksha Cave on Arunachala Hill, one Sivaprakasam Pillai met him and sought answers to questions relating to the Self. Ramana was twenty-three years old then and was not talking, because he had no inclination to speak. However, he answered in writing the thirteen questions Pillai gave him on a piece of paper. This record was first published in 1923 in the original Tamil and then later an English translation of it came out. The book was titled *Nan Yar*—'Who Am I?'

Who Am I?

In a sense, all of Ramana Maharshi's teachings till the end revolved around the question 'Who Am I?' It was the pivot on which his words rested and turned, throwing light on all the deeper questions of life, the world and living. Simple and direct, he answered questions and then typically tagged the answers with a counter-question: 'Who is asking the question?'

Who am I? The question might smack of the Upanishadic method, which assured seekers that through self-enquiry and persistent negation, you would come into the awareness that 'I am Brahman'—*aham Brahmasmi*, or, 'Thou art That'—*tat tvam asi*. In imitation of this method many swamijis today offer this technique of enquiry to their disciples. But what Ramana suggested was different. He said that as each thought arises, one should enquire with diligence, 'To whom has this thought arisen?' The answer that would emerge would be 'to me'. Thereupon one enquires, 'Who am I?' And this self-enquiry, 'Who Am I?' he warned, is a different technique from the meditation on 'I am He', 'I am Brahman'. In his words:

I rather emphasize Self-Knowledge, for you are first concerned with yourself before you proceed to know the world or its Lord. The 'I am He' or 'I am Brahman' meditation is more or less mental, but the quest for the Self of which I speak is a direct method. For, the moment you get into the quest for the Self and begin to go deeper, the real Self is waiting there to receive you and then whatever is to be done is done by something else and you, as an individual, have no hand in it. (Godman 1992)

In simpler terms, we could say that there is no answer to the question: 'Who am I?' The seeker, the 'I', could be a man, woman, teacher, driver, banker and so on. Or, we could say, 'I' am my thought, the body, the senses, and so on. But soon, we run out of answers or realize that no answer is the real answer. We may also find that the answer we arrive at is only a relative, constructed, conditioned answer. So, in effect, Ramana Maharshi was actually trying to stop the questioner, corner and stun him, throw him into that state where there is no question and therefore no answer, and no questioner, either. For, like the stick used for stirring the burning pyre would itself in the end get destroyed, the questioner would also get annihilated at the end of the questioning.

In 1949, a small nodule appeared below Ramana Maharshi's left elbow and very soon it flared up and turned into a tumour, which was diagnosed as a cancer. Radium treatment and three surgeries only aggravated the disease. 'There is no cause for alarm,' Ramana Maharshi said. 'The body itself is a disease; let it have its natural end.'

People were amazed at his indifference to pain. Death was a problem and a riddle to the devotees, but not to Ramana Maharshi: 'Have I ever asked for any treatment?' he asked. 'It is you who want this and that for me, so it is for you to agree about it among yourselves. If I were asked I should always say, as I have said from the beginning, that no treatment is necessary. Let things take their course.' (Cohen 1998)

Two days before his passing, he refused all medication. He died on
the evening of 14 April 1950. He was seventy years old. The evening
he breathed his last, although it had been quite late, the devotees had
hung about outside the room where he had been laid, and they had
begun singing 'Arunachala-Siva'. Minutes later hundreds reported
seeing a bright star shooting across the sky and disappearing behind
the peak of Arunachala Hill.

The Teaching

The individual being that identifies its existence with that of the
life in the physical body as 'I', is called the ego. The Self, which
is pure Consciousness, has no ego-sense about it. Neither can the
physical body, which is inert in itself, have this ego-sense. Between
the two, that is between the Self or pure Consciousness and the
inert physical body, there arises mysteriously the ego-sense or 'I'
notion, the hybrid which is neither of them, and this flourishes
as an individual being. This ego or individual being is at the root
of all that is futile and undesirable in life. Therefore it is to be
destroyed by any possible means; then That, which ever is alone,
remains resplendent. This is Liberation or Enlightenment or Self-
Realization.

~

The enquiry: 'Who am I?' really means trying to find the source
of the ego or of the 'I'-thought. Seeking the source of the 'I'
serves as a means of getting rid of all other thoughts. You should
not allow any scope for other thoughts, but should keep the
attention fixed on finding the source of the 'I'-thought by asking,
when any other thought arises, to whom it occurs; and if the
answer is 'to me', you then resume the thought: 'What is this 'I'
and what is its source?'

~

All religions postulate the three fundamentals: the world, the soul
and God; but it is the One Reality that manifests itself as these

three. One can say: 'The three are really three' only so long as the
ego lasts. Therefore to inhere in one's own Being, when the ego is
dead is the perfect state.

'The world is real', 'No, it is mere illusory appearance', 'The
world is conscious,' 'No', 'The world is happiness', 'No,'—What
use is it to argue thus? That state is agreeable to all wherein, having
given up the objective outlook, one knows one's Self and loses all
notions either of unity or duality, of oneself and the ego.

If one has form oneself, the world and God will also appear to
have form; but if one is formless, who is to see these forms, and
how? Without the eye can any object be seen? The seeing Self is
the Eye, and that Eye is the Eye of Infinity. Brahman is not to be
seen or known. It is beyond the threefold relationship of seer, sight
and seen, or knower, knowledge and known. The Reality remains
ever as it is. The existence of ignorance or the world is due to our
illusions. Neither knowledge nor ignorance is real; what lies beyond
them, as beyond all other pairs of opposites, is the Reality. It is
neither light nor darkness but beyond both, though we sometimes
speak of it as light and of ignorance as its shadow.

~

'Sannyasa' means renouncing one's individuality, not shaving one's
head and putting on ochre robes. A man may be a householder but
if he does not think he is one, he is a sannyasin.

~

Although the scriptures proclaim 'Thou art That,' it is only a sign
of weakness to meditate 'I am That, not this,' because you are
eternally That. What has to be done is to investigate what one
really is and remain That.

'I am Brahman' is only a thought. Who says it? Brahman
himself does not say so. What need is there for him to say it? Nor
can the real 'I' say so. For 'I' always abides as Brahman. So it is
only a thought. Whose thought is it? All thoughts come from the
unreal 'I', that is the 'I'-thought. Remain without thinking. So long
as there is thought, there will be fear.

~

There are no stages in Realization or *Mukti*. There are no degrees of Liberation. So there cannot be one stage of Liberation with the body and another when the body has been shed.

There is no difference between the dream, and waking states except that the former is short and the latter long. Both are the product of the mind.

In truth, there is no bondage. Our real nature is Liberation, but we imagine that we are bound and we make strenuous efforts to get free, although all the while we are free.

Aphorisms

Help yourself and you will help the world. You are not different from the world nor is the world different from you.

~

It is impossible for you to be without effort. When you go deeper, it is impossible for you to make effort.

~

So long as the ego lasts, effort is necessary. When the ego ceases to exist, actions become spontaneous.

~

Realization or real awakening are all parts of the dream. When you attain realization you will see there was neither the dream during sleep nor the waking state, but only yourself and your real state.

~

Grace is not something outside you. In fact your very desire for grace is due to grace that is already working in you.

~

Self-reform automatically results in social reform. Attend to self-reform and social reform will take care of itself.

~

Why should you worry about the future? You don't even know the present properly. Take care of the present and the future will take care of itself.

~

Non-action is unceasing activity. The Sage is characterized by
eternal and incessant activity. His stillness is like the apparent
stillness of a fast rotating top.

~

The charred ashes of a rope look like a rope but they are of no use
to tie anything with.

✍

Nisargadatta Maharaj

Nisargadatta Maharaj was one of the most popular non-dual teachers
of modern times. He was a fiery sage of liberating wisdom, who spoke
directly from his 'beingness' rooted in non-dual reality. Once, when
asked about his past, he dismissed it as 'dead matter', and then added,
'there is no such thing as the past—nothing has really happened'. Living
in the ever-burning present, in the vivid realization of the oneness of
reality, he challenged, probed, goaded and guided all those who sought
his spiritual advice. 'Consciousness is the same in all,' used to be his
often repeated mantra:

> It is the same Consciousness in Lord Krishna, a human being, a
> donkey, or an ant ... There is only one Consciousness. ... Discard
> all you are not and go ever deeper. Just as a man digging a well
> discards what is not water, until he reaches the water-bearing
> strata, so must you discard what is not your own. ... You are Pure
> Awareness. You are that witness only. (Frydman 1987)

Nisargadatta Maharaj, named Maruti Shivrampant Kambli, was
born on 17 April 1897 to a deeply religious couple Shivrampant Kambli
and Parvatibai, in Bombay (now Mumbai). Shivrampant worked for a
merchant in Colaba in Bombay. In 1896, when the plague broke out

in the district, Shivrampant went back to his home town Revandi, bought a piece of land in Kandalgaon, a small village in Ratnagiri district in Maharashtra, and turned into a small-time farmer. It was in Kandalgaon village that Maruti Shivrampant Kambli grew up, along with his two brothers and four sisters.

Maruti studied only up to class four at a local school. After that he dropped out and took to tending cattle and working on their land. It is said that even as a boy he was friendly and helpful and mixed freely with boys from lower castes. And that he was full of questions about the mysteries of life and nature.

In 1915, his father died. The income from the land was hardly sufficient for the large growing family. A year later, his elder brother left for Bombay in search of a job. Two years later, in 1918, Maruti too joined him to support the family back home. He worked as a junior clerk at an office and joined a night school to learn English. He was not happy with his job as a clerk, so after a couple of months he left the job and turned to business. He opened a small general store. The turnover was good and within that year, he opened a string of eight retail shops and started making good money. About thirty to forty employees worked under him.

In 1924, he married Sumatibai and they had three daughters and a son. Maruti read religious texts in Marathi, followed the usual religious practices and even learnt yogic exercises from a yogi by the name of Sri Athavale. In 1933, his friend Yashwantrao Baagkar introduced him to Siddharameshwar Maharaj, the head of the Inchegiri branch of the Navanath *Sampradaya* in Bijapur district of Karnataka. The Maharaj saw that Maruti was already an adept in spiritual matters and initiated him into the *panth marg* by giving him a '*nama mantra*'. Thus began Maruti's self-enquiry and spiritual sadhana and soon he was a transformed being. Years later, as Nisargadatta Maharaj, he recounted the momentous occasion thus:

> My Guru told me: 'Go back to that state of pure being, where the "I am" is still in its purity before it got contaminated. Abandon

your false self-identifications. You are Divine. Take it as the
absolute truth.' I soon realized how true his words were. I followed
his instruction, which was to focus the mind on pure being, 'I am,'
and stay in it. Soon the peace and joy and deep all-embracing love
became my normal state. In it all disappeared—myself, my guru,
the life I lived, the world around me. Only peace remained, and
unfathomable silence. (Gogate and Phadol)

A year after his guru's death in 1936, Nisargadatta resolved to
renounce the 'material' world, left Bombay and travelled across India.
First he went on foot south-east to the holy Maharashtraian holy
temple town of Pandharpur. There he gave up his costly clothes, put
on an ochre robe, and with just two small pieces of loin cloth and a
coarse woollen, he began the life of a *jangama*, wanderer. He walked
all the way to Gangapur and then wandering through many towns and
villages of Maharashtra, he turned to the south, visited Rameshwar
(in the state of Tamil Nadu), and then walked through (present-day)
Karnataka. After nearly eight months, he returned a changed man to
his family in Bombay in 1938.

His zest for business having waned, he let go the tottering chain
of shops he had maintained all these years. He kept for himself
only the original small retail shop, for it was absolutely necessary to
keep the business going even if it was on a small scale, to sustain the
family. But now he had more time on hand to pursue his spiritual
practices. He followed a strict and regulated routine, spent several
hours in meditation, observed religious practices, read spiritual texts
such as *Yoga Vashista*, the Bhagavad Gita, Upanishads, *Amritanubhava*,
Dhyaneshwari and so on. He loved singing devotional songs and often
found himself lost in ecstasy for long periods.

A mezzanine floor in his small flat in Khetwadi in Bombay was
used for daily chanting, meditation sessions, and talks. His instructions
happened not so much through talks as through dialogues, through
question and answer assemblies, most of which were recorded and

then later published as books. He also wrote lyrical poetry, *Abhangas*, which were later published as a book. During this phase (1934–35), poems used to flow out him, and once, he simply added 'Nisargadatta' at the end of a poem and the name stuck. *'Nis-arga'* literally means 'natural', and *'datta'* means 'given'; together, 'Nisargadatta' means 'one who dwells in the natural state.' The word 'Maharaj' which means the 'great monarch', rather, in the given context, the 'great luminary', which he was, came to be added to his name later.

It would be fair to state here that inwardly he was a 'finished' man as far as the spiritual pursuit was concerned. In his words, 'Nothing was wrong anymore'. He had finally awakened to the Absolute Reality or Oneness of Reality. All attachment, aversion and delusion had ended. Nevertheless, outwardly he kept his business and religious practices going. But he stopped going to temples and meeting gurus and saints. Once, a spiritual guru, one Tikka Baba, sent him a message: 'I am dropping my mortal body, do come and receive my spiritual powers.' Nisargadatta replied: 'My contract has already been finalized once and for all time' (Gogate and Phadol, 'Meet the Sage', n.d.).

He suffered two personal losses during the years 1942–48—first the death of his wife, followed by the death of his daughter—but unruffled he carried on with his routine. He was a witness to the horrible violence and birth pangs of India's Independence. Soon spiritual seekers started gathering around him. He gave talks and answered questions in a style, plain, direct and uninhibited, which was all his own. In the words of Maurice Frydman, his long-time disciple and friend, he was 'warm-hearted, tender, shrewdly humorous, fearless and true; inspiring, guiding and supporting all who came to him'. To some, however, he seemed a 'tiger'!

It is said that once Nisargadatta had remarked to his fellow siddha, Bhainath Maharaj: 'You are very cool like Lord Vishnu. Look at me! I am like the fiery Lord Rudra.' And Rudra he was, direct and candid and fiery. David Godman, a close associate and also author of books on Ramana Maharshi, recalled the fiery yet cleansing days thus:

We all got shouted at on various occasions, and we all got told
off from time to time because of things we did or said. We
were all a little fearful of him because we never knew when
the next eruption would come. We had all come to have the
dirt beaten out of us, in the same way that the dhobis clean
clothes by smashing them on rocks. Maharaj smashed our
egos, our minds and our concepts on the immovable rock
of the Self because he knew that in most cases that was the
only way to help us. (Godman, 'Remembering Nisargadatta
Maharaj', n.d.)

In his dialogues, Nisargadatta usually emphasized the importance
of self-enquiry, but he was quite critical of intellectual approaches
to non-dual Truth. Indeed the path of knowledge or *jnana* yoga was
important but it was not the only approach to Truth. And so for many he
suggested the path of devotion, the bhakti yoga: love of guru and God,
the practice of mantra repetition and singing devotional songs. In 1951,
after a personal revelation from his guru, Siddharameshwar Maharaj,
he started to give initiations by way of giving *nama* mantra.

During the course of these talks and conversations, on and off, he
smoked beedis—a habit he did not give up until his last days—because
of which he was sometimes referred to as 'Beedi Baba'. But there never
was a dull moment, and his words, burning and cleansing, transformed
hundreds of seekers, who now came from far-off places and even from
outside the country. Seated on the mezzanine floor, abiding in the 'I
Am–ness', puffs of smoke from his beedi mingling with the aroma of
burning scented sticks, his penetrating eyes scanning the little crowd,
he dialogued with the seekers from different walks of life for twenty-
five long years until his death on 8 September 1981, at the age of
eighty-four, of throat cancer. A few months before he died, talking
about his illness to friends, he said:

Doctors have diagnosed that this body has cancer. The world is
your direct experience, your own observation. All that is happening
is happening at this level, but I am not at this level.

The ultimate state in spirituality is called nirvana, *nirguna*, that which is the Eternal and Ultimate Truth. The essence and sum total of this whole talk is called *Satguru Parabrahman*.

I remain ever untouched. I am the principle which survives all the creations, all the dissolutions. This is my state, and yours, too, but you don't realize it because you are embracing your beingness. (Dunn 2003)

The Teaching

People come here for knowledge. I talk because the words naturally come out. There is no intention behind my talk that you should get knowledge. Others come here because they are in difficulties. I make no determination that those difficulties should go away, but the fact remains that in many cases they do go away. I merely sit here, people come and go, I am not concerned. They come here from long distances because the consciousness feels the need to come here.

~

In the end you know that there is no sin, no guilt, no retribution, only life in its endless transformations. With the dissolution of the personal 'I', personal suffering disappears. What remains is the great sadness of compassion, the horror of the unnecessary pain.

~

Realize that every mode of perception is subjective, that what is seen or heard, touched or smelt, felt or thought, expected or imagined, is in the mind and not in reality, and you will experience peace and freedom from fear.

~

You cannot be conscious of what does not change. All consciousness is consciousness of change. But the very perception of change— does it not necessitate a changeless background?

~

The person is merely the result of a misunderstanding. In reality, there is no such thing. Feelings, thoughts and actions race before the watcher in endless succession, leaving traces in the brain and creating an illusion of continuity. A reflection of the watcher in the mind creates the sense of 'I' and the person acquires an apparently independent existence. In reality there is no person, only the watcher identifying himself with the 'I' and the 'mine'.

~

You see yourself in the world, while I see the world in myself. To you, you get born and die, while to me the world appears and disappears.

~

Once you realize that the world is your own projection, you are free of it. You need not free yourself of a world that does not exist, except in your own imagination!

~

The final answer is this: nothing is. All is a momentary appearance in the field of the universal consciousness. Continuity as name and form is a mental formation only, easy to dispel.

~

Awareness is primordial; it is the original state, beginningless, endless, uncaused, unsupported, without parts, without change. Consciousness is on contact, a reflection against a surface, a state of duality. There can be no consciousness without awareness, but there can be awareness without consciousness, as in deep sleep.

~

In reality things are done to you, not by you. Your desire just happens to you along with its fulfilment or non-fulfilment. You can change neither. All is in the picture exposed on the cinema screen, nothing in the light, including what you take yourself to be, the person. You are the light only.

~

Aphorisms

I am not an object in Consciousness but its source, its Witness, pure shapeless Awareness.

~

Whatever has a form is only limitations imagined in my consciousness.

~

The world is but a show, a make-believe world.

~

Desire and fear come from seeing the world as separate from my-Self.

~

I am not even Consciousness, which is dual and perceivable: I am the unknown Reality beyond.

~

In reality there are no others, and by helping yourself you help everybody else.

~

Ultimately nothing is mine or yours, everything is ours. Just be one with yourself and you will be one with all, at home in the entire universe.

~

To act from desire and fear is bondage, to act from love is freedom.

~

I do not know bad people, I only know myself. I see no saints nor sinners, only living beings.

~

You will receive everything you need when you stop asking for what you do not need.

Jiddu Krishnamurti

There is no way we can measure the impact of Jiddu Krishnamurti's teaching on the world. But he surely marked a major departure in religious thinking and the philosophy of religion in modern times. His criticism of religious traditions and authority has changed the way we look at religious thought and even at reports of mystical experiences today. He was notably the first 'deconstructionist', so to speak, who blazed a scorching new path to analyse the intriguing nature and functioning of the mind, much before the post-modernist thinkers would take on the mega-narratives and 'deconstruct' the 'hallowed ideas' of Western philosophy.

Born in a Telugu-speaking Brahmin family on 12 May 1895, in the small town of Madanapalle in Andhra Pradesh, Jiddu Krishnamurti was the eighth child of Jiddu Narayaniah and Sanjeevamma and was named after the Hindu god Krishna. His mother Sanjeevamma died when he was ten. His father Jiddu Narayaniah, an official in the colonial British administration, retired at the end of 1907. He had been a Theosophist since 1882 and after retirement sought employment at the Headquarters of the Theosophical Society at Adyar. He was hired by the Society as a clerk and in January 1909 the family moved to Madras (now Chennai).

By this time the Theosophical Society, started by Ukraine-born Helena Petrovna Blavatsky, was nearly forty-three years old. The Brotherhood of Theosophists had caught the imagination of people, and Theosophy as a complete philosophy was increasingly seen as a great religious alternative in a war-torn world. The organization in the meanwhile had been on a long search for the likely 'vehicle for the Lord Maitreya' (in Theosophical doctrine, an advanced spiritual entity periodically appearing on Earth as a World Teacher to guide the evolution of humankind).

In April 1909, Charles Leadbeater spotted fourteen-year-old Jiddu Krishnamurti—a lean, morose-looking lad with rather vacant eyes—squatting on the sands of Adyar Beach. By April 1911, Annie Besant had adopted both Krishnamurti and his brother Nityananda and they were taken to England to get an education. Nitya did well in his studies, but Krishnamurti failed to pass. His strength lay elsewhere—he was now the head of the Order of the Star, which had been formed to facilitate the coming of the World Teacher. And Krishnamurti, accompanied by Nitya, quite earnestly embarked on a series of lectures, meetings and discussions around the world.

Life-Altering Experiences

At Ojai, California, in 1922, Krishnamurti underwent an intense, 'life-changing' experience. This happened while he sat beneath an old pepper tree. He had complained of pain in the back of his neck and exhibited symptoms of illness three days earlier. His close associate Rosalind, and brother Nitya reported the episode in glowing terms. They said that they felt a great mighty presence descend over the place. Later, Krishnamurti himself described the experience thus:

> I was supremely happy, for I had seen. Nothing could ever be the same. I have drunk at the clear and pure waters at the source of the fountain of life and my thirst was appeased. Never more could I be thirsty, never more could I be in utter darkness. I have seen the Light. I have touched compassion which heals all sorrow and suffering: it is not for myself, but for the world … I have drunk at the fountain of Joy and eternal Beauty. I am God-intoxicated. (Lutyens 1997)

In a letter to a close associate he was less poetic and simply said: 'I am happy beyond human happiness … I can never be the same— 'But it was not all pure happiness and bliss, for, over the next few days he suffered spinal and neck pain, loss of appetite, occasional delirious ramblings, an unbearable sensation of heat in the body and the occasional lapse into unconsciousness. It was said this was a spiritual transformation brought on by the awakening of Kundalini power. These episodes were later followed by what was called the 'process', which would recur, at frequent intervals and with varying intensity, until his last days. These experiences were accompanied, or followed, by what was interchangeably described by Krishnamurti as the 'presence', 'benediction', 'immensity', 'sacredness', 'vastness' and 'otherness'.

In 1922–23, as news of his mystical experiences spread, the belief concerning his messianic status was further strengthened. There were great expectations of spiritually significant happenings. But, as his fate would have it, in 1925, while he was on his way to Adyar to attend the Theosophical Society's Jubilee Convention in Madras, he received the news of his brother Nitya's death.

Nitya had persistent health problems and had died on 13 November, aged twenty-seven, at Ojai, from complications of influenza and tuberculosis. Nitya's death shook Krishnamurti's belief in Theosophy and his faith in the masters and the leaders of the Theosophical Society. The masters had promised to protect Nityananda against all danger and let Nitya work shoulder to shoulder with him in his career as the World Teacher. How could he die on him now? How could it happen? It seemed nothing short of a terrible betrayal, and 'the ideological edifice in which he had come to believe so passionately and with such certainty, now began to crumble' (Vernon 2002).

In many ways Nitya's death marked a turning point in Krishnamurti's life, changing him in many ways. Over the next few years there was a radical shift in his outlook and this was manifested in his new concepts that appeared in his talks, discussions, and correspondences, which were now free of Theosophical terminology. In point of fact, Krishnamurti was disenchanted with the infighting in the Society by then, disturbed enough to move away from the likes of Leadbeater, Arundale and his camp. The death of his beloved brother further impelled him to question and re-examine the ideology and practices of the Theosophical Society. In 1927, in a gathering of Theosophists, he declared: 'I hold that doubt is essential for the discovery and the understanding of the Truth—' And he reprimanded his followers for their blind beliefs and invited them to reject all spiritual authorities, including his own, and practise doubt as a method of enquiry, and 'scrutinize the very knowledge which you are supposed to have gained. For I tell you that orthodoxy is set up when the mind and the heart are in decay.'

Two years later, on 3 August 1929, now completely disillusioned with the Theosophical Society and its doctrine, he dissolved the Order of the Star and severed all his connections with the Society. He said:

> I maintain that truth is a pathless land, and you cannot approach it by any path whatsoever, by any religion, by any sect. Truth, being limitless, unconditioned, unapproachable by any path whatsoever, cannot be organized; nor should any organization be formed to lead or coerce people along a particular path. ... This is no magnificent deed, because I do not want followers, and I mean this. The moment you follow someone you cease to follow Truth. I am not concerned whether you pay attention to what I say or not. I want to do a certain thing in the world and I am going to do it with unwavering concentration. I am concerning myself with only one essential thing: to set man free. I desire to free him from all cages, from all fears, and not to found religions, new sects, nor to establish new theories and new philosophies. (Rao 2005)

Following the dissolution of the Order of the Star, prominent Theosophists turned against Krishnamurti, including Leadbeater, who declared, 'the Coming had gone wrong'. Krishnamurti resigned from the various trusts and other organizations that were affiliated with the now defunct Order of the Star. He returned the donated monies and properties of the Order to their donors. From then on Krishnamurti was on his own, holding dialogues and giving public talks around the world. He spoke on the nature of belief, truth, sorrow, freedom, death, and the quest for a spiritually fulfilled life.

Doubt as a Method of Enquiry

Doubt as a method of enquiry was the strong point of Krishnamurti's teaching. The persuasive yet the insistent way he questioned, doubted, probed tested and negated the established and sacred beliefs and ideas of religious traditions of the East and West, the manner in which he opened new ways of seeing and experiencing life was something new.

It was a voice, deep, profound and cathartic, a voice that had not been heard for a long time.

This way, for over sixty years, with doubt as his method, he tried to awaken people from their slumber and goad them into questioning everything, all truths that had been accepted as given. And, with what may be called boddhisattvic zeal, he wanted to create a new order, a new way of living and being in the world. To bring about this new order, this new way of living, he declared repeatedly, doggedly:

> We must understand disorder. It is only through negation that you understand the positive, not by the pursuit of the positive ... out of negation comes the right discipline, which is order ... Negation can only take place when the mind sees the false. The very perception of the false is the negation of the false ... The total negation of that (old) road is the new beginning, the other road. This other road is not on the map, nor can it ever be put on any map. Every map is the map of the wrong road, the old road. (Vernon 2002)

Almost until his death, he held that 'the idea of the teacher and the taught is basically wrong'. What he was trying to do was not teaching, but 'sharing', 'merely acting as a mirror' in which others could see themselves clearly and then discard the mirror. Or, at the most, he was only trying to 'awaken' people from their slumber and see for themselves the truth, 'truth not at the top of the ladder; truth is where you are, in what you are doing, thinking, feeling, when you kiss and hug, when you exploit—you must see the truth of all that, not a truth at the end of innumerable cycles of life' (Ibid.).

His epic career as a Teacher came to a dramatic end with his last three talks in January 1986, at Adyar, Madras, from where he had begun his life as the World Teacher. Despite high fever he had managed to speak for three days. When the discomfort and fatigue increased, all the programmes, including the talks in Bombay were cancelled and he was flown to California.

Back in Ojai, at Arya Vihar, his home for several decades now, he could not relax. He was admitted into Santa Paula Hospital. His condition was diagnosed as cancer of the pancreas. His condition deteriorated rapidly and on 17 February 1986, less than thirty days after his last talk, Jiddu Krishnamurti passed away. He was ninety-one years old.

Ten years before his death, at a meeting with close associates in Ojai, Krishnamurti had asked:

> If people come here and ask, 'What was it like to live with this man?', would you be able to convey it to them? If any of the Buddha's disciples were alive would not one travel to the ends of the earth to see them, to find out from them what it had been like to live in his presence? (Lutyens 1999)

Krishnamurti believed that his very coming and his teaching was a major departure from all the religious teachings of the world, and that his teaching, far from being outdated, would last at least for five hundred years, before another Maitreya would come and finish it. And so in 1986—after living through two world wars, through great historical upheavals and unprecedented changes in the world, and teaching his 'pathless path' for over sixty years—ten days before he breathed his last, one of the Trustees of Krishnamurti Foundation, gazing at the wasted and shrunken body of the teacher, asked: 'What really happens to that extraordinary focus of understanding and energy that is K. after his death?'

Krishnamurti replied: 'It is gone. If you only knew what you had missed—that vast emptiness.'

The Teaching

> You and the world are not two different entities with separate problems; you and the world are one. You may be the result of certain tendencies, on environmental influences, but you are not

different fundamentally from another. Inwardly we are very much alike; we are all driven by greed, ill will, fear, ambition, and so on.

~

If we would bring about a sane and happy society we must begin with ourselves and not with another, not outside of ourselves, but with ourselves.

And as we are—the world is. That is, if we are greedy, envious, competitive, our society will be competitive, envious, greedy, which brings misery and war. The State is what we are. To bring about order and peace, we must begin with ourselves and not with society, not with the State, for the world is ourselves ... If we would bring about a sane and happy society we must begin with ourselves and not with another, not outside of ourselves, but with ourselves.

~

It seems to me that the real problem is the mind itself, and not the problem which the mind has created and tries to solve. If the mind is petty, small, narrow, limited, however great and complex the problem may be, the mind approaches that problem in terms of its own pettiness. So the question is: Can the mind that is small, petty, be transformed into something which is not bound by its own limitations?

~

Organized religion separates man from man. You are a Muslim, I am a Hindu, another is a Christian or a Buddhist—and we are wrangling, butchering each other. Is there any truth in that?

~

These *Mahavakyas*: *prajnanam Brahma* (consciousness is infinite), *aham Brahmasmi* (I am that infinite), *tat tvam asi* (Thou art That), what do they mean? Why do we always attach ourselves to something which we suppose to be the highest? Why not say: I am the river, I am the poor man? Why don't we say 'I am that also'?

Can a conditioned mind, can a mind that is small, petty, narrow, living on superficial entertainments, can that know or conceive, or understand, or feel, or observe the unconditioned?

What is Vedanta? The end of the Vedas, the end of knowledge! Therefore, leave it. Why proceed from there to describe what is not? If Vedanta means the end of knowledge ... the ending of Vedas, which is knowledge—then why should I go through all the laborious process of acquiring knowledge, and then discarding it? Why should not I, from the very beginning, see what knowledge is and discard it? Why did the traditionalists, the professionals, the scriptures, the spiritual leaders not see this? Was it because authority was tremendously important—the authority of the Gita, the experience, the scriptures? Why? Why did they not see this?

~

Man has throughout the ages been seeking something beyond himself, beyond material welfare—something we call truth or God or reality, a timeless state—something that cannot be disturbed by circumstances, by thought or by human corruption. Man has always asked the question: what is it all about? Has life any meaning at all? He sees the enormous confusion of life, the brutalities, the revolt, the wars, the endless divisions of religion, ideology and nationality, and with a sense of deep abiding frustration he asks, what is one to do, what is this thing we call living, is there anything beyond it?

~

The first step is the last step. The first step is to perceive, perceive what you are thinking, perceive your ambition, perceive your anxiety, your loneliness, your despair, this extraordinary sense of sorrow, perceive it, without any condemnation, justification, without wishing it to be different. Just to perceive it, as it is. When you perceive it as it is, then there is a totally different kind of action taking place, and that action is the final action. Right? That is, when you perceive something as being false or as being true, that perception is the final action, which is the final step. Now listen to it. I perceive the falseness of following somebody else, somebody else's instruction—Krishna, Buddha, Christ, it does not matter who it is. I see, there is the perception of the truth that following somebody is utterly false. Because your reason, your logic and everything points out how absurd it is to follow somebody. Now that perception is the final step, and when you have perceived, you leave it, forget it, because the next minute you have to perceive anew, which is again the final step.

Aphorisms

To die every day to every problem, every pleasure, and not carry over any problem at all; so the mind remains tremendously attentive, active, clear.

~

People need to be awakened, not instructed.

~

When all authority of every kind is put aside, denied, then you can find out for yourself.

~

To be vulnerable is to live. To withdraw is to die.

~

Beware of the man who offers you a reward in this world or the next.

~

The state of the mind that questions is much more important than the question itself.

~

Truth is an eternal movement, and so cannot be measured in words or in time.

~

When our hearts are empty, we collect things.

~

Freedom from desire for an answer is essential to the understanding of a problem.

~

The craving for experience is the beginning of illusion.

~

Knowledge prevents listening.

~

Relationship surely is the mirror in which you discover yourself.

~

The ideal is always what is not.

U.G. Krishnamurti

With neither guru nor initiation,
with no discipline, and no duty to perform,
like the formless sky, self-existent purity,
the *avadhuta* lives alone in an empty hut;
with a pure, even mind, he is always content,
he moves about, naked and free,
in the burning and bright awareness.

(Avadhuta Gita)

In 1986, after the death of Jiddu Krishnamurti, U.G. Krishnamurti went public with what he had to say. It was time to dismantle the old spiritual discourses or teachings, but not erect or construct anything new in its place. It would not be a new interpretation, amplification or clarification of the old teachings, whether J. Krishnamurti's or Ramana Maharshi's, the Buddha's or the Upanishads'. Religious dross had to be cleared, the slate had to be wiped clean. So it would be a negation of all approaches.

He made clear that there was no 'method' implied in either his negation or rejection of things; it could not be made into yet another approach. In point of fact, it would be neither a negation nor an assertion of anything. No apocalypse! No Kingdom of God cometh! No Atman, no Brahman, no moksha, no nirvana! No *sunyata* either.

If the Upanishads quickened our minds, the Buddha urged and nudged us into enquiring the cause of sorrow, if Ramana teased and pressed us to find out who the questioner was, if J. Krishnamurti drove us to doubt and question all forms of authority and belief systems and come to truth through a process of rigorous negation, U.G. Krishnamurti took us deeper into the waters of self-enquiry, into the very heart of the problem itself, to reveal how even our so-called enquiry, our questions, even our negations, are shaped by the answers or solutions we already have.

Born on 9 July 1918 in Masulipatnam, a town in coastal Andhra Pradesh, U.G. grew up in a peculiar milieu of both Theosophy and Hindu religious beliefs and practices. With all the religious practices and exposure to Theosophy he had at quite an early age, U.G. grew up to be a passionate yet rebellious character, but with a strong spiritual streak in him. It was while pursuing an undergraduate honours course in philosophy and psychology at the University of Madras that his spiritual quest gained momentum.

During this three-year degree course, he spent his summers in the Himalayas studying yoga and practising meditation. Though he had certain mystical experiences, he realized that deep within him there was no transformation. He was still caught up in conflict and found himself burning with anger all the time. It seemed that he had meditated and performed penance to no avail. He quit university as well, he wanted nothing less than moksha. One day, in 1939, a friend suggested he meet Sri Ramana Maharshi. U.G. agreed and went to meet him.

He asked Ramana, 'Is there anything like moksha? Can you give it to me?'

Ramana said, 'I can give it, but can you take it?'

The counter-question struck U.G. like a thunderbolt. And he realized that nobody could *give* that state to him and he had to *find* it for himself. But the meeting with Ramana had only deepened his anguish. The quest, of course, did not end there, but he was going nowhere. The Theosophical Society seemed to be the only way out and he took up a job as a press secretary to the president of the society.

In 1943, at twenty-five years of age, he got married and started on a new assignment as a lecturer for the Theosophical Society in Madras (now Chennai). Travelling extensively in India and Europe he gave talks on Theosophy, but quit the post by the end of his seventh year. From 1953, he began interacting with J. Krishnamurti at a personal level, holding long and deep conversations with him on several occasions. It was during this period that he underwent a 'near-death experience' that altered his perception of life and eventually lead him up to the 'final death' and awakening into the 'natural state' in 1967.

The period between 1953 and 1964 was a period of great changes and the beginning of the metamorphosis he would undergo in 1967. In brief, he went to USA to get medical treatment for his polio-stricken son; took to lecturing to earn a living; broke away from his family; visited parts of Europe and then began to drift aimlessly in London, like a dry leaf blown hither and thither. Eventually he landed up in Saanen, Switzerland. The quest had come to an end now, his body had turned into something like rice chaff—burning, smouldering within, the fire slowly and steadily moving in circles towards the outer surface, as it were, preparing itself for the 'metamorphoses' that would challenge the very foundation of human thought built over centuries. He held out in a state of 'masterly inactivity' and 'watchful expectancy' and on 13 August 1967, on the completion of his forty-ninth year, biological changes began to manifest.

For the next seven days, these bewildering changes catapulted him into what he called the 'natural state'. The whole chemistry of his body, including the five senses, was transformed. His eyes stopped blinking; his skin turned soft; and when he rubbed any part of his body with his palm, it produced a sort of ash. His senses started functioning independently and at the peak of their sensitivity. And the hitherto dormant ductless glands, such as the thymus, the pituitary, the pineal, which Kundalini Yoga calls the chakras or energy centres, were activated. And on the eighth day, he 'died'.

He felt a tremendous burst of energy and all these energies seemed to draw themselves to a focal point from different parts of his body. The terrific movement of the life force continued and it seemed to be converging at some point in his body. It was the sign of approaching death. He stretched himself on his bed ready to die. Then a point arrived when it seemed as though the aperture of a camera was trying to close, but something was trying to keep it open—that was the 'I', the residue of 'thought' (the fear of death, fear of the unknown, the void, dramatized as Mara in Buddhist literature), refusing to die. Then, after a while, there was no 'will' to do anything, not even to prevent the aperture closing itself. And, it closed. His hands and feet turned cold, the body became stiff, the heartbeat slowed down, and he started gasping for breath and he 'died', only to be reborn in the state of 'undivided consciousness'. For about forty years thereafter, and until his final departure from the body and this world, U.G. travelled the globe and wherever he stayed, people came to see him and to listen to his 'anti-teaching'. He talked openly of the 'natural state' and responded to people's queries and answered their questions candidly, holding back nothing, 'revealing all the secrets'.

His first (and last) public talk was given at the Indian Institute of World Culture in Bangalore (now Bengaluru), in May 1972. He never again gave a public talk, nor would he accept invitations to talk at universities or institutions. He gave no lectures or discourses but he could not stop people from meeting and talking to him.

Though U.G. usually stayed with friends or in small rented apartments, he never stayed in one place for more than three or a maximum of six months. He had no organization, no office, no secretary, and no fixed address. Despite his endless repetition that he had 'no message for mankind', thousands of people the world over felt otherwise and flocked to see and listen to his 'anti-teaching'. The 'shop' was kept open from early morning to late evening for people to feel free to come without any prior appointment, and feel free to go whenever they wanted. 'This is how it should be. There should be no special duration, prior appointment, and such,' U.G. would say, and his hosts everywhere maintained the rule without fail.

He often insisted, preferring the term 'natural state' over 'enlightenment', that whatever transformation he had gone through was within the structure of the human body and not in the mind at all. And, avoiding religious terms, he described the 'natural state' as a pure and simple physical and physiological state of being. It was 'undivided state of consciousness', where all desires and fear, and the search for happiness and pleasure, God and truth, came to an end. And he never tired of pointing out that 'this is the way you, stripped of the machinations of thought, are also functioning'.

The Saints Go Marching Out

In the 'natural state' of undivided or pure consciousness, even the so-called good thoughts, holy thoughts, mystical experiences, including visions of God or gods, are only 'contaminations' and therefore have to be flushed out. U.G. dubbed this experience as 'the saints go marching out'.

It is interesting to note here that in the reports of experiences of sages, we are told about their visions of gods and goddesses and of enlightened masters such as the Buddha and so on, and how these spiritual entities affected the sages. Sri Ramakrishna, for instance, talked about visions of spiritual entities and how they merged in his being. Anandamayi Ma also often talked of visions of spiritual entities. At one time, during the early period of his career as the World Teacher, J. Krishnamurti, too, talked of feeling the great presence of the Buddha and how his being was filled by that presence. But in U.G.'s case, he reiterated that all these visions were flushed out. This is how he described the experience:

> There are no purificatory methods necessary, there is no *sadhana* necessary for this kind of a thing to happen. The consciousness is so pure that whatever you are doing in the direction of purifying that

consciousness is adding impurity to it. Consciousness has to flush itself out: it has to purge itself of every trace of holiness, every trace of unholiness, everything. ... It's not a vision outside there or inside of you; suddenly you yourself, the whole consciousness, takes the shape of Buddha, Jesus, Mahavira, Mohammed, Socrates—only those people who have come into this state; not great men, not the leaders of mankind—it is very strange—but only those people to whom this kind of a thing happened. One of them was a coloured man, and during that time I could tell people how he looked. Then some women with flowing hair—naked. I was told that there were two saints here in India—Akkamahadevi and Lalleswari—they were naked women. Suddenly you have these two breasts, the flowing hair—even the organs change into female organs. But still there is a division there—you, and the form the consciousness has assumed, the form of Buddha, or Jesus Christ or God knows what.

But that division cannot stay long; it disappears and something else comes. Hundreds of people—probably something happened to so many hundreds of people. This is part of history—so many *rishis*, some Westerners, monks, so many women, and sometimes very strange things. All that people have experienced before you is part of your consciousness. I use the expression 'the saints go marching out'; in Christianity they have a hymn 'When the Saints Go Marching In.' But here, they run out of your consciousness because they cannot stay there any more. This flushing out of everything good and bad, holy and unholy, sacred and profane has got to happen, otherwise your consciousness is still contaminated, still impure. Once it has become pure, of and by itself, then nothing can touch it, nothing can contaminate that any more. All the past up to that point is there, but it cannot influence your actions any more. All these visions and everything were happening for three years after the 'calamity'. Now the whole thing is finished. The divided state of consciousness cannot function at all anymore; it is always in the undivided state of consciousness—nothing can touch that. You are back in that primeval, primordial, pure state of consciousness—call it 'awareness' or whatever you like.' (Arms [Ed.] 1982)

How do we understand this experience, which is actually no experience in the ordinary sense of the term? Does this mark the end of spiritual adventure, or do we see it as the end product of evolution, resulting in the emergence of a new human being in the state of pure awareness? Or, in other words, should we understand this as the final play of consciousness, wherein the consciousness empties itself of all its content and returns to its primal state? Could this really be the non-dual state of being? The state of Brahman, of moksha or nirvana?

When the Buddha said, 'The eye, ear, nose, tongue, the body (all sense experiences) and ideas, or intellect consciousness are empty of a self or of anything pertaining to a self. Thus it is said that the world is empty', was he describing the state of being wherein the consciousness had emptied itself of all ideas and images? Was Allama's *vachana*—emptiness sown in emptiness, growing in emptiness, emptiness emptying itself turns into emptiness—a poetic rendering of the same phenomenon?

'You are back in that primordial, pure state of consciousness,' said U.G. and described it simply as the 'Natural State'. He often said that it was not a state of mind, rather it was a state of being where the binary mind was absent, where the search had come to an end, and the continuity of all kinds had ceased. A pure and simple physical and physiological state of being, where the body was in tune with the cosmos. A state of being where evolution had come to fruition. It was finished, complete.

To better appreciate this state of being, you'll recall here the reports of how Sri Ramakrishna had visions of Rama, Sita, Christ and Muhammad, and that all these spiritual entities entered into him and created different states of *bhava*. And then, later, having finished with all the possible modes of *bhava*, under the guidance of Totapuri, Ramakrishna entered the state of *nirvikalpa* samadhi. In his words:

... as soon as the gracious form of the Divine Mother appeared
before me, I used my discrimination as a sword and with it severed
it in two. There remained no more obstruction to my mind, which
at once soared beyond the relative plane, and I lost myself in
nirvikalpa samadhi. (Nikhilananda 2008)

But, later, by Ramakrishna's own admission, as per the command
from the Mother Kali, he opted out of *nirvikalpa* samadhi and decided
to remain in *bhavamukha*—a state of being intermediate between
samadhi and normal consciousness.

All images, which are products of the mind or rather the mind itself,
create the division, duality. Without duality there is no relationship,
no devotion, no quest and no love. For reasons even sages cannot
explain, some of them remain on the threshold short of the final step
as it were; perhaps they are meant to stay in the state of *bhava*, of
compassion, and as good boatmen to lead earnest questers to the other
shore. There is no choice exercised in this matter, rather these things
happen by themselves. It's an enigma! But rarely do we see a sage
completely dissolve into the state of absolute non-duality. Even here it
is not a matter of choice. It has to happen! However, U.G.'s vision of
'the saints marching out' seems to hold the key to understanding U.G.
He was cleansed of all the images embedded in human consciousness
from time memorial and was thrown into the state of primordial
consciousness, or the state of perfect non-duality.

Non-duality is a burning awareness, it burns up all forms of
division, all frames of thought that are trapped in binaries. This should
explain why U.G. often dismissed, rejected and exploded all questions
thrown at him, why he dismissed even the Buddha and other sages,
too. To many he sounded cynical, negative, even jealous, because with
apparent disdain he rejected them all. Nothing can be far from truth.
He was a living embodiment of non-duality in action. 'You are unique,'
said U.G. 'You are far ahead of the Buddha, Jesus and all these religious
teachers put together. But this uniqueness cannot express itself unless

the limitations are destroyed'; unless 'you touch life at a point never touched before' (Rao [Ed.] 2007).

The Way It Is

We may roughly discern three phases in U.G.'s life and his 'anti-teaching'. The first lasted from 1967 to almost the late '70s, when his approach may be characterized as raw, soft, tender and obliging. At this time, U.G. talked approvingly, though cautiously, of other sages and their teachings and certain religious texts. This was, in a sense, a different U.G., who was 'open' and persuasive, taking along or leading his listeners, ever so sympathetically and caringly, on a journey into the exploration of the functioning of the mind and the body. He would point out to them the irrelevance of methods and techniques for 'self-realization', the unnatural state and its problems, the natural state as a physiological state of being and how it could impact or change the world consciousness and so on.

During the second phase in the 1980s and '90s, he looked a sage in rage. His words were deep and explosive and cathartic. He was like fire that burned everything to ash so that a new beginning could be made, without the touch of sorrow. This was also the time when he went 'public' by way of giving TV interviews and radio talks in order to reach out to people in the wider world. All grand narratives and symbols of various religions and cultures, ideologies and philosophies were subverted or dismissed as so much garbage. There was nothing sacred or sacrosanct, nothing unquestionable and incontestable: subversion was the way, then subversion too was subverted and demolished. He was the 'primordial being', 'unconverted member of the human race', blasting every frame of thought, challenging the very foundation of human culture.

During this phase people would call him, especially in the media, 'a sage in rage', a cosmic Naxalite, anti-guru and so on, and this image of him as a raging sage somehow got overemphasized and sort of fixed even in the minds of U.G. admirers, not to speak of the media and

those who had only a vague idea of who he was and his teaching.
It only showed how difficult it was to understand the non-dual truth
he was trying to convey, caught up as we are in a dualistic mode of
thinking and being and wedded to some ideal or the other. Like the
Buddha—who knocked off all narratives as mere mental constructs
and a hindrance to entering the state of nirvana—U.G., by exploding
all our ideas and ideals, did not merely pull the carpet out from under
our feet, but also destroyed the very ground, apparently secure but
false, on which we stood. He would not allow us to cling to any lie,
because a lie is a lie and falsified our lives. The truth, howsoever hard,
shattering and shocking, had to be brought to us.

The last ten years before U.G.'s death may be characterized as the
phase of playfulness and laughter. Since all expressions were false,
even to say something was false was false, there was only rejection
wholly and totally, and there was laughter. There were the sweet and
delightful giggles of Krishna, the drinker of milk, and the *attahasa* or
apocalyptic laughter of Siva, the drinker of poison. From the heights
of Kailasa everything turned comical. 'Comedy,' wrote Lee Siegel,

> challenges notions of meaning, strives to undermine all
> hermeneutics and epistemologies, and exposes the ambiguities
> inherent in any knowing and feeling. In the world of comedy,
> absurdity itself is the logos. The senselessness of the universe
> makes comic sense. Laughter expresses the comic understanding
> that nothing is ever really understood. (Siegel 1989)

However, the essential thrust in his approach was always the same.
He described the way we functioned in the unnatural state, caught in a
world of opposites, constantly struggling to become something other
than what we are, and in search of non-existent gods and goals. How
we all are thinking and functioning in a 'thought sphere', just as we all
share the same atmosphere for breathing. How and why the self, which
is self-protective and fascist in nature, is not the instrument to help us
to live in harmony with the life around us. Preferring the term 'natural

state' over 'enlightenment', he insisted that whatever transformation he had gone through was within the structure of the human body and not in the mind at all. And he described the natural state as a pure and simple physical and physiological state of being. It is the state of 'primordial awareness without primitivism', or the 'undivided state of consciousness', where all desires and fear, and the search for happiness and pleasure, God and truth, have come to an end. It is an a causal state of 'not-knowing' (Rao [Ed.] 2010).

If on the one hand he marked a creative continuity of the enlightenment traditions of the Buddha, the Upanishadic and later sages of India, on the other hand, U.G. marked a radical departure from the enlightenment traditions in the way he de-psychologized and demystified the notion of enlightenment, and redefined it as the 'natural state' in physical and physiological terms. More importantly, by knocking off all grand narratives and epistemologies, he offered us not only release from the tyranny of sacred symbols and ideas, gods and goals, but also a foretaste of that vast emptiness.

The Last Days

He died on 22 March 2007 in Vallecrosia, Italy, on the Mediterranean coast close to the French border. In many ways, the way U.G. died, rather the way he decided to pass away, reminds us of the way the Buddha died, by going away from the cities and towns where he taught, in a remote place called Kusinara, with only Ananda as his companion and witness. Perhaps the Buddha went away to this far-off place because he was finished with his teaching, because he did not wish all his words to be converted into sacred mantras, into a religion, and himself converted into a god. But that was not to be, and that is quite another story.

After he came into the natural state, U.G. had said, 'This is the way to live.' And the way he lived and moved in the world for the next forty years was a living example of the natural state, or what may be called non-duality in action. Responding to questions on death, U.G. would often say, 'Life and death cannot be separated. When what you call clinical death takes place, the body breaks itself into its constituent elements and that provides the basis for the continuity of life. In that sense the body is immortal' (Newland 1988). And true enough, during his last days, he said, 'This is the way to die', and he died the way he lived, with no fear, no anxiety, with no self in operation there. He withered like a tree, like a leaf turning yellow and falling off. He was eighty-nine years old.

Anti-Teaching

There is no teaching of mine, and never shall be one. 'Teaching' is not the word for it. A teaching implies a method or a system, a technique or a new way of thinking to be applied in order to bring about a transformation in your way of life. What I am saying is outside the field of teachability; it is simply a description of the way I am functioning. It is just a description of the *natural state* of man—this is the way you, stripped of the machinations of thought, are also functioning.

~

The natural state is not the state of a self-realized, God-realized man, it is not a thing to be achieved or attained, it is not a thing to be willed into existence; it is *there*—it is the living state. This state is just the functional activity of life. By 'life' I do not mean something abstract; it is the life of the senses, functioning naturally without the interference of thought. Thought is an interloper, which thrusts itself into the affairs of the senses. It has a profit motive: thought directs the activity of the senses to get something out of them, and uses them to give continuity to itself.

~

Your natural state has no relationship whatsoever with the religious states of bliss, beatitude and ecstasy; they lie within the field of experience. Those who have led man on his search for religiousness throughout the centuries have perhaps experienced those religious states. So can you. They are thought-induced states of being, and as they come, so do they go. Krishna Consciousness,

Buddha Consciousness, Christ Consciousness, or what have you, are all trips in the wrong direction: they are all within the field of time. The timeless can never be experienced, can never be grasped, contained, much less given expression to, by any man. That beaten track will lead you nowhere.

Is There a Beyond or Timelessness?

Is there a beyond? Because you are not interested in the everyday things and the happenings around you, you have invented a thing called the 'beyond', or 'timelessness', or 'God', 'Truth', 'Reality', 'Brahman', 'enlightenment', or whatever, and you search for that. There may not be any beyond. You don't know a thing about that beyond; whatever you know is what you have been told, the knowledge you have about that. So you are projecting that knowledge. What you call 'beyond' is created by the knowledge you have about that beyond; and whatever knowledge you have about a beyond is exactly what you will experience. The knowledge creates the experience, and the experience then strengthens the knowledge. What you know can never be the beyond. Whatever you experience is not the beyond. If there is any beyond, this movement of 'you' is absent. The absence of this movement probably is the beyond, but the beyond can never be experienced by you; it is when the 'you' is not there. Why are you trying to experience a thing that cannot be experienced?

~

In the natural state the movement of self is absent. The absence of this movement probably is the beyond but that can never be experienced by you. It is when the 'you' is not there. The moment you translate, the 'you' is there. You look at something and recognize it. Thought interferes with the sensation by translating. You are either thinking about something which is totally unrelated to the way the senses are functioning at the moment or else labelling. That is all that is there. The word separates you from what you are looking at, thereby creating the *you*. Otherwise, there is no space between the two.

Mind Is a Myth

The separation between mind and body must come to an end. Actually, there is no separation. I have no objection to the word mind but it is not in one particular location or area. Every cell in your system has a mind of its own and its functioning or working is quite different from that of the other cells.

~

Mind or thought is not yours or mine. It is our common inheritance. There is no such thing as your mind and my mind (it is in that sense mind is a myth). There is only mind, the totality of all that has been known, felt and experienced by man, handed down from generation to generation. We are all thinking and functioning in that thought sphere just as we all share the same atmosphere for breathing.

~

Thought in its birth, in its origin, in its content, in its expression, and in its action is very fascist. When I use the word 'fascist' I use it not in the political sense but to mean that thought controls and shapes our thinking and our actions. So it is a very protective mechanism. It has no doubt helped us to be what we are today. It has helped us to create our high-tech and technology. It has made our life very comfortable. It has also made it possible for us to discover the laws of nature. But thought is a very protective mechanism and is interested in its own survival. At the same time, thought is opposed fundamentally to the functioning of this living organism.

~

It is thought that has invented the ideas of cause and effect. There may not be any such thing as a cause at all. Every event is an individual and independent event. We link up all these events and try to create a story of our lives. But actually every event is an independent event. If we accept the fact that every event is an independent event in our lives, it creates a tremendous problem of maintaining what we call identity. And identity is the most important factor in our lives. We are able to maintain this identity through the constant use of memory, which is also thought. This constant use of memory or identity, or whatever you call it, is consuming a tremendous amount of energy, and it leaves us with no energy to deal with the problems of our living. Is there any way that we can free ourselves from the identity? As I said, thought can only create problems; it cannot help us to solve them. Through dialectical thinking about thinking itself we are only sharpening that instrument. All philosophies help us only to sharpen this instrument.

~

Thought is very essential for us to survive in this world. But it cannot help us in achieving the goals that we have placed before ourselves. The goals are unachievable through the help of thought. The quest for happiness, as you mentioned, is impossible because there is no such thing as permanent happiness. There are moments of happiness, and there are moments of unhappiness. But the demand to be in a permanent state of happiness is the enemy of this body. This body is interested in maintaining its sensitivity of the sensory perceptions and also the sensitivity of the nervous system. That is very essential for the survival of this body. If we use that instrument of thought for trying to achieve the impossible goal of permanent happiness, the sensitivity of this body is destroyed. Therefore, the body is rejecting all that we are interested in—permanent happiness and permanent pleasure. So, we are not going to succeed in that attempt to be in a permanent state of happiness.

~

Thought can never capture the movement of life, it is much too slow. It is like lightning and thunder. They occur simultaneously, but sound, travelling slower than light, reaches you later, creating the illusion of two separate events. It is only the natural physiological sensations and perceptions that can move with the flow of life.

~

You have, through ideation and mentation, created your own thoughts which you consider to be yours, just as when different colours are mixed into various hues, but all of them can be reduced to the seven basic colours found in nature. What you think are your thoughts are actually just combinations and permutations of the thoughts of others.

Knowledge and Experience

Whatever you experience—peace, bliss, silence, beatitude, ecstasy, joy, God knows what—will be old, second-hand. You already have knowledge about all of these things. The fact that you are in a blissful state or in a state of tremendous silence means that you know about it. You must know a thing in order to experience it. That knowledge is nothing marvellous or metaphysical; 'bench', 'bag', 'red bag', is the knowledge. Knowledge is something which is put into you by somebody else, and he got that from somebody else; it is not yours. Can you experience a simple thing like that bench that is sitting across from you? No, you only experience the knowledge you have about it. And the knowledge has come from some outside agency, always. You think the thoughts of your society, feel the feelings of your society and experience the experiences of your society; there is no new experience.

~

Knowledge is not something mysterious or mystical. You know that you are happy, and you have theories about the working of the fan, the light—this is the knowledge we are talking about. You introduce another knowledge, 'spiritual knowledge', but— spiritual knowledge, sensual knowledge—what is the difference? We give the names to them. Fantasies about God are acceptable, but fantasies about sex are called 'sensual', 'physical'. There is no difference between the two; one is socially acceptable, the other is not. You are limiting knowledge to a particular area of experience, so then it becomes 'sensual', and the other becomes 'spiritual'? Everything is sensual.

Desire and Selfishness

Man is *always* selfish, and he will remain selfish as long as he practices selflessness as a virtue. I have nothing against selfish people. I don't want to talk about selflessness—it has no basis at all. You say 'I will be a selfless man tomorrow. Tomorrow I will be a marvellous man'—but until tomorrow arrives (or the day after tomorrow, or the next life) you will remain selfish. What do you mean by 'selflessness'? You tell everybody to be selfless. What is the point? I have never said to anybody 'Don't be selfish.' Be selfish, stay selfish!—that is my message. Wanting enlightenment is selfishness. The rich man's distributing charity is also selfishness: he will be remembered as a generous man; you will put up a statue of him there.

~

You have been told that you should practice desirelessness. You have practised desirelessness for thirty or forty years, but still desires are there. So something must be wrong somewhere. Nothing can be wrong with desire; something must be wrong with the one who has told you to practice desirelessness. This (desire) is a reality; that (desirelessness) is false—it is falsifying you. Desire is there. Desire as such can't be wrong, can't be false, because it is there.

~

You hope that you will be able to resolve the problem of desire through thinking, because of that model of a saint who you think has controlled or eliminated desire. If that man has no desire as you imagine, he is a corpse. Don't believe that man at all! Such a man builds some organization, and lives in luxury, which you pay for. You are maintaining him. He is doing it for his livelihood. There is always a fool in the world who falls for him. Once in a while he allows you to prostrate before him. You will be surprised if you live with him. You will get the shock of your life if you see him there. That is why they are all aloof—because they are afraid you will catch them some time or the other. The rich man is always afraid that you will touch him for money. So too the religious man—he never, never comes in contact with you. Seeing him is far more difficult than seeing the President of your country—that is a lot easier than seeing a holy man. He is not what he says he is, not what he claims he is.

The Body Is Immortal

It is the body which is immortal. It only changes its form after clinical death, remaining within the flow of life in new shapes. The body is not concerned with 'the afterlife' or any kind of permanency. It struggles to survive and multiply NOW. The fictitious 'beyond', created by thought out of fear, is really the demand for more of the same, in modified form. This demand for repetition of the same thing over and over again is the demand for permanence. Such permanence is foreign to the body. Thought's demand for permanence is choking the body and distorting perception. Thought sees itself as not just the protector of its own continuity, but also of the body's continuity. Both are utterly false.

~

The moment you die, the body begins to decay, returning back to other, differently organized forms of life, putting an end to nothing. Life has no beginning and no end. A dead and dying body feeds the hungry ants there in the grave, and rotting corpses give off soil-enriching chemicals, which in turn nourish other life forms. You cannot put an end to your life, it is impossible. The body is immortal and never asks silly questions like, 'Is there immortality?' It knows that it will come to an end in that particular form, only to continue on in others. Questions about life after death are always asked out of fear.

~

The human body, when broken into its constituent elements, is no different from the tree out there or the mosquito that is sucking your blood. Basically, it is exactly the same. The proportions of the elements may be higher in one case and lesser in the case of the others. You have eighty percent of water in the body, and there is eighty percent of water in the trees and eighty percent on this planet. So that is the reason why I maintain that we are nothing but a fortuitous concourse of atoms. If and when death takes place, the body is reshuffled, and then these atoms are used to maintain the energy levels in the universe. Other than that, there is no such thing as death to this body.

~

Thought is only a response to stimuli. The brain is not really a creator; it is just a container. The function of the brain in this body is only to take care of the needs of the physical organism and to maintain its sensitivity, whereas thought, through its constant interference with sensory activity, is destroying the sensitivity of the body. That is where the conflict is. The conflict is between the need of the body to maintain its sensitivity and the demand of thought to translate every sensation within the framework of the sensual activity. I am not condemning sensual activity. Mind, or whatever you want to call it, is born out of this sensuality. So, all activities of the mind are sensual in their nature, whereas the activity of the body is to respond to the stimuli around it. That is really the basic conflict between what you call the mind and the body.

You Stand on Your Own

You are lost in a jungle and you have no way of finding your way out. Night is fast approaching. The wild animals are there including the cobras and still you are lost. What do you do in such a situation? You just stop. You don't move. As long as there is that hope that you can somehow or the other get out of the jungle, so long will you continue what you are doing, searching, and so long you feel lost. You are lost only because you are searching. You have no way of finding your way out of the jungle.

~

You can stop it in you. Free yourself from that social structure that is operating in you without becoming anti-social, without becoming a reformer, without becoming anti-this, anti-that. You can throw the whole thing out of your system and free yourself from the burden of this culture, for yourself and by yourself. Whether it has any usefulness for society or not is not your concern. If there is one individual who walks free, you don't have any more the choking feeling of what this horrible culture has done to you. It's neither East nor West, it's all the same. Human nature is exactly the same—there's no difference.

~

I am telling you to stand on your own. You can walk. You can swim. You are not going to sink. That's all that I can say. As long as there is fear, the danger of your sinking is almost certain. Otherwise, there is a buoyancy there in the water that keeps you afloat. The fear of sinking is the very thing that makes it impossible for you to let the movement happen in its own way. You see, it has no direction. It is just a movement with no direction. You are trying to manipulate and channel that movement along a particular direction so that you can have some benefits. You are just a movement without a direction.

~

Courage is to brush aside everything that man has experienced and felt before you. You are the only one, greater than all those things. Everything is finished, the whole tradition is finished, however sacred and holy it may be—then only can you be yourself—that is individuality. For the first time you become an individual.

Briefly Telling It Like It Is

A messiah is the one who leaves a mess behind him in this world.

~

Religions have promised roses but you end up with only thorns.

~

Anything you want to be free from for whatever reason is the very thing that can free you.

~

God and sex go together. If God goes sex goes, too.

~

When you know nothing, you say a lot. When you know something, there is nothing to say.

~

All experiences however extraordinary they may be are in the area of sensuality.

~

Man cannot be anything other than what he is. Whatever he is, he will create a society that mirrors him.

~

Inspiration is a meaningless thing. Lost, desperate people create a market for inspiration. All inspired action will eventually destroy you and your kind.

~

Love and hate are not opposite ends of the same spectrum; they are one and the same thing. They are much closer than kissing cousins.

~

By using the models of Jesus, Buddha, or Krishna we have destroyed the possibility of nature throwing up unique individuals.

~

As long as you are doing something to be selfless, you will be a self-centred individual.

~

Life has to be described in pure and simple physical and physiological terms. It must be demystified and de-psychologized.

~

Society is built on a foundation of conflict, and you are society. Therefore you must always be in conflict with society.

~

The peak of sex experience is the one thing in life you have that comes close to being a first-hand experience; all the rest of your experiences are second-hand, somebody else's.

~

Food, clothing and shelter—these are the basic needs. Beyond that, if you want anything, it is the beginning of self-deception.

~

The day man experienced the consciousness that made him feel separate and superior to the other forms of life, at that moment he began sowing the seeds of his own destruction.

~

You eat not food but ideas. What you wear are not clothes, but labels and names.

~

If you do not know what happiness is, you will never be unhappy.

~

Thoughts come in waves, it is all over, you pick only thoughts you want.

~

Cause and effect are not two different things, they are one. It is the mind that separates the two.

~

You formulate questions from the answers you already have.

~

You are not at peace with yourself then how can you create peace in the world?

~

There is no relationship between what you are thinking and how you are living and it is this that isolates you from the movement of life and causes pain and suffering.

~

You never listen to anybody, you are always listening to yourself. You translate everything in terms of your own knowledge and experience.

~

All moral absolutes, all moral abstractions are falsifying you.

~

It is the search that is creating the disturbance, the division in your state of consciousness. That is violence. Your holy thoughts are same as the thoughts of a fascist dictator.

~

To become somebody else you need time, to be yourself it doesn't need time.

~

Throw away all the crutches, you don't need any help, you can walk by yourself.

Acknowledgements

Narayana Moorty's encouraging words on reading an early draft and Udayan Mitra backing the work gave me the much-needed impetus to complete the book which had been on the anvil for quite some years. I am immensely grateful to both of them. I have drawn heavily on the non-dual philosophical works, biographies of saints and sages, and translations of non-dual spiritual texts, and I remain deeply indebted to all the authors of these works. And grateful I am to Chandra Shekar Babu for his unstinting support, Suyasheii A. for her editorial assistance and the creative and editorial team of HarperCollins for producing the book so well.

References

Preface

Bhikkhu, Thanissaro (Trans.), 'Alagaddupama Sutta: The Raft Simile', in *Majjhima Nikaya*, Pali Text Society, 2004; accessible at: https://www.accesstoinsight.org/tipitaka/mn/mn.022.than.html.

Krishna, Daya, *Indian Philosophy: A Counter perspective*, Oxford University Press, New Delhi, 1996.

Ramanujan, A.K., *Speaking of Siva*, Penguin India, New Delhi, 1973.

Rao, Mukunda (Ed. and with Introduction), *The Biology of Enlightenment: Early Conversation of U.G. Krishnamurti with Friends after He Came into the Natural State (1967–71)*, HarperCollins Publishers India, Noida, 2010.

One: The Word and the Birth of the Self

Basham, A.L., *The Wonder That Was India*, Rupa & Co., New Delhi, 1967.

Campbell, Joseph, *Oriental Mythology*, a Condor Book, Souvenir Press, London, 2000.

Panikkar, Raimundo, *The Vedic Experience: Mantramañjari: An Anthology of the Vedas for the Modern Man and Contemporary Celebration*, All India Books, Puducherry, 1983.

Rao, Mukunda, *In Search of Shiva: A Novel*, Dronequill Publishers Pvt. Ltd, Bengaluru, 2010.

Tagore, Rabindranath, *Gitanjali and Fruit-Gathering*, Macmillan and Co., Limited, London, 1919; also accessible at: http://tagoreweb.in.

The Holy Bible, King James Version, 'The Gospel According to St John', Chapter 1: Verse 1, Cambridge University Press, Cambridge.

Two: The Upanishads

Panikkar, Raimundo, *The Vedic Experience: Mantramañjari: An Anthology of the Vedas for the Modern Man and Contemporary Celebration*, All India Books, Puducherry, 1983.

Nikhilananda, Swami (Transl.), *The Upanishads*, Advaita Ashrama, Kolkata, 1986.

Prabhavananda, Swami and Manchester, Frederick (Trans.), *The Upanishads: Breath of the Eternal* (Selections), Sri Ramakrishna Math, Chennai, 1968.

Rao, Mukunda, *The Buddha: An Alternative Narrative of His Life and Teaching*, HarperCollins Publishers India, Noida, 2018.

_____(Ed.), *The Biology of Enlightenment: Early Conversations of U.G. Krishnamurti with Friends after he came into the Natural State (1967–71)*, HarperCollins Publishers India, Noida, 2010.

Three: The Coming of the Buddha

Armstrong, Karen, *Buddha*, Phoenix, London, 2006.

Bhikkhu, Thanissaro (Trans.), *Majjhima Nikaya*, Pali Text Society; accessible at www.acesstoinsight.org.

Burtt, Edwin A. (Ed.), *The Teachings of the Compassionate Buddha*, Mentor Books, New York, 1982.

Campbell, Joseph, *Oriental Mythology: The Masks of God*, Souvenir Press Ltd, London, 2000.

Carus, Paul (Ed.), *Gospel of the Buddha*, Pilgrims Publishing, Varanasi, 2003.

Conze, Edward, *Further Buddhist Studies*, Bruno Cassirer Ltd, Oxford, UK, 1976.

Oldenberg, Hermann, *Buddha: His Life, His Doctrine, His Order*, William Hoey (Trans.), Williams and Norgate, London, 1882.

Panikkar, Raimundo, *The Vedic Experience: Mantramañjari: An Anthology of the Vedas for the Modern Man and Contemporary Celebration*, All India Books, Puducherry, 1983.

Rao, Mukunda, *The Buddha*, HarperCollins Publishers India Ltd, 2018.

Rhys Davids, T.W. (Trans.), *Dialogues of the Buddha*, Volumes 1, 2 and 3, The Pali Text Society, London, 1971–73.

Four: One Source, Two Streams

Batchelor, Stephen, *Verses from the Center: A Buddhist Vision of the Sublime*, Riverhead books, New York, 2000; accessible at http:www. stephenbatchelor.org/index.php/en/verses-from-the-center.

Bhikku, Thanissaro, Andrew Olendzki and Buddharakkhita (Trans.), *Samyutta Nikaya* 35-85; *Sunna Satta*; accessible at: www. accesstoinsight org.

Satchidananda Murty, K., *Nagarjuna*, National Biography Series, National Book Trust, New Delhi, 1971.

Nikhilananda, Swami (Trans.), *Mandukya Upanishad with Gaudapada's Karika*, 1949; accessible at: archive.org.

Gambirananda, Swami (Trans.), *Gaudapada: Mandukya Karika*, Ramakrishna Math, Kolkata, 1987.

Five: Songs in Dualism and Non-Dualism

Bhagavad Gita

Davies, Paul, *The Origin of Life*, Penguin Books, London, 2003.

Dharwadker, Vinay (Ed.), *The Collected Essays of A.K. Ramanujan*, Oxford University Press, New Delhi, 2001.

Dunn, Jean (Ed.), *Prior to Consciousness: Talks with Sri Nisargadatta Maharaj*, 1980; accessible at: http://prahlad.org/gallery/nisargadatta/books/Nisargadatta.

Menon, Ramesh, *Srimad Bhagavad Gita*, Rupa Publications India, Delhi, 2007, 2012, 2016.

Krishnananda, Swami (Trans.), *Katha Upanishad*, Divine Life Society, Shivanandnagar; accessible at: www.swami-krishnananda.org.

Rao, Mukunda (Ed.), *The Biology of Enlightenment*, HarperCollins India Publishers Ltd, Noida, 2010.

Sivananda, Swami (Trans.), *Bhagavad Gita*, The Divine Life Society, Shivanandnagar, 1995; accessible at: http://www.dlshq.org/download/bgita.pdf.

Sri Aurobindo, *Essays on the Gita*, ninth edition, Sri Aurobindo Ashram Press, Puducherry, 2003.

____*The Life Divine*, Sri Aurobindo Ashram Press, Puducherry, 1998.

Ashtavakra Gita

Arms, Rodney (Ed.), *The Mystique of Enlightenment: The Unrational Ideas of a Man Called U.G. Krishnamurti* published by Dinesh Vaghela, Goa, India, 1982.

Chinmayananda, Swami (Trans. with commentary), *Discourses on Ashtavakra Gita*, Central Chinmaya Mission Trust, Mumbai, 1985.

Marshall, Bart, *Ashtavakra Gita*, translated e-book, 2005; accessible at: https://www.holybooks.com/wp-content/uploads/Ashtavakra-Gita-ebook.pdf.

Nityaswarupananda, Swami (Trans. with commentary), *Ashtavakra Samhita*, Advaita Ashrama, Kolkata, 2006.

Avadhuta Gita

Abhayananda, Swami (Trans. and with Introduction), *Dattatreya Song of the Avadhut: An English Translation of the Avadhut Gita (with Sanskrit Transliteration)* Sri Satguru Publications, 2000; also accessible at: https://www.holybooks.com/wp-content/uploads/Song-of-the-Avadhut-by-Dattatreya.pdf.

Ashokananda, Swami (Trans. and annotated), *Avadhuta Gita of Dattatreya*, Sri Ramakrishna Math, Chennai, 1988.

Chetananda, Swami (Trans.), *Avadhuta Gita of Dattatreya*, Advaita Ashrama, Kolkata, 2005.

Frydman, Maurice (Trans.), *I Am That: Talks with Sri Nisargadatta Maharaj*, Chetana, Mumbai, 1987.

Six: Jnana Yajna

Adi Shankara

Tapasyananda, Swami (Trans.), *Sankara Digvijaya: The Traditional Life of Sri Sankaracharya*, Madhava-Vidyaranya (fourteenth-century Sanskrit text), Sri Ramakrishna Math, Chennai, 1980.

Central Chinmaya Mission Trust, *Sankara the Missionary*, Central Chinmaya Mission Trust, Mumbai, 1978.

Jagadananda, Swami (Trans. with explanatory Notes), *Upadeshasahasri: A Thousand Teachings of Sri Sankaracharya*, Sri Ramakrishna Math, Chennai, 1949.

Allama Prabhu

Basavaraju, Dr L. (Ed.), *Allamana Vachanagalu: Selected Vachanas of Allama Prabhu*, Geetha Book House, Mysuru, 1997.

Hiremath, Dr R.C. (Ed.), *Sunya Sampadane*, Gummalapurada Siddalingadevaru, Kannada Study Centre, Karnataka University, Dharwad, 1972.

Nagaraj, D.R., *Allama Prabhu Mattu Shaiva Pratibhe: A Critical Study of Allama Prabhu and the Shaiva Imagination*, Akshara Prakashana, Sagar, Karnataka, 1999.

Ramanujan, A.K., *Speaking of Siva*, Penguin India, New Delhi, 1973.

Rao, Mukunda, *In Search of Shiva: A Novel* Dronequill Publishers Pvt. Ltd, Bengaluru, 2010.

Vidyashankar, Prof. S. and Prof. G.S. *Siddaligaiah* (Eds.) *Halageyaryana Sunya Sampadane*, Priyadarshini Prakashana, Bengaluru, 1997.

Vidyashankar, Dr S. (original with prose rendering), *Chamarasan Prabhulinga Leele*, Kannada Sahitya Parishath, Bengaluru, 2014.

Kabir

Dharwadker, Vinay (Trans., with Introduction and Notes), *Kabir: The Weaver's Songs*, Penguin Books India, New Delhi, 2003.

Shah, Ahmad (Trans.), *The Bijak of Kabir*, Asian Publication Services, New Delhi, 1977.

Tagore, Rabindranath (Trans.), *Songs of Kabir*, Macmillan Co. Ltd, New York, 1915.

Seven: Beyond Gender

Akka Mahadevi

Bhoosnurmath, Prof. S.S., *Sunyasampadaneya Paramarse*, Directorate of Kannada and Culture, Bengaluru, 1983.

Chandrasekhar, Laxmi, *The Sign: Vachanas of the 12th Century*, O.L. Nagabhushana Swamy (Ed.), Prasaranga, Kannada University, Hampi, 2007.

Hiremath, Dr R.C. (Ed.), *Sunya Sampadane*, Gummalapurada Siddalingadevaru, Kannada Study Centre, Karnataka University, Dharwad, 1972.

His Holiness Mahatapsvi Shri Kumarswamiji, *Prophets of Veerashaivism*, 1992; accessible at: http://www.virashaiva.com/akka-mahadevis-vachanas/.

Menezes, Armando, *Songs from the Saranas and Other Poems*, Karnataka University, Dharwad, 1973.

Ramanujan, A.K., *Speaking Of Siva*, Penguin Books India, New Delhi, 1973.

Rao, Mukunda, *In Search of Shiva: A Novel*, Dronequill Publishers Pvt. Ltd. Bengaluru, 2010.

_____*Sky-clad: The Extraordinary Life and Times of Akka Mahadevi*, Westland Publications Pvt. Ltd, Chennai, 2018.

Sreekantaiya, T.N., 'Akka Mahadevi', in Ghanananda, Swami and Sir John Stewart Wallace (Eds), *Women Saints: East and West*, Vedanta Press, California, 1979.

Lalleshwari

Hoskote, Ranjit (Trans. with Introduction and Notes), *I, Lalla: The Poems of Lal Ded*, Penguin Books India, New Delhi, 2013. Lal Ded's *Vakhs* accessible at: http://www.koausa.org/Saints/LalDed/Vakhs2.html.

Ramanujan, A.K., *Speaking Of Siva*, Penguin Books India, New Delhi, 1973.

Rao, Mukunda, *Sky-Clad: The Extraordinary Life and Times of Akka Mahadevi*, Westland Publications Pvt. Ltd, Chennai, 2018.

Razdan, P.N. (Mahanori), *Gems of Kashmiri Literature and Kashmiriyat: The Trio of Saint Poets*, Smakaleen Prakashan, New Delhi, 1998.

Anandamayi Ma

Lipski, Dr Alexander, *Life and Teaching of Sri Anandamayi Ma*, Motilal Banarasidass, New Delhi, 2000.

Dasgupta, Ganga Charan (Trans.), *Mother as Revealed to Me*, Shree Shree Anandamayee Sangha, Kankhal, Haridwar, 2004 (English translation of *Matridarshan* by Bhaiji in Bengali).

Yogananda, Paramahansa, *Autobiography of a Yogi*, Philosophical Library, New York, 1946.

The Mother

Alfassa, Mirra, *Collected Works of the Mother*, Sri Aurobindo Ashram, Puducherry, 1978.

_____*Words of the Mother I, II and III*, Sri Aurobindo Ashram, Puducherry, 2004; accessible at: http://www.collectedworksofsriaurobindo.com.

Joshi, Kireet, *Sri Aurobindo and the Mother: Glimpses of Their Experiments, Experiences and Realisations*, The Mother's Institute of Research (Delhi) in association with Motilal Banarasidass, New Delhi, 1996.

Satprem (Ed.), *Mother's Agenda 1951–1973*, 13 volumes (English translation), Institute for Evolutionary Research, New York, 1979.

_____*The Mind of the Cells: Or Willed Mutation of Our Species*, Institute for Evolutionary Research, New York, 1982.

Eight: Modern Sages

Sri Ramakrishna Paramahamsa

Chetanananda, Swami (Trans. and Ed.), *Ramakrishna as We Saw Him*, Advaita Ashram, Kolkata, 1999.

Nikhilananda, Swami (Trans.), *The Gospel of Sri Ramakrishna*, Sri Ramakrishna Math, Chennai, 2002; originally written in Bengali by Mahendranath Gupta.

_____*Life of Sri Ramakrishna*, Advaita Ashrama, Uttarakhand, 2008.

Sri Aurobindo

Paranjape, Makarand (Ed.), *The Penguin Sri Aurobindo Reader*, Penguin Books India, New Delhi, 1999.

Purani, A.B., *Evening Talks with Sri Aurobindo (1938–50)*, Sri Aurobindo Ashram, Puducherry, 1987.

Sri Aurobindo, *The Supramental Manifestation & Other Writings*, Sri Aurobindo Ashram, Puducherry, 1971a.

_____*The Life Divine*, Sri Aurobindo Ashram, Puducherry, 1971b.

Sri Ramana Maharshi

Brunton, Paul, *The Maharshi and His Message*, Sri Ramanasramam, Thiruvannamalai, 2007.

Cohen, S.S., *Guru Ramana*, Sri Ramanasramam, Thiruvannamalai, 1998.

Godman, David (Ed.), *Be As You Are: The Teachings of Sri Ramana Maharshi*, Penguin Books India, 1992.

————*Living by the Words of Bhagvan*, Sri Ramanasramam, Thiruvannamalai, 1999.

Osborne, Arthur, *The Teachings of Ramana Maharshi in His Own Words*, Sri Ramanasramam, Tiruvannamalai, 2010.

Nisargadatta Maharaj

Dunn, Jean (Ed.), *Consciousness and the Absolute: The Final Talks of Sri Nisargadatta Maharaj*, Chetana, Mumbai, 2003, published in arrangement with the Acorn Press, Durham, NC, 1994.

Frydman, Maurice (Trans.), *I Am That*, Sri Nisargadatta Maharaj, Chetana, Mumbai, 1987.

Godman, David, *Remembering Nisargadatta Maharaj*, (David Godman interview; n.d.); accessible at: http://www.davidgodman.org/interviews/nis1.shtml.

Gogate, Shrikant and Phadol, P.T., *Meet the Sage Sri Nisargadatta*, Sri Nisargadatta Maharaj Amrit Mahotsav Samiti, Mumbai, n.d.; accessible at: http://sri-nisargadatta-maharaj.blogspot.com/2014/11/meet-sage-sri-nisargadatta.html..

Powell, Robert (Ed.), *The Nectar of Immortality: Sri Nisargadatta Maharaj's Discourses on the Eternal*, Motilal Banarasidass, New Delhi, 2008.

J. Krishnamurti

Krishnamurti, J., *The Awakening of Intelligence*, Penguin Books India, New Delhi, 2000.

_____*Total Freedom: The Essential Krishnamurti*, Krishnamurti Foundation India, Chennai, 2002.

Lutyens, Mary, *Krishnamurti: The Years of Fulfilment*, Avon Books, New York, 1983.

_____*Krishnamurti: The Years of Awakening*, John Murray Ltd., London, 1975; Shambhala Publications, reprint edition, 1997.

_____*Life and Death of Krishnamurti*, John Murray Ltd London, 1990; Srishti Publishers & Distributors, New Delhi, 1999.

Vas, Luis S.R. (Ed.), *The Mind of J. Krishnamurti*, Jaico Publishing House, Mumbai, 1973.

Vernon, Roland, *Star in the East: Krishnamurti the Invention of a Messiah*, Penguin Books India, New Delhi, 2002.

Rao, Mukunda *The Other Side of Belief: Interpreting U.G. Krishnamurti*, Penguin India, New Delhi, 2005.

U.G. Krishnamurti

Arms, Rodney (Ed.), *The Mystique of Enlightenment: The Unrational Ideas of a Man Called U.G.*, published by Dinesh Vaghela, Goa, 1982.

Babu, Chandrasekhar, *Stopped in Our Tracks*, Volumes I, II and III, Smriti Books, New Delhi, 2002.

Kelker, Shanta, *The Sage and the House Wife*, Sowmya Publishers, Bengaluru, 1990.

Newland, Terry (Ed.), *Mind Is a Myth: Disquieting Conversations with the Man Called U.G.*, Dinesh Publications, 1988.

Nikhilananda, Swami, *Life of Sri Ramakrishna*, by Advaita Ashrama, Uttarakhand, 2008.

Krishnamurti, U.G., *Thought Is Your Enemy: Conversations with U.G. Krishnamurti*, Frank Noronha and Naryana Moorty (Eds), Smriti Books, New Delhi, 2002.

Rao, Mukunda (Ed. and with Introduction), *The Penguin U.G. Krishnamurti Reader*, Penguin Books India, New Delhi, 2007.

_____(Ed. and with Introduction), *The Biology of Enlightenment: Early Conversations of U.G. Krishnamurti with Friends after He Came into the Natural State (1967–71)*, HarperCollins Publishers India Ltd, Noida, 2010.

Siegel, Lee, *Laughing Matters: Comic Tradition in India*, Motilal Banarasidass, New Delhi, 1989.

A Reading List

Abhayananda, Swami (Trans. and with Introduction), *Dattatreya Song of the Avadhut: An English Translation of the Avadhut Gita (with Sanskrit Transliteration)*, Sri Satguru Publications, 2000; also accessible at: https://www.holybooks.com/wp-content/uploads/Song-of-the-Avadhut-by-Dattatreya.pdf.

Alfassa, Mirra, *Collected Works of the Mother*, 17 volumes, Sri Aurobindo Ashram, Puducherry, Centenary Edition, 1978.

____*Rays of Light, Sayings of the Mother*, Sri Aurobindo Ashram, Puducherry, 1997.

Arms, Rodney (Ed.), *The Mystique of Enlightenment: The Unrational Ideas of a Man Called U.G.*, published by Dinesh Vaghela, Goa, 1982.

Armstrong, Karen, *Buddha*, Phoenix, London, 2006.

Arnold, Edwin, *The Light of Asia and the Indian Song of Songs*, Jaico Publishing House, Kolkata, 1949.

Ashokananda, Swami (Trans. and annotated), *Avadhuta Gita of Dattatreya*, Sri Ramakrishna Math, Chennai, 1988.

Auro Publications, *The Mother, A Short Biography*, Auro Publications, Sri Aurobindo Society, Puducherry, 2014.

Babu, Chandrasekhar, *Stopped in Our Tracks*, Volumes I, II and III, Smriti Books, New Delhi, 2002.

Basavaraju, Dr L. (Ed. with Introduction), *Akkana Vachanagalu* (selected *vachanas* of Akka Mahadevi), Manasa Gangotri, University of Mysore, Geetha Book House, Mysuru, 1995.

Basham, A.L., *The Wonder That Was India*, Rupa & Co., New Delhi, 1967.

Basrur, Subba Rao, *Allama Prabhu: A Study in Philosophy with Translation of Poems*, Shri Mangesh Publishers, Bengaluru, 2007.

Batchelor, Stephen, *Verses from the Centre: A Buddhist Vision of the Sublime*, Riverhead, New York, 2000.

Bhatt, Mahesh, *A Taste of Life: The Last Days of U.G. Krishnamurti*, Penguin Books India, New Delhi, 2009.

Bharati, Agehananda, *The Light at the Centre: Context and Pretext of Modern Mysticism*, Bell Books, Vikas Publishing House, 1977.

Bhikkhu, Thanissaro (Trans.), '*Samadhanga Sutta:* The Factors of Concentration', *Anguttara Nikaya*, 1997; accessible at: https://www.accesstoinsight.org/tipitaka/an/an05/an05.028.than.html.

_____(Trans.), *Majjhima Nikaya: The Middle Collection*, accessible at: https://www.dhammatalks.org/suttas/MN/index_MN.html.

Bhoosnurmath, Prof. S.S., *Sunyasampadaneya Paramarse*, Directorate of Kannada and Culture, Bengaluru, 1983.

Blomfield, Vishvapani, *Gautama Buddha: The Life and Teachings of the Awakened One*, Quercus, Great Britain, 2011.

Brawley, Louis, *Goner: The Final Travels of U.G. Krishnamurti*, Non-Duality Press, Salisbury, 2011.

Brunton, Paul, *The Maharshi and His Message*, Sri Ramanasramam, Thiruvannamalai, 2007.

Burton, David, *Emptiness Appraised: A Critical Study of Nagarjuna's Philosophy*, Motilal Banarasidass, New Delhi, 2001.

Burtt, Edwin A. (Ed.), *The Teachings of the Compassionate Buddha*, Mentor Books, New York, 1982.

Calasso, Robert, *Ka*, Vintage, London, 1999.

Campbell, Joseph and Bill Moyers, *The Power of Myth*, Anchor Books, New York, 1991.

Campbell, Joseph, *The Masks of God: Oriental Mythology*, Souvenir Press Ltd, London, 2000.

Carus, Paul, *Gospel of the Buddha*, Pilgrims Publishing, Varanasi, 2003.

Central Chinmaya Mission Trust, *Sankara the Missionary*, Central Chinmaya Mission Trust, Mumbai, 1978.

Chakravarty, Uma, 'The World of the Bhaktin in South Indian Traditions: The Body and Beyond', *Manushi*, Number 50-51-52 (January–June 1989).

Chandrasekhar, Laxmi, Vijaya Guttal, and Nagabhusan Swami, *The Sign: Vachanas of 12th Century*, Prasaranga, Kannada University, Hampi, 2007.

Channabasavanka, *Mahadeviyakkana Purana*, B.N. Chandraiah (Ed.), Sharath Prakashana, Mysuru, 1967.

Chaudhuri, Haridas, *The Philosophy of Integralism: The Metaphysical Synthesis in Sri Aurobindo's Teaching*, Sri Aurobindo Ashram, Puducherry, 1967.

Chaudhuri, Narayan, *That Compassionate Touch of Ma Anandamayee*, Motilal Banarasidass, New Delhi, 2006.

Chetanananda, Swami (Trans. and Ed.), *Ramakrishna as We Saw Him*, Advaita Ashram, Kolkata, 1999.

_____(Transl.), *Avadhuta Gita of Dattatreya*, Advaita Ashrama, Kolkata, 2005.

Chidananda Murthy, M., *Allamana Vachanagalu: Selected Vachanas of Allama Prabhu*, Dr L. Basavaraju (Ed.), Geetha Book House, Mysuru, 1997.

Chinmayananda, Swami (Trans. with Commentary), *Discourses on Ashtavakra Gita*, Central Chinmaya Mission Trust, Mumbai, 1985.

Cohen, S.S., *Guru Ramana*, Sri Ramanasramam, Thiruvannamalai, 1998.

Cole, Colin A., *A Study of Gaudapada's Mandukya Karika*, Motilal Banarasidass, Delhi, 2004.

Coward, Harold G. (Ed.), *Studies in Indian Thought: Collected Papers of Prof. T.R.V. Murti*, Motilal Banarasidass, New Delhi, 1983.

Das, Nolima (Ed.), *Glimpses of the Mother's Life*, Sri Aurobindo Ashram, Puducherry, 1978.

Dasgupta, Surendranath, *A History of Indian Philosophy*, Volume I and II, Motilal Banarasidass Publishers, Delhi, 1975.

de Bary, W.T. (Ed.), *The Buddhist Tradition in India, China and Japan*, Vintage, Random House, New York, 1972.

Dharwadker, Vinay (Ed.), *The Collected Essays of A.K. Ramanujan*, Oxford University Press, New Delhi, 2001.

_____(Trans.) and with Introduction and Notes), *Kabir: The Weaver's Songs*, Penguin India, New Delhi, 2003.

Doniger, Wendy, *The Hindu: An Alternative History*, Penguin/Viking, New Delhi, 2009.

Dunn, Jean (Ed.), *Consciousness and the Absolute: The Final Talks of Sri Nisargadatta Maharaj*, Chetana, Mumbai, 2003, published in arrangement with the Acorn Press, Durham, NC, 1994.

Frydman, Maurice (Trans.), *I Am That*, Sri Nisargadatta Maharaj, Chetana, Mumbai, 1987.

Gambirananda, Swami (Trans.), *Gaudapada: Mandukya Karika*, Ramakrishna Math, Kolkata, 1987.

Garfield, J.L., *Empty Words: Buddhist Philosophy and Cross-cultural Interpretation*, Oxford University Press, Oxford, 2002.

Ghanananda, Swami and Sir John Stewart Wallace (Eds), *Women Saints: East and West*, Vedanta Press, California, 1979.

Godman, David (Ed.), *Be As You Are: The Teachings of Sri Ramana Maharshi*, Penguin Books India, 1992.

_____*Living by the Words of Bhagavan*, Sri Ramanasramam, Tiruvannamalai 1999.

Gogate, Shrikant and Phadol, P.T., *Meet the Sage Sri Nisargadatta*, Sri Nisargadatta Maharaj Amrit Mahotsav Samiti, Mumbai, n.d.; accessible at: http://sri-nisargadatta-maharaj.blogspot.com/2014/11/meet-sage-sri-nisargadatta.html.

Goodall, Dominic (Ed. and with new Trans.), *Hindu Scriptures*, Phoenix Giant, London, 1996.

Hiremath, Dr R.C. (Ed.), *Sunya Sampadane*, Gummalapurada Siddalingadevaru, Kannada Study Centre, Karnataka University, Dharwad, 1972.

_____*Mahadeviyakkana Vachanagalu*, Karnataka University, Dharwar, 1973.

Hiriyanna, M., *An Introduction to Indian Philosophy*, Oxford University Press, New Delhi, 1978.

Hoskote, Ranjit (Trans. with Introduction and Notes), *I, Lalla: The Poems of Lal Ded*, Penguin Classics, New Delhi, 2011.

Huxley, Aldous, *The Perennial Philosophy*, Perennial Classics edition, HarperCollins, New York, 2004.

Jagadguru Sri Annadaeeswara Mahaswamiji, *Mahadeviakkana Vachana-Chintana*, Sri Shivarathreeshwara Granthamale, 2001.

Jagadananda, Swami (Trans. with explanatory Notes), *Upadeshasahasri: A Thousand Teachings of Sri Sankaracharya*, Sri Ramakrishna Math, Chennai, 1949.

Joshi, Kalidas, *Understanding J. Krishnamurti*, Rupa & Co., New Delhi, 2002.

Joshi, Kireet, *Sri Aurobindo and the Mother: Glimpses of Their Experiments, Experiences and Realisations*, The Mother's Institute of Research (Delhi) in association with Motilal Banarasidass, New Delhi, 1996.

Isherwood, Christopher, *Ramakrishna and His Disciples*, Vedanta Press, California, 1965.

Kalupahana, David, *Mulamadhyamakakarika of Nagarjuna: The Philosophy of the Middle Way*, Motilal Banarasidass, New Delhi, 2005.

Katz, Jerry (Compiler and Ed.), *The Nisargadatta Song of I Am*, n.d.; accessible at: http://www.nonduality.com/iam.htm.

Kaul, Jayalal, *Lal Ded*, Sahitya Akademi, New Delhi, 1973.

Kelker, Shanta, *The Sage and the Housewife*, Sowmya Publishers, Bengaluru, 1990.

Koestler, Arthur, *Janus: A Summing Up*, Picador Books, London, 1979.

Krishna, Daya, *Indian Philosophy: A Counter Perspective*, Oxford University Press, New Delhi, 1996.

Krishnamurti, J., *Krishnamurti's Notebook*, Victor Gollancz Ltd, London, 1976; Harper & Row, New York, 1976.

_____*The Awakening of Intelligence*, Penguin Books India, New Delhi, 2000.

_____*Total Freedom: The Essential Krishnamurti*, Krishnamurti Foundation India, Chennai, 2002.

Krishnamurti, U.G., *Thought Is Your Enemy: Conversations with U.G. Krishnamurti*, Frank Noronha and Naryana Moorty (Eds), Smriti Books, New Delhi, 2002.

Krohnen, Michael, *The Kitchen Chronicles: 1001 Lunches with J. Krishnamurti*, Penguin Books, India, 1997.

Lipski, Dr Alexander, *Life and Teaching of Sri Anandamayi Ma*, Motilal Banarasidass, New Delhi, 2000.

Loy, David R., 'The Deconstruction of Buddhism', in Coward and Foshay (Eds), *Derrida and Negative Theology*, Suny Press, 1992 (see pp. 227–53 for a very learned analysis and understanding of the problematic of the notion of *Sunyata* in the light of postmodern philosophy); accessible at: http://enlight.lib.ntu.edu.tw/FULLTEXT/JR-ENG/loy10.htm.

Lutyens, Mary, *Krishnamurti: The Years of Fulfilment*, Avon Books, New York, 1983.

____*Life and Death of Krishnamurti*, John Murray Ltd, London, 1990; Srishti Publishers & Distributors, New Delhi, 1999.

Mabbett, Ian W., 'Naagaarjuna and Deconstruction', in *Philosophy East and West* Volume 45(2), University of Hawaii Press (see pp. 203–25 for a very learned analysis and understanding of the problematic of the notion of *Sunyata* in the light of postmodern philosophy); accessible at: http://enlight.lib.ntu.edu.tw/FULLTEXT/JR-PHIL/mabbet1.htm.

Mahadevan, T.M.P., *Gaudapada: a Study in Early Vedanta*, University of Madras, Chennai, 1960.

Mangalananda, Swami, *A Goddess among Us: The Divine Life of Anandamayi Ma*, Yogi Impressions Books Pvt. Ltd, Mumbai, 2016.

Marshall, Bart, *Ashtavakra Gita*, translated e-book, 2005; accessible at: https://www.holybooks.com/wp-content/uploads/Ashtavakra-Gita-ebook.pdf.

Max Muller, F. (Trans.), *The Dhammapada: A Collection of Verses*, The Sacred Books of the East, Clarendon Press, 1884.

____(Trans.), *The Thirteen Principal Upanishads*, Wordsworth Classics, London, 2000.

McDaniel, June, *The Madness of the Saints: Ecstatic Religion in Bengal*, University of Chicago Press, 1989.

Mehta, Rohit, *The Intuitive Philosophy: Krishnamurti's Approach to Life*, Chetana, Mumbai, 1950.

Menezes, Armando, *Songs from the Saranas and Other Poems*, Karnataka University, Dharwar, 1973.

Metcalf, Stephen (Ed.), *Selected Writings: Friedrich Nietzsche*, Srishti Publishers, New Delhi, 2001.

Mishra, Pankaj, *An End to Suffering: The Buddha in the World*, Picador Books, London, 2004.

Murti, T.R.V., *The Central Philosophy of Buddhism: A Study of Madhyamika System*, Munshiram Manoharlal Publishers Pvt. Ltd, New Delhi, 2010.

Nagaraj, D.R., *Allama Prabhu Mattu Shaiva Pratibhe: A Critical Study of Allama Prabhu and the Shaiva Imagination*, Akshara Prakashana, Heggodu, Sagar, 1999.

Nandimath, S.C., *A Handbook of Virasaivism*, Motilal Banarasidass, New Delhi, 1942.

Newland, Terry (Ed.), *Mind Is a Myth: Disquieting Conversations with the Man Called U.G.*, Dinesh Publications, 1988.

Nikhilananda, Swami (Trans.), *The Upanishads*, Volumes I to IV, Sri Ramakrishna Math, Chennai, 1980.

_____(Trans.), *Mandukya Upanishad with Gaudapada's Karika*, Sri Ramakrishna Math, Chennai, 2002a.

_____(Trans.) *The Gospel of Sri Ramakrishna*, Sri Ramakrishna Math, Chennai, 2002b; originally written in Bengali by Mahendranath Gupta.

_____*Life of Sri Ramakrishna*, Advaita Ashrama, Uttarakhand, 2008.

Nityaswarupananda, Swami (Trans. with Commentary), *Ashtavakra Samhita*, Advaita Ashrama, Kolkata, 2006.

Odin, Steve, 'Derrida & the Decentered Universe of Chan/Zen Buddhism', *Journal of Chinese Philosophy* 17(1): 61–86, 1990 (for a very learned analysis and understanding of the problematic of the notion of *Sunyata* in the light of postmodern philosophy).

Oldenberg, Hermann *Buddha: His Life, His Doctrine, His Order*, William Hoey (Trans.), Williams and Norgate, London, 1882.

Osborne, Arthur, *Ramana Maharshi and the Path of Self-Knowledge*, Sri Ramanasramam, Tiruvannamalai, 1997.

_____*The Teachings of Ramana Maharshi in His Own Words*, Sri Ramanasramam, Tiruvannamalai, 2010.

Osborne, Katya, 'How I Came to Bhagavan', *Mountain Path*, January–March 2003.

Osho, *Buddha: His Life and Teachings and Impact on Humanity*, Random House India, New Delhi, 2007.

Panikkar, Raimundo, *The Vedic Experience Mantramañjari: An Anthology of the Vedas for the Modern Man and Contemporary Celebration*, All India Books, Puducherry, 1983.

Paranjape, Makarand (Ed.), *The Penguin Sri Aurobindo Reader*, Penguin Books India, New Delhi, 1999.

Parimoo, B.N., *The Ascent of Self: A Reinterpretation of the Mystical Poetry of Lalla-Ded*, Motilal Banarasidass, Delhi, 1978.

Powell, Robert (Ed.), *The Nectar of Immortality: Sri Nisargadatta Maharaj's Discourses on the Eternal*, Motilal Banarasidass, New Delhi, 2008.

Purani, A.B., *Evening Talks with Sri Aurobindo (1938–50)*, Sri Aurobindo Ashram, Puducherry, 1987.

Prabhavananda, Swami and Frederick Manchester (Trans.), *The Upanishads: Breath of the Eternal*, Sri Ramakrishna Math, Chennai, 1979.

Radhakrishnan, S. (Trans.), *The Dhammapada*, translated by S. Radhakrishnan, Oxford University Press, Oxford, 1950.

_____*Indian Philosophy*, Volumes 1 and II, Oxford University Press, New Delhi, 1989.

_____*Eastern Religions and Western Thought*, Oxford University Press, 1977.

Rajagopal, D. (Ed.), *Commentaries on Living*, Three Series, B.I. Publications, 1984.

Ramachandran, V.S., *The Tell-Tale Brain: Unlocking the Mystery of Human Nature*, Random House India, 2010.

Ramanujan, A.K., *Speaking Of Siva*, Penguin Books India, 1973.

Ramaswamy, Vijaya, *Walking Naked: Women, Society, Spirituality in South India*, Indian Institute of Advanced Studies, Shimla, 2007.

Rao, Dr K.B. Ramakrishna, *The Bhagavad Gita: As the Philosophy of Loka-Samgraha or Cosmic Consolidation, An Exposition*, Darpan (an imprint of Prism Books Pvt. Ltd), Bengaluru, 2016.

Rao, Mukunda, *The Other Side of Belief: Interpreting U.G. Krishnamurti*, Penguin India, New Delhi, 2005.

_____(Ed. and with Introduction), *The Penguin U.G. Krishnamurti Reader*, Penguin Books India, New Delhi, 2007.

_____*In Search of Shiva: A Novel*, Dronequill Publishers Pvt. Ltd, Bengaluru, 2010a.

_____(Ed. and with Introduction), *The Biology of Enlightenment: Early Conversations of U.G. Krishnamurti with Friends after He Came into the Natural State (1967–71)*, HarperCollins Publishers India Ltd, Noida, 2010b.

_____*Between the Serpent and the Rope: Ashrams, Traditions, Avatars, Sages and Con Artists*, Harper Element, HarperCollins Publishers India, New Delhi, 2014.

_____*The Buddha: An Alternative Narrative of His Life and Teaching*, HarperCollins Publishers India Ltd, 2016.

Razdan, P.N. (Mahanori), *Gems of Kashmiri Literature and Kashmiriyat: The Trio of Saint Poets*, Smakaleen Prakashan, New Delhi, 1998.

Rhys Davids, T.W., *Buddhism*, Motilal Banarasidass, New Delhi, 1882, 1987.

_____(Trans.), *Mahaparinibbana Sutta: The Last Days and Teaching*, Clarendon Press, Oxford, 1880s; reissued by Lotus Press, New Delhi, 2006.

Richards, John (Trans.), *Ashtavakra Gita*, n.d.; retrieved 20 July 2012 and accessible at: https://realization.org/p/ashtavakra-gita/richards. ashtavakra-gita/richards.ashtavakra-gita.html.

Roebuck, Valeri J. (Trans. and with Introduction), *The Upanishads*, Penguin Books India, New Delhi, 2000.

Sastry, Alladi Mahadeva (Trans.), *The Bhagavad Gita*, with a Commentary by Sri Sankaracharya, Samata Books, Chennai, 1981.

Satprem, *Sri Aurobindo, or the Adventure of Consciousness*, Sri Aurobindo Ashram, 1973.

_____(Ed.), *Mother's Agenda* 1951-1973, 13 volumes, (English translation), Institute for Evolutionary Research, New York, 1979.

_____(Ed.), *The Mind of the Cells: Or Willed Mutation of Our Species*, Institute for Evolutionary Research, New York, 1982.

_____*Mother or the New Species*, Mira Aditi Centre, Mysuru, 1976, 2005.

Schoch, Manuel, *Bitten by the Black snake: The Ancient Wisdom of Ashtavakra*, Sentient Publications, Boulder, CO, 2007.

Shah, Ahmad (Trans.), *The Bijak of Kabir*, Asian Publication Services, New Delhi, 1977.

Shree Shree Anandamayee Sangha, *Mother, as Seen by Her Devotees*, Shree Shree Anandamayee Sangha, Haridwar, 1995.

Sreekantaiya, T.N., 'Akka Mahadevi', in Ghanananda, Swami and Sir John Stewart Wallace (Eds), *Women Saints: East and West*, Vedanta Press, California, 1979.

Sri Aurobindo, *The Supramental Manifestation & Other Writings*, Sri Aurobindo Ashram, Puducherry, 1971a.

_____*The Life Divine*, Sri Aurobindo Ashram, Puducherry, 1971b.

_____*Essays on the Gita*, Sri Aurobindo Ashram, Puducherry, 2000.

Sri Ramana Maharshi, 'Hridaya Vidya', in Sankaranarayanan (Trans.), *Sri Ramana Gita: The Teachings Of Bhagavan Sri Ramana Maharshi, with a Commentary by Kapali Sastriar*, Sri Ramanasramam Book Depot, Tiruvannamalai, 1997.

Sri Sri Ravi Shankar, *Ashtavakra Gita*, Sri Sri Publications Trust, Bengaluru, 2010.

Tagore, Rabindranath (Trans.), *Songs of Kabir*, Macmillan Co. Ltd, New York, 1915.

Tapasyananda, Swami (Trans.), *Sankara Digvijaya: The Traditional Life of Sri Sankaracharya*, Madhava-Vidyaranya (fourteenth-century Sanskrit text), Sri Ramakrishna Math, Chennai, 1980.

Tarikere, Rahamath (Ed.), *Akka Mahadevi Vachanagalu: Saamskrutika Mukhaamukhi*, Prasaranga, Kannada University, Hampi, 2005.

Temple, Sir Richard Carnac, *The Word of Lalla the Prophetess*, Cambridge 1924.

Vas, Luis S.R. (Ed.), *The Mind of J. Krishnamurti*, Jaico Publishing House, Mumbai, 1973.

Vernon, Roland, *Star in the East: Krishnamurti, the Invention of a Messiah*, Penguin Books India, New Delhi, 2002.

Vidyashankar, Prof. S., and Prof. G.S. Siddaligaiah (Eds.), *Halageyaryana Sunya Sampadane*, Priyadarshini Prakashana, Bengaluru, 1997.

Vidyashankar, Dr S. (original; with prose rendering), *Chamarasan Prabhulinga Leele*, Kannada Sahitya Parishath, Bengaluru, 2014.

Zaehner, R.C., *The Bhagavad Gita*, with Commentary based on the original sources, Oxford University Press, Oxford, 1969.

Copyright Acknowledgements

Grateful thanks to

Ramesh Menon and Rupa Publications India Pvt. Ltd for the permission to reproduce translated verses from *Srimad Bhagavad Gita*, 2007;

Krishna Shauri Ramanujan and Estate of A.K. Ramanujan for the permission to reproduce poems from *Speaking of Siva*, 1973;

Vinay Dharwadker and Penguin Random House India Pvt. Ltd for the permission to reproduce poems from the book *Kabir: The Weaver's Song*, 2003;

Ranjit Hoskote and Penguin Random House India Pvt. Ltd for the permission to reproduce poems from the book *I, Lalla: The Poems of Lal Ded*, 2013.